CU00894808

The Practitioner's Guide to Working with Families

Edited by

Margaret Bell and Kate Wilson

Selection, editorial matter and Introduction © Margaret Bell and Kate Wilson 2003
Other chapters (in order) © Christine Skinner; Nick Frost and Brid Featherstone;
Liza Bingley Miller and Arnon Bentovim; Dorothy Heard; Una McCluskey;
Christopher Clulow and Chistopher Vincent; Jane Batchelor; Stephanie Petrie;
Margaret Bell; Dorota Iwaniec; Kate Wilson and Ian Sinclair 2003

All rights reserved. No reproduction, copy or transmission of
this publication may be made without written permission.

No paragraph of this publication may be reproduced, copied or
transmitted save with written permission or in accordance with
the provisions of the Copyright, Designs and Patents Act 1988,
or under the terms of any licence permitting limited copying
issued by the Copyright Licensing Agency, 90 Tottenham Court
Road, London W1T 4LP.

Any person who does any unauthorised act in relation to this
publication may be liable to criminal prosecution and civil
claims for damages.

The authors have asserted their rights to be identified
as the authors of this work in accordance with the
Copyright, Designs and Patents Act 1988.

First published 2003 by
PALGRAVE MACMILLAN
Houndmills, Basingstoke, Hampshire RG21 6XS and
175 Fifth Avenue, New York, N.Y. 10010
Companies and representatives throughout the world

PALGRAVE MACMILLAN is the global academic imprint of the Palgrave Macmillan
division of St. Martin's Press, LLC and of Palgrave Macmillan Ltd. Macmillan® is a
registered trademark in the United States, United Kingdom and other countries.
Palgrave is a registered trademark in the European Union and other countries.

ISBN 0–333–92264–6

This book is printed on paper suitable for recycling and
made from fully managed and sustained forest sources.

A catalogue record for this book is available from the British Library.

10 9 8 7 6 5 4 3 2 1
12 11 10 09 08 07 06 05 04 03

Printed and bound in Great Britain by
Creative Print & Design (Wales), Ebbw Vale

Contents

Notes on the Contributors

Jane Batchelor is Senior Lecturer in Social Work at the University of Bath. She is a qualified social worker with a long-standing interest in stepfamily issues. She was a founder member of the National Stepfamily Association and in 1994 co-authored *Understanding Families* with Donna Smith and Brian Dimmock.

Margaret Bell is Senior Lecturer in Social Work and Director of Graduate Social Work Research Studies at the University of York. She is author of the book, *Child Protection: Families and the Conference Process*, and her teaching and research interests are in child care and protection, multidisciplinary work, domestic violence and looked-after children. She has worked as a senior social worker in the health field, more recently as a children's guardian.

Arnon Bentovim is a child and family psychiatrist. He also trained as a psychoanalyst and a family therapist. He worked at the Great Ormond Street Children's Hospital in London and the Tavistock Clinic in London for many years until 1994, when he founded the London Child and Family Consultation Service. Here he introduced a family approach to child mental health problems, researching and developing approaches to assessment and therapeutic work.

Liza Bingley Miller is a social worker now working independently and is involved with a number of projects including Making Research Count (University of York), the Attachment Research Group, the PQ in Child Care and the Systems-Centred Therapy Training Programme at the University of York. She is Chair of the City of York Adoption and Permanency Panel and a UKCP-registered family therapist.

Christopher Clulow is Director of the Tavistock Marital Studies Institute, where he works as a senior couple psychotherapist, teacher and researcher. He has directed action research projects on the transitions to parenthood and out of marriage, and published extensively on marriage and couple work for professional and lay readers.

Brid Featherstone is the NSPCC Reader in Applied Childhood Studies at the University of Huddersfield and is a qualified social worker. She has published in the areas of gender relations and child welfare. She is currently writing a book on *Family Life and Family Support: A Feminist Analysis* to be published by Palgrave in 2003.

Nick Frost is Senior Lecturer in Continuing Education at the University of Leeds. He has been a social worker, project leader and a policy officer in a number of social services settings. He is also active in the voluntary child-care sector. He has published extensively in the fields of child welfare, family support and continuing professional education.

Dorothy Heard is a psychoanalytic psychotherapist in private practice and Honorary Research Fellow in the Department of Psychology at the University of Leeds. She trained under John Bowlby as a child psychiatrist at the Tavistock Clinic in London, where she worked with parents of disturbed children and developed Bowlby's attachment theory. She has a number of publications in the fields of immunohaematology and psychotherapy and in the development of attachment theory, including *The Challenge of Attachment for Caregiving* in collaboration with Brian Lake.

Dorota Iwaniec is Professor of Social Work and Director of the Institute of Child Care Research at Queen's University Belfast. Her main research interests are in neglect, emotional abuse, behaviour management, and the whole area of parenting including parent training. She has been involved in research for over 25 years and has finished a 20-year follow-up study on 'children who faild to thrive'. She has published extensively in the area of child care.

Una McCluskey is Senior Lecturer in Social Work and Director of the group psychotherapy programme at the University of York. Her practice, research and publications focus on the dynamics of interaction between couples, families and groups. She has been involved in the York University Attachment Research Group since the 1980s and is currently looking at the dynamics of attachment as they manifest in group interaction.

Stephanie Petrie is Lecturer in Social Work at the University of Liverpool. She has worked as a social worker and manager in the statutory and independent sectors. Her research interests lie in examining the impact of mixed-economy welfare policies, funding and structures on services for children and their families. She is currently involved in a Department of Health funded research project into teen pregnancy.

Ian Sinclair worked in the steel industry, probation, the Home Office research unit, social work and counselling before becoming Director of Research at the National Institute of Social Work. He moved from there to be Professor of Social Work at the University of York, where he is currently co-director of the Social Work Research and Development Unit.

Christine Skinner is Lecturer in Social Policy at the University of York. Her recent research has explored how parents coordinate childcare with employment commitments and she is currently writing a report for the Joseph Rowntree Foundation. She is interested in all aspects of policy relating to families with children including social security benefits and tax credits, welfare to work agenda, and parental obligations following relationship breakdown.

Christopher Vincent is a senior couple psychotherapist and clinical lecturer in marital studies at the Tavistock Marital Studies Institute, where he coordinates the Institute's research and publications activities. His clinical and research interests have focused on work with individuals and couples who are separating or divorcing, and he currently is part of the research team looking at the relationship between attachment patterns and couples' conflict management tactics.

Kate Wilson is Professor of Social Work at Nottingham University, where she directs the Centre for Social Work. She has published widely in the field of child welfare and therapeutic work with children and adults. Her books include two jointly authored books *Play Therapy*, and an edited second edition (with Adrian James) of *The Child Protection Handbook*. She has worked as a probation officer, social worker and as a mediator and counsellor.

Introduction

Margaret Bell and Kate Wilson

The idea for this book came from our recognition, as teachers and researchers in the field of social care, of the range of situations in which practitioners become involved in working with families, and the substantial developments which have taken place in this work in the last decade. Equally, we were conscious that despite specialist books on particular methods of intervention (approaches to family therapy being the most obvious) we lacked a book which would bring together policy and practice accounts of these different approaches and place them within a framework of developments in contemporary family policy. The present edited book is an attempt to fill this gap.

It is intended as a practice guide for practitioners and trainees from social work, health and related professions who work with children and families and who do not have specialist training in, for example, family or couples therapy. It brings together policy, legal and theoretical and practice approaches to working with families in a variety of forms and contexts. Part I of the book considers broad policy issues in relation to understanding families, and some of the theoretical accounts and structural changes in the family which have informed these, and which have buttressed developments in working with families. In Part II, theoretical frameworks are offered for understanding, assessing and working with families. The third part then considers policies, theories and practice skills involved in working with families in different contexts and with different problems. These have been chosen either because they are clearly areas where there have been considerable recent developments in policy and practice (such as working with stepfamilies or in the field of domestic violence), or because from our experience in working with students and practitioners the problems themselves pose particular challenges for practice (such as those addressed by Petrie in her chapter on working with families where there are child protection issues). The chapters in this third part focus on situations commonly encountered in practice. These reflect diverse family structures and problems and consider the impact on family members of these, whether arising from parental conflict, the need to negotiate new family structures, or the need to work with neglect, abuse or domestic violence.

Historical Background to Family Services

Historically, the primary aim of those who implemented the recommendations of the Seebohm committee in 1971 was the creation of a *family* social work service. The original conception of the larger, wide-ranging local authority social service departments envisaged a progressive, universal service 'available to all and with wide community support' (Parton, 2001). It depended on cooperation between local authorities and parents, and reflected the view that State and family could work together to ensure children had the appropriate conditions in which to develop. The era was one of considerable optimism both about the strength and formative power of families and, where families were deficient, about the ability of judicious professional interventions to effect improvements in the lives of children and families.

This optimism in the power of the State to intervene effectively, either in enabling children and families to remain together or by bringing the individual child into State care, began increasingly to falter from the mid-1970s onwards in the face of a variety of different critiques. These emerged in part from the growth of the women's movement and the recognition that families could be places where women and children suffered a range of abuse at the hands of men, which might make them not havens but places to take refuge from. Much of the initial concern around domestic violence in fact centred on the position of women, and it was not until roughly a decade later that attention began to focus on the plight of children, first through well-publicised cases of physical and emotional abuse and neglect (the subject of over 30 inquiries in the 1980s) and then from growing recognition of sexual abuse, highlighted in the Cleveland Inquiry (Secretary of State for Social Services, 1988).

These critiques, as Freeman (1983) and Franklin (1995) variously point out, suggested the need to disaggregate the interests of individual family members from those of the family as a whole, and saw the development of a range of practice and practical initiatives which focused on, for example, the need for women to be protected from domestic violence (an issue explored by Bell in Chapter 9). Greatest attention, however, during this period was paid to the need to improve the skills of childcare professionals, particularly social workers, who were seen as having failed to protect children through a mixture of incompetence, naiveté and a failure to concentrate on the interests of children as opposed to their parents. Recommendations in a number of well-publicised inquiries emphasised the importance of using the legal mandate to protect children, and the need to improve the recognition of signs and symptoms of abuse and skills in interdisciplinary working.

A rather different set of concerns and approaches to interpreting events emerged in the Cleveland Inquiry, in which in addition to the failures of social service practitioners and the inadequacies of inter-professional cooperation the diagnostic techniques and approaches of the medical profession came under criticism for the first time. Not only did events suggest that sexual abuse could occur in 'ordinary' families, not just those marginalised by poverty and inadequacy, but also the power of the State to intervene in family life came powerfully into question. Events in Cleveland thus triggered 'a major set of debates around patriarchy and male power' (Parton, 2001) and opened up for the first time political arguments around gender and the need for a greater emphasis on individual rights within a reformed statutory framework. From the early 1990s on, the dominant discourse began to be framed less in socio-medical and more in socio-legal terms.

These developments form the backdrop for the major legislative changes which were taking place, culminating in the Children Act 1989. They also have a significant impact on practice developments in working with families, and the new range of initiatives and approaches to working which have occurred in the last decade. Much research and practice concern has focused on the need to ensure the care and protection of children while at the same time recognising and enhancing family autonomy and parental responsibility, a tension to which Petrie returns in Chapter 8. The broader implications of the changes in the priorities and boundaries of the welfare state have also affected practice with individuals within families, as the first two chapters in the book suggest (Skinner, Chapter 1; Frost and Featherstone, Chapter 2) through, for example, the involvement in family breakdown. We consider first the legislative framework, before discussing the common themes of the different approaches to working with families and explaining how the book is organised.

The legislative framework

The legislative framework for working with families with children is very broad. However, the Children Act 1989 is focal in determining policy and provision for children and families in need. It consolidated earlier childcare legislation, and marked a shift in policy from a preoccupation with prevention of reception into care to a broader concept of family support. In the words of Wendy Rose:

> The Children Act places a duty on local authorities to safeguard and promote the welfare of children in their area who are in need and, subject to that duty, to promote the upbringing of such children by their families. The new emphasis in sec. 17 is for local authorities to work with or facilitate the work of others. (Rose, 1991, p. ix)

The Act has been described as 'the most radical legislative reform to children's services this century' (Lord Mackay, 1991). It is based on the principle of promoting children's welfare, and marks the bringing together of public and private law to ensure that children's welfare is paramount, and that their needs are approached in the same way. Healthy child development is seen as being the key to their welfare, and local authorities are required to take a corporate approach to providing services. The guidance supporting the Act (*Working Together*, DoH, 1991) stressed the importance of working collaboratively across agencies. Sec. 27 specifically refers to the need for Social Service Departments to cooperate with education, housing and health to develop imaginative and flexible services and recent research has advocated the greater use of this section (see Brandon *et al.*, 1999).

Another fundamental principal of the Act is that children are best looked after by their families. Parents are seen as having continuing responsibility for the care of their children, and the aim is, wherever possible, to maintain their care at home. Compulsory proceedings should be avoided and parents should be involved in all decision-making processes, such as reviews and child protection conferences, and involved as partners in any intervention within their families. The children should also be consulted and their religion, culture, ethnicity and language given due attention. In Chapter 2 Frost and Featherstone describe in detail some of the ways in which family structures are changing, and the need to work with diversity in relation to ethnicity, as well as changing family structures, has been and continues to be a challenge to local authorities and practitioners.

Despite the focus on children's welfare needs, mainstream social work with children in the early part of the 1990s was dominated by Sec. 47 enquiries relating to concerns about protecting children from harm. The publication of *Child Protection: Messages from Research* (DoH, 1995a) drew widespread attention to the fact that the preoccupation with significant harm meant that large numbers of children in need were not being offered help. Also, there was continuing uncertainty about how to work in partnership with families – especially where abuse was taking place – and the Challenge of Partnership (DoH, 1995b) was issued to provide a more detailed framework for working in partnership with families. Research evaluating the involvement of parents in decision-making has broadly supported partnership attempts (Thoburn *et al.*, 1995), although the difficulties of working in partnership in child protection have increasingly received attention (Bell, 1999; Corby *et al.*, 1996).

The introduction of Children's Services Plans in 1996 urged local authorities to reconsider their use of scarce resources, and the ensuing debate resulted in a sharper focus on Sec. 17(10) of the Act which states that a child is 'in need' if

(a)   he is unlikely to achieve or maintain, or have the opportunity of achieving or maintaining, a reasonable standard of health or development without the provision for him of services by a local authority;

(b)   his health or development is likely to be significantly impaired, or further impaired, without the provision for him of such services; or

(c)   he is disabled.

At the same time as the refocusing debate was taking place, New Labour came to power, adding their momentum to a broad policy shift to family support and early intervention. One feature of New Labour's family policy has been the recognition of the important role of poverty in family dysfunction, and accordingly their term of office has witnessed a number of attempts to eradicate child poverty by, for example, the new Children's Tax Credit and by measures to encourage employment (including of lone mothers). Another has been a preoccupation with promoting stable (married) families through good parenting and community regeneration. Attempts to address social exclusion – especially of young people disaffected by school – are increasingly being accorded high priority as problems in schools escalate. In 1998 the *Quality Protects* (DoH, 1998a) programme was launched, designed to raise the standards of care for children who are vulnerable and/or looked-after children by specifying eight objectives for local authorities to meet. These objectives include ensuring that children are securely attached to their caregivers, gain maximum life-chance benefits from educational opportunities, that they enter adulthood adequately prepared, and so on. The clear intention is that health, education and social care organisations should work together to achieve these objectives, and agencies only receive money if they evidence that they achieve targets – including joint work. To further this 'joined-up agenda', the White Paper *Modernising Health and Social Services* (DoH, 1998b) increased the original eight children's services objectives to eleven.

There is some evidence that *Quality Protects* is raising expectations and improving practice. For example, in the first year of the programme more young people were maintained in the system until aged 18, looked-after children had fewer moves in the care system, and more were adopted. By 2000 new arrangements to develop community-based preventive services to give vulnerable children and young people the stability and support they need were put in place, including the new Children's Fund to support new partnerships to provide preventative services for 5–13-year-olds in deprived communities, Sure Start to support pre-school children in deprived neighbourhoods, and the Connexions Service to provide teenage children with focused one-to-one personal support in making the transition to parenthood. Some of these initiatives, such as the National Childcare Strategy and Sure Start are discussed by Skinner in Chapter 1. Wilson and Sinclair, in the concluding chapter of this book, describe some of the ways in which the needs of looked-after children are being supported. However, as Iwaniec and Hill (2000) pointed out, although family support is the primary policy matter facing child welfare in the twenty-first century, there continues to be debate about what is meant by the concept and whether it works in practice. Attempts to evaluate family support still fail to evidence the effectiveness of programmes by examining the outcomes for children, although there is evidence to suggest that, at the very least, the families appreciate some family support interventions, such as family centres (McDonald and Williamson, 2002). Clearly there is a need for a rigorous evaluation of what works for which children in what circumstances, including what is cost-effective.

One of the key requirements of *Quality Protects* is the proper assessment of children and families, and so new guides for assessment and working together have become an important part of the work of the Department of Health in developing practice guidance. In relation to practice with children and families, the recent documents *Working Together* (DoH, 2000), and the *Framework for Assessment* (DoH, 2001) have reiterated the need for a child-centred, inter-agency approach to assessments and intervention taking into account the wishes and feelings of the child. Good assessments are seen as being a key aspect of the decision-making process, enabling quicker decisions to be made on the basis of an early initial assessment (within seven days of referral), with more detailed core assessments being reserved for the more complex work. In this way children in need can be identified and provided with preventative services within the community, while the needs of children in danger of suffering significant harm will be formally assessed by all the agencies involved. Core assessments, to be completed in 35 days, will be based on judgments of children's needs across seven dimensions – health, education, emotional and behavioural development, identity, family and social relationships, social presentation and self-care skills and upon the domains of parenting capacity – ensuring safety, stimulation, emotional warmth and guidance and boundaries and environmental and family factors, such as housing, income and community resources. The importance of an underpinning knowledge base in child development and the theoretical framework of attachment theory is emphasised, and this forms the theoretical base of this book and of the practice initiatives presented in the practice section.

The assessment documents commissioned by the Department of Health are being refined so that they can also be used for looked-after children to replace the existing LAC (Looked after Children) materials. The new records will comprise the Integrated Children's System and should be available in electronic form for practitioners and agencies to access and use. Their existence, of course, does not ensure that they will be used, or that the quality of assessments will improve – but having a common framework with agreed dimensions of development and domains of capacity has to be a step forward. A number of assessment tools have been designed to encourage and enable practitioners to develop their assessment skills within the domains of the new framework, and one of these, The Family Assessment, is presented by Miller and Bentovim in Chapter 3.

Working Together (DoH, 2000) further develops the framework for inter-agency work, paying particular attention to ways in which agencies should work together before and after the initial child protection conference, and to alternative methods for working with families where children's protection can be guaranteed (Horwarth, 2001). Where children's safety is assured, family support meetings or family group conferences are seen as more appropriate decision-making fora than child protection conferences. These meetings place an emphasis on inter-agency involvement in the ongoing intervention, and on the role of families in determining what the issues are for them, and what resources they want to help them with their parenting (see Marsh and Crow, 1998; Wilson and Bell, 2001.) The emphasis on a welfare-based service, it is hoped, will promote opportunities for preventive and therapeutic work, and will be experienced by families as supportive. While the focus on involving families in assessments and interventions is welcome, stepparents (whether resident or non-resident) are rarely referred to in the framework, other than by occasional references to caregivers and significant adults. This is an omission, given the changing structure of families discussed in the first section of this book, and we redress the balance by including two chapters on working with families experiencing partner breakdown. In Chapter 6 , Clulow and Vincent explore some of the issues in working with families who are divorcing, and in Chapter 7 Bachelor highlights the importance of working with stepparents, and suggests some ways forward.

A number of questions still remain. One is about how adequately the developments in family support are being resourced (Tunstill, 1996) and, related to this, the basis on which decisions are made about appropriate service provision. Even though child protection services remain chronically underfunded they have to receive priority, and, within that, priority is accorded to cases of physical and sexual abuse.Wilding and Thoburn's (1997) study found that although physical neglect was the largest category of maltreatment, such cases were the lowest in resource allocation for family support. The lack of attention accorded to emotional abuse and neglect is a further area of concern, and is discussed by Iwaniec in Chapter 10 of this book. Finally, also of concern is the degree to which social workers can feel safe in relinquishing their investigative policing role in the light of media criticism (see for example the inquiry into the death of Victoria Climbie) allied to the lack of skills they feel they have in providing family support. In Chapter 8, Petrie discusses some of the practice issues for practitioners working in the field of child protection.

In addition to the legislation specifically laying out statutory responsibilities for childcare and protection, in particular the Children Act 1989, other recent legislative changes are having considerable impact upon the organisation and provision of services to children and families. The implications for social work of the National Health Service and Community Care Act 1990, and the Health and Social Care Act 2001, requiring local authorities to draw up plans of services for the community in conjunction with health authorities and trusts have yet to be felt. The injunction to work in partnership should lead to more joint-funded projects, and to greater involvement of health professionals in completing the core assessment and in ongoing child protection work. Legislation relating to services for people with disabilities, such as the Carers and Disabled Children Act 2000, has enhanced their opportunities for involvement in assessments and for choice in the provisions of services. The provisions of the Education Acts of 1981 and 1997 in relation to assessing and statementing children with special needs and in promoting joint working initiatives in school inclusion schemes should also lead to closer working relationships and to schools taking an enhanced role in community regeneration. In the field of criminal justice, the Family Law Act, 1996, is impacting particularly on families where there is domestic violence, and the Housing Act, 1996, (sec. 18.9) is relevant in entitling people who are homeless and in priority to temporary accommodation. Bell in Chapter 9 comments on some of the issues for families experiencing domestic violence. In so far as looked-after children are concerned, the Children Leaving Care Act 2000 requires local authorities to make provision for young people leaving care, and the Adoption Bill currently before Parliament is requiring local authorities and adoption agencies to undertake a number of reforms to reduce delay, increase the numbers of children adopted and make the process of assessment more transparent. A feature of much of the legislation mentioned is the emphasis on rights – rights for information, for involvement in decision-making in both the planning and delivery of services, for choice and to be heard. The rights agenda is underpinned by the Data Protection Act 1998, and the Human Rights Act 1998, the implications of which are yet to be felt but are likely to be far-reaching in the areas of personal health and social services.

Having considered the legislation which informs policy and practice in working with families, we now consider briefly the theoretical frameworks for understanding and working with families, and how these in turn have formed the basis for the selection of chapters in the book.

Key issues in working with families

Virtually all approaches to working with families see the family as an interactive system, consisting of a group of people which includes at least two generations who are related by biological and/or legal ties and expectations of loyalty and trust. All Western societies (and most worldwide) share the expectation that the family performs certain tasks, for example taking responsibility for the emotional, educational, social and physical development of children, and providing for the emotional well-being and personal growth of the adults. The tasks relating to the fulfilment of these responsibilities alter depending on the life-cycle of the family. In a family with young children, for example, attention is likely to focus on nurturing and ensuring their safety, while with adolescents, attention will shift to helping them establish a secure sense of self and to making a successful transition into adulthood. This developmental perspective means also that particular events, such as a child running away from home, or mismanagement of diet, will have different implications, and be interpreted differently, depending on the family's life stage and the age of the child.

The way in which families carry out these tasks, functions and responsibilities varies according to the individual family's culture, ethnic group and religion, the balance of power within the family, and the values, attitudes, traditions and past experiences of the adult members of it. These functions are carried out in a social context, and are buttressed by other people and networks of extended family and friends and a wider framework of educational, statutory and medical services (issues addressed in the first section of this book). All families have properties which include the structure, boundaries, patterns and processes of communication of the particular family; the relationship between the different subsystems within the family, and between it and the wider world; and family rules and the way in which individual family members give meaning to their experiences. People within the family are involved in a continual series of negotiations in which the response of one individual to another will in turn influence that person (Barker, 1990; Bentovim, 2001).

This systemic framework informs, whether explicitly or implicitly, all the forms of intervention described in this book, and is used to make sense of the problems and difficulties encountered by individuals, sub-groups or the family as a whole. They are also based, as some of the above implies, on a developmental perspective. This suggests that change in families is inevitable as families move through different stages of their life-cycle. It is also axiomatic that some way of conceptualising these processes is necessary for practitioners to make sense of this developmental momentum and to understand both how these changes are understood and experienced at an emotional level within the family and the processes involved in family dissolution and reconstruction. Theoretical perspectives which have been found to be helpful in understanding families are therefore set out in Part II of the book.

The three chapters in this part suggest a theoretical framework which can provide the basis for understanding and conceptualising the emotional experiences of families at different stages of their life-cycle, and the ways in which assessments of families may be helpfully and supportively carried out. Practitioners will be familiar with the main tenets of attachment theory, and accustomed to applying these to their work with children and families. What is less familiar is how attachment theory can be extended to an understanding of adult relationships within the family. Heard in her chapter on the attachment dynamic (Chapter 4) builds on Bowlby's original concept of two goal-directed systems of care-seeking and care-giving, which essentially focus on adult–child interactions. She identifies two further goal-directed systems of sexuality and companionable interaction as the other main motivational forces which bring adult human beings into relationship with each other. McCluskey in the following chapter (Chapter 5) integrates this into a framework of understanding the emotional dynamics of family life and the way in which themes and concerns are carried forward transgenerationally.

Although, as we suggest above, there are common themes in working with families, the extent to which individual chapters in the final third part emphasise one or more inevitably varies depending on the context in which the intervention is taking place. The application of the more familiar concepts of attachment theory is considered more or less explicitly through-out the chapters in the third part. Wilson and Sinclair, for example, in Chapter 11 develop a model of successful fostering which includes an analy-sis of how, in showing 'responsive parenting', foster carers must handle the attachment behaviour of foster children appropriately. The chapters by Clulow and Vincent, and that by Batchelor (Chapters 6 and 7), focus on the interactive processes between the adult couple, the importance of under-standing the impact on current relationships of past experiences and the need to clarify issues of family history and boundaries in working with step-families. Family boundaries are also at the core of much of the work in foster care, where issues of contact between foster children and their birth and foster families are a key focus of concern. Chapter 10 by Iwaniec considers, as well as diagnosis and assessment, intergenerational issues in working with neglect. Petrie in Chapter 8 and Bell in Chapter 9 consider developments in working with families, and the way in which different perspectives (for example a feminist or systems perspective) may have an impact on the way in which the intervention is conducted.

How the parts and chapters are organised

Part I presents the policy context within which work with families is under-taken, and discusses some of the impacts on practice of changing family structures. Skinner in the opening chapter provides an account of the devel-opment of New Labour's family policy, describes the major shifts that have taken place and raises some questions about the possible implications for social work practice. She tracks some of the ways in which New Labour's policy developed from strengthening marriage and families to one more firmly embedded in improving the life chances and opportunities for chil-dren. A significant focus is on child poverty, and she describes how the promotion of work, changes to the tax and benefit system and ways of reconciling work and family life are seen as the best route out of poverty. She then outlines the means by which the government makes support avail-able to all families with children, such as children's tax credit, the national childcare strategy and parental leave, before looking at the measures aimed specifically at poor families and children who are socially excluded. Her account of the benefits and community initiatives available provide a valu-able source of information for practitioners working with families in need by describing specific benefits such as income support, and initiatives such as Sure Start.

In Chapter 2, Frost and Featherstone develop and flesh out the social context within which practitioners operate by introducing some theoretical accounts of family which have influenced political thinking, and by provid-ing more detailed information about family and household structure and social inequality. Three contemporary approaches are presented: communi-tarianism, as developed by Etzioni; the risk theories of Giddens and Beck and Beck-Gernsheim, and feminist theories. The theoretical debate about family and parenting, about family roles and the respective responsibilities of men and women is threaded throughout, with useful commentary on the ways in which political thinking and New Labour policies have been developed in response. The second half of the chapter brings together a range of material collated from official statistics which vividly portrays the extent of changes in household structure and formation which have a major impact upon the social environment and family patterns within which practitioners operate. This is followed by an account of the extent of social inequalities and poverty, a serious problem which is correlated with other dimensions of difference – notably ethnicity and lone parenthood.

Part II develops the theoretical frameworks for understanding and assessing families, concluding with a discussion and case illustration of a model of therapeutic intervention. Taken as a whole, the three chapters show the integration of theory into family assessment and intervention. The first chapter by Bingley Miller and Bentovim presents a well-developed model for assessing families which is built upon and takes further the new Assessment Framework. They begin by locating the family within the wider social context and exploring some of the social and economic factors which need to be considered as an integral part of making that assessment. They then outline the model of family functioning on which this assessment is structured, based upon systemic thinking, describe the skills and methods for working with families during the assessment process, and then outline the Recording Form they have devised which forms the central instrument for making a systemic assessment.

The second chapter in this part, that by Heard, describes significant developments of Bowlby's attachment theory. This was extended by the author and Lake (Heard and Lake, 1986, 1987) in order to give practitioners within the caring professions guidance when working with adult clients who are in parental roles, or with adults more interested in life with their peers than with their parents or those of their parents' generation. Having reviewed some of the earlier work on attachment theory, she describes the part played in adulthood by companionable and exploratory interest sharing relationships with peers, and by affectional sexual relationships, through a detailed discussion of the features of the concept of the attachment dynamic and the different instinctive systems of which it is composed. This includes a consideration of some of the defensive strategies by which individuals maintain relationships which are experienced as conflict and fear-driven, and are shown to be insecure. The final section of the chapter focuses on different ways in which practitioners can apply the theory in their work with families.

McCluskey's chapter describes in detail a way of working with families which she has devised and used successfully in conjunction with Bingley Miller. Theme-focused family therapy addresses the emotional world of families by organising family sessions around a central key theme, determined by information provided by the family members themselves. The process of doing this, and the skills required are carefully described in a way which makes the method accessible to practitioners working with disturbed families in a range of settings and situations. A case study, and the format by which information is recorded and used, illustrate the method. Theme-focused family therapy derives its theoretical foundation from attachment theory and the attachment dynamic and the theory of living systems, and in discussing this and applying it to the case, McCluskey provides an excellent model for using theory to underpin practice.

Part III considers policies, theories and practice skills involved in working with different families and different problems. Each chapter considers relevant policy and research, discusses practice issues in working with families in these differing circumstances, and contains a brief case study or scenario to illustrate the discussion.

The section begins with two chapters focusing on adult partnerships and repartnering. Clulow and Vincent (Chapter 6) suggest that many of the disputes about children which professionals become involved with, such as contact and residence disputes, are centrally related to the adult partners' unresolved feelings about the ending of their relationship. They discuss the nature of the anxiety affecting adults who are going through separation and divorce, and draw on attachment theory and object relations theory to provide a conceptual base for working with couples in difficulty. Like others, such as McCluskey in this book, they see the way in which past losses have been experienced as highly relevant to how they are managed in the present, illustrating the impact of past trauma through a brief case vignette.

Batchelor in the next chapter discusses some of the difficulties in evaluating the research on stepfamilies, especially in relation to two key questions which concern policy-makers and professionals, namely outcomes for children who grow up in stepfamilies and the prevalence of child abuse by step-parents. The difficulties arise in part at least from problems in agreeing definitions of what a stepfamily is and the increased visibility of stepfamilies. She discusses seven key ways in which stepfamilies differ from nuclear families, some of the tasks which stepfamilies face as a result of these differences, and some of the ways in which practitioners can help both children and families. She stresses particularly the need for practitioners to remember the significance of stepfamily relationships when assessing children, in part because of the cursory mention given to steprelationships in the Framework of Assessment to which we referred earlier.

The remaining four chapters of this part focus on areas where practitioners are involved with families because of their statutory role. Petrie in Chapter 8 discusses the way in which the change of emphasis in child protection policies and practice is taking place in a system of welfare which has moved away from welfare state provision to a mixed economy of welfare. However, she argues that the elements of effective work with families where there are child protection concerns have been emerging through practice research and professional debate during the last three decades and remain relevant. This requires childcare professionals to focus on the child through direct communication and comprehensive ongoing development and attachment observations. The quality of the work with parents is also important, especially how to work openly and honestly in situations where adults may be threatening and aggressive. Finally, she suggests that the quality of inter-agency communication and joint work is especially critical in the current context of the fragmentation of the welfare state. These issues are illustrated in a case study which illustrates some of the elements of effective work in the current context.

Bell in Chapter 9 outlines the policy and legislative background to working with families who are experiencing domestic violence and presents research on the serious impacts on women and children. The ways in which the dominant theoretical frameworks – of feminism, systems theory and psychopathology – have informed practice are then discussed, with a useful account of current practice initiatives. The need for agencies to work together at primary, secondary and tertiary levels is well made, as is the welcome attention paid to the need to develop ways of working with men. A detailed account of some key issues in assessing safety, need and motivation to change in situations of domestic violence provides valuable guidance to practitioners, as do suggestions about the range of practice initiatives that are proving to work most effectively in preventing and addressing the problem.

Iwaniec, in Chapter 10, discusses issues in working with families who neglect their children. Apart from the pioneer work which she has undertaken in researching and working with families where there is neglect, this topic was chosen because it tends, as the author stresses, to be the most understudied and consequently the least understood of all forms of child maltreatment. The chapter considers some of the difficulties in definitions of neglect as a complex and multifaceted phenomena, practice issues which face professionals working with neglectful families, and concludes with a case study which illustrates some of the methods and services used in parent training and the processes involved in dealing with cases of neglect.

Finally, in Chapter 11, Wilson and Sinclair consider a rather different form of family, that of the foster family. They review the service, practice and professional considerations which need to be kept in mind in providing foster care, focusing on the needs of foster children and the perspectives of foster children and birth families, and consider the evidence which examines how successfully foster care meets its tasks. Some of the practice issues for professionals involved in working with foster families are explored, and a model of successful foster care developed from the authors' research (Sinclair *et al.*, in press; Wilson *et al.*, in press) is presented and illustrated by a brief case study.

References

Barker, P. (1990) *Basic Family Therapy*. Oxford: Blackwell Scientific.

Bell, M. (1999) 'Working in Partnership in Child Protection', *British Journal of Social Work*, vol. 29, pp. 437–55.

Brandon, M., Thoburn, J., Lewis, A. and Way, B. (1999) *Safeguarding children with the Children Act*. London: Stationery Office.

Bentovim, A. (2001) 'Working with Abusing Families', in K. Wilson and A. James, (eds), *The Child Protection Handbook*, London: Balliere Tindall.

Corby, B., Miller, M. and Young, L. (1996) 'Parental participation in child protection work; rethinking the rhetoric', *British Journal of Social Work*, 26, 4. pp 475–93.

Department of Health (DoH) (1991) *Working Together under the Children Act 1989: A Guide to Arrangements for Inter-Agency Cooperation for the Protection of Children from Abuse*. London: HMSO.

— (1995a) *Child Protection: Meassages from Research*. London: HMSO.

— (1995b) *The Challenge of Partnership in Child Protection: Practice Guide*. London: HMSO.

— (1998a) *Quality Protects: Framework for Action*. London: HMSO.

— (1998b) *White Paper: Modernising Health and Social Services*. London: HMSO.

— (2000) *Working Together to Safeguard and Promote the Welfare of Children*. London: HMSO.

— (2001) *Framework for the Assesment of Children in Need and their Families*. London: HMSO.

Franklin, B. (ed.) (1995) *A Comparative Handbook of Children's Rights*. London: Basil Blackwell.

Freeman, M. (1983) *The Rights and Wrongs of Children*. London: Francis Pinter.

Heard, D. H. and Lake, B. (1986) 'The Attachment Dynamic in Adult Life', *British Journal of Psychiatry*, vol. 149, pp. 430–9.

— (1997) *The Challenge of Attachment for Caregiving*. London: Routledge.

Howarth, J. (2001) (ed.) *The child's world: assessing children in need*. London: Jessica Kingsley.

Iwaniec, D. and Hill, M. (2000) *Child Welfare Policy and Practice*. London: Jessica Kingsley.

Marsh, P. and Croe, G. (1997) *Family group conferences in child welfare*. Oxford: Blackwell.

McDonald, G. and Williamson, E. (2002) *Against the Odds; an Evaluation of Child Family Support Services*. London: National Childrens Bureau and Joseph Rowntree Foundation.

Parton, N. (2001) 'Protecting Children: A Socio-Historical Analysis', in K. Wilson and A. James (eds), *The Child Protection Handbook*. London: Balliere Tindall.

Rose, W. (1992) *Patterns and outcomes in child placement: messages from research*. London: HMSO.

Secretary of State for Social Services (1988) *Report of the Inquiry into Child Abuse in Cleveland*. Cmnd 412, London: HMSO.

Sinclair, I., Gibbs, I. and Wilson, K. (in press) 'Matches and Mismatches: the contribution of carers and children to the success of foster placements', *British Journal of Social Work*.

Thoburn, J., Lewis, A., Shemmings, D. (1995) *Paternalism or partnership? Family involvement in the child protection process*. London: HMSO.

Tunstill, J. (1996) 'Family Support: Past, Present and Future Challenges', *Child and Family Social Work*, 1, 3, pp. 151–158.

Wilding, J. and Thoburn, J. (1997) 'Family Support Plans for Neglected and Emotionally Maltreated Children', *Child Abuse Review*, vol. 6(5), pp. 343–56.

Wilson, K. and Bell, M. (2000) *An evaluation of family group conferences*. York: University of York.

Wilson, K., Sinclair, I. and Gibbs, I. (in press) 'A Kind of Loving: a model of effective foster care', *British Journal of Social Work*.

PART I

The Social, Political and Welfare Context for Working with Families

1

New Labour and Family Policy

Christine Skinner

Introduction

Labour became the first government in the UK ever to set out an *explicit* family policy. Their aspirations and plans were contained within a 1998 discussion document *Supporting Families* (Home Office, 1998). However, some of the plans were already launched or under consultation (FPSC, 1999; Fox-Harding, 2000) and, overall, a coherent approach to family policy was not presented. Rather, the strength of the document lay in its demonstration that family policy is a new and important agenda for Labour. What has followed is a series of cross-cutting initiatives directed at families with children and an explicit commitment made in 1999 to eradicate child poverty.

This is an important time to be considering family policy as Labour's welfare strategy makes it clear that they are willing to partly share the costs and burdens of parenthood. Moreover, the Labour government has been highly active in reforming welfare systems to the advantage of families with children. Consequently, there have been many fast and frequent changes. The changes are now at an interim stage and the most radical reforms to the tax and benefit systems are about to be put in place setting the format for delivering social assistance for the foreseeable future.

This chapter will describe policies that are specifically targeted at families with children. These include financial support for families in general as well as for poorer families, initiatives to reconcile work and family life and welfare-to-work policies. The aim is to set the family policy context, describe the major shifts that have taken place under the Labour government and raise questions about possible implications for social work practice. Before giving an account of family policy, the chapter will briefly discuss family change and the underpinning ideological stance of the previous Conservative and current Labour governments. Labour's family policies will then be outlined from two perspectives, general support for all families with children and support specifically aimed at poorer families with children. Finally, the possible implications for social work practice will be discussed.

The context of family change

In the last half of the twentieth century, the way in which families with children are constituted and the ways in which they live their lives have changed dramatically. The 'golden age' of the traditional two-parent family with the father a full-time earner and the mother a full-time carer has gone (McRae, 1999). There are now more lone-parent families as a result of high levels of relationship breakdown, more 'reordered' or 'stepfamilies' and considerable diversity in family forms and in relation to ethnicity, all requiring continuing attention from policy makers and practitioners. Later in this book, Chapters 6 and 7 by Clulow and Vincent and by Bachelor address the implications for practitioners of family breakdown. Yet, while family structures have changed, so too have the ways in which families earn money and provide care. The majority of mothers of working age are now in paid employment (65 per cent), though most are in part-time (60 per cent) rather than full-time work (40 per cent) (Twomey 2002, p. 121). Mothers are also returning to work earlier following the birth of a child (McRae, 1999; Dex, 1999; Daycare Trust, 1999). These changes are described more fully by Frost and Featherstone in the next chapter, but they form the important context within which government approaches to families with children can be understood and to which we now turn.

The Conservative governments' approach

Conservative governments under Thatcher and Major were committed to an ideology of 'traditional family values' and to non-interference in family life. They were also determined to cut the costs of state expenditure, to encourage self-help and independence from the State and to cut crime. In the late 1980s attention turned to lone-parent families as they seemed to exemplify a threat to both family values and to these policy objectives. For example, the numbers of lone-parent families were increasing but their dependency on social security benefits was rising even faster incurring considerable expenditure costs. Right-wing theorists such as Charles Murray also singled them out as prime candidates for the creation of a 'dependency culture'. It was argued that lone-parents' children were learning to rely on state benefits rather than learn the values of self-help and independence, and also that father absence in these families accounted for rises in crime rates and incivility in young men (Murray, 1990). Conservative politicians were heavily swayed by such arguments and, according to Lister (1996), an 'orgy of lone-parent bashing' took place at the 1993 Conservative Party Conference in which politicians held them responsible for inflating the costs of welfare, for damaging family values, for undermining marriage and for raising juvenile crime rates.

This hostility to lone-parent families characterises the Conservatives' family policy of the 1990s, but solving the 'problem' created a dilemma (Lister, 1996). Encouraging lone mothers into employment would help cut expenditure costs and promote independence from the State. However, this would conflict with upholding traditional family values. Consequently, a neutral stance on mothers' employment was adopted and despite some changes to the in-work benefit Family Credit, little was achieved to facilitate lone-parents' employment. Moreover, European Union initiatives to improve parental leave were actively blocked and calls by the Equal Opportunities Commission to develop a national childcare strategy were ignored (Bagilhole and Byrne, 2000). Consequently, the public nursery daycare provision that was available in England was allowed to reduce by nearly a half, from approximately 33,000 places to 17,000 places between 1989 and 1999 (Harker, 2000, p. 174). Legislative intervention into the working lives of families was vehemently opposed because of a desire to preserve a *laissez-faire* economic philosophy of open competition and unfettered and unregulated labour markets (Bagilhole and Byrne, 2000; Lister, 1996). Consequently, the UK lagged behind many EU countries in supporting parents to reconcile work and family life. Moreover, during the 18 years of Conservative government there was a dramatic increase in child poverty unique to the UK among Western industrial countries (Bradshaw, 2001; HM Treasury, 1999). Bradshaw argues this was a direct result of Conservative economic policies and the desire to reduce public expenditure costs. In 1995 the publication of *Messages from Research* (DoH, 1995) drew further attention to the lack of family support services for children in need. As described in the Introduction, the research studies presented in the publication were seminal in persuading local authorities to refocus children and family services away from a focus on child protection, to one addressing preventive work and family support. At the same time, awareness of the need to include environmental factors, such as poverty, in assessments of family need was being addressed by the Department of Health in their new *Framework for Assessment* (DoH, 2001). Later in the book, Iwaniec discusses the factors contributing to child neglect and explores some of the issues raised for practitioners in working with families who neglect their children.

Conservative policies therefore shifted the boundary of responsibility from the State to families, and where families failed to support themselves, family obligations tended to be enforced upon them (Lister, 1996; Fox-Harding 1996, 2000). This is exemplified in the enforcement of child support payments, the measures in the criminal justice system which held parents responsible for their children's misdemeanours, and to some extent within the Children Act 1989 where parental rights were replaced with parental responsibilities (Fox-Harding, 2000). Despite promoting family values, Conservative governments did very little to directly help families with children. Indeed, additional financial support available to the poorest lone-parent families dependent upon Income Support was withdrawn. However, it fell to the new Labour government to enact this policy (discussed below). As Lister (1996) states, it was 'Family politics rather than family policies' which thrived throughout the early 1990s. As will be shown, the same critique cannot be so easily made of the Labour government's approach to families with children.

The Labour Government's approach

Historically, the Labour Party has not promoted 'the family' nor has it been part of their political identity, although in a 1989 Labour policy review proposals were made to help women return to work and to reconcile work and family life (Coote *et al.*, 1990). While many of these proposals are evident in current Labour policy, it is not a simple matter to identify any consistent ideological approach to families. It has been argued that Labour adopted a similar stance to the Conservatives in that, in the mid-1990s, their ideological approach contained a 'family values-type rhetoric' in which there was a preoccupation with promoting stable (married) families and good parenting (Fox-Harding, 2000). Certainly, plans to strengthen marriage and parenting were contained within the *Supporting Families* document (Home Office, 1998). These were underpinned by a belief in the importance of stable 'married' families to the rearing of children and to building strong communities (*ibid.*, para. 4.1). As the Home Secretary Jack Straw stated in the Foreword to *Supporting Families*:

> Family life is the foundation on which our communities, our society and our country are built. Families are central to this Government's vision of a modern and decent society.

This emphasis on building stronger families and communities was also one of the key objectives identified for the Sure Start programme to support disadvantaged families with very young children (aged under three) (HM Treasury, 1999, p. 27) and, as described in the Introduction, became a focus for developing policy in Children's Services departments.

Whilst this demonstrates some coherence in thinking, proposals to strengthen marriage have been watered down over time and programmes to support good parenting have primarily been handed over to the voluntary sector. For example, Part II of the 1996 Family Law Act which aimed to save marriages was repealed for being ineffective (Press Release, Lord Chancellor's Department, 16 January 2001) and only minimal changes have been implemented to the Marriage Act (HO, 1999). The Married Couples Tax Allowance was also withdrawn in April 2000 and no policies on marriage were outlined in the 2001 Labour Party manifesto. Less rhetorical use is also being made of the link between strengthening families to create stronger communities. As Tony Blair stated in the manifesto, one aim for the second term is to ensure that 'all families are safe *in* their communities by tackling crime and its causes' (emphasis added).

Other similarities between Labour and Conservative ideological approaches have been identified in welfare policy. For example, Burden *et al.*, (2000) have argued that 'other-than' traditional families (such as lone parents) are pathologised by Labour in similar ways to the Conservatives through their political rhetoric and policies on welfare-to-work. Implicitly, therefore, it is not poverty *per se* that is the problem, but rather the failure of individuals to take advantage of the 'right' opportunities to be self-supporting and independent from the state. This has led others to argue that Labour's family support policies, such as welfare-to-work, were primarily a means of relieving pressure on the State (Bagilhole and Byrne, 2000; Land, 1999b; Daniel and Ivatts, 1998). Recent changes in adoption policy can also be viewed as a means of both relieving the State from permanent responsibility for children and of reducing the costs of care. The implications of such policies for working with families is considerable.

Certainly, an attack on child poverty started very badly with Labour carrying through the Conservative's plans to abolish extra social security benefits for lone parents. This was despite the fact that the UK had the highest rate of child poverty in the European Union, and internationally only the USA and Russia had higher rates (Bradshaw, 2001). Moreover, the government was slow to take any direct action (Bradshaw, 2000). It was not until March 1999, two years after entering office, that Tony Blair announced a commitment to eradicate child poverty in 20 years. The Treasury followed with a commitment to halve it in 10 years' time, and in 2000 a further commitment was made in a Public Service Agreement to reduce it by a quarter by 2004 (DWP, 2002). This commitment appears to have driven a clearer more focused rhetoric which has moved away from strengthening marriage and families *per se* to one more firmly embedded in improving the life chances and opportunities for children. As Tony Blair stated in the 2001 manifesto:

> My passion is to continue the modernisation of Britain in favour of hard-working families, so that all our children, wherever they live, whatever their background, have an equal chance to benefit from the opportunities our country has to offer and to share in its wealth.

The welfare agenda in relation to poorer families with children may therefore be altering in favour of a more traditional Labour position, the redistribution of wealth and resources, at least to children. Indeed, in 2001 the government expected that tax and benefit changes made in their first term (1997–2001) would lift 1.2 million children out of relative poverty. The latest evidence, however, shows that only 0.5 million children have been lifted out of relative poverty, a reduction from 4.4 million in 1996–97 to 3.9 million in 2000–01 (DWP, 2002; Brewer *et al.*, 2002). The reasons for this apparent lack of success are complex, but non-take-up of benefits and the fact that increases in benefit levels in 2000 have not yet been picked up in survey data are important factors (Bradshaw, 2002). That a large number of families continue to live in poverty presents serious issues for practitioners in relation to both family support and child protection, and the implications of this are discussed further by Iwaniec in Chapter 10.

Despite these changes, a consistent Labour ideology on 'the family' remains elusive. The diversity and the continuing uncertainty of family and working life have raised new questions about collective and individual responsibility and about the appropriate division between them for personal and social welfare (Land, 1999b, p. 17) Arguably, Labour have embarked on a project of attempting to rebalance public and private responsibilities and so it is futile to reduce family policies into a single ideological perspective. Rather, it is better to examine swathes of family policies on their own merits. The next section will provide a broad framework through which Labour's family policy agenda can be viewed. This will be from two distinct perspectives – supporting families with children in general, and specific initiatives for supporting poor families. This is not a fully comprehensive list and some of the initiatives can be seen to overlap.

General support for all families with children

As described, family policy is a new and important agenda for Labour and the focus on child poverty is particularly significant. Evidence shows that the risk of child poverty increases when a child lives in a lone-parent family, a workless family, a large family, a family with a disabled person, a family/household that is headed by someone from an ethnic minority community, a family where the mother is aged 30 or below, or aged 54 years and above, or a family where the youngest child is under five years' of age (DWP, 2002). Some of these issues are being tackled in policy initiatives which are promoting work as the best route out of poverty. These include, major changes to the tax and benefit system which offer higher levels of monetary support at the same time as building-in work incentives. There are also policies making it easier for parents to work and to reconcile work and family life. The next section outlines the support available to all families with children, followed by that for poor families. It is important to consider general policies because these will help stop more families falling into poverty, whereas policy targeted at poor families aims to lift them out of poverty.

Child Benefit

Universal Child Benefit (CB) is a direct payment by government to *all* families with children. Importantly, this benefit is normally paid to mothers and a review of the evidence over 20 years show that mothers tend to earmark this money to be spent on child-related expenditures (such as children's clothing and shoes) or that it is used for household items such as food and fuel which also benefit children as household members (Bradshaw and Stimson, 1997). Child Benefit is also valued by mothers as an independent income from husbands/partners (*ibid.*). Labour have increased the value of CB by over a quarter for the first child, and in April 2001 it was worth £15.50 per week for the first child and £10.35 for subsequent children. Labour's commitment to CB is part of the strategy on child poverty, as is the Children's Tax Credit.

Children's Tax Credit

The Children's Tax Credit replaced the Married Couples Tax Allowance in 2001. It is available to all families with children where the main earner is paid less than £40,000 per year. It is worth up to £520 per year and is paid by the Inland Revenue via the wage packet to the highest earning parent – most likely to be the father. By 2002, families with a child under the age of one will also be eligible for a 'Baby Tax Credit' (also worth up to £520 per year) (HM Treasury, Budget 2001).

This Children's Tax Credit has strengths and weaknesses. A strength is that it provides additional financial support specifically for families with children and is given irrespective of parents' marital or partnership status. In this respect it is more inclusive than Married Couples Tax Allowance and some five million families are estimated to be eligible (Labour Manifesto, 2001). Its weakness is that unlike Child Benefit it is not universal and therefore not all families with children will benefit. The eligibility criteria are that at least one parent has to be a taxpayer and families have to actively apply for it, the effect of which is that one million eligible families have not applied (*Observer*, Cash, 11 March 2001). More importantly it is an interim measure which will be subsumed within a new second generation of tax credits to be introduced in 2003. These new credits will significantly alter the ways in which families receive financial support in the future (see HM Treasury, 1999, 2000; Inland Revenue, 2001); this is discussed further in the next section.

National childcare strategy

The Labour government's 1998 consultation document *Meeting the Childcare Challenge* marked a sea-change in the status of childcare provision in the UK. The aim is to develop a national childcare strategy to improve the availability, affordability and quality of childcare in order to increase prosperity through employment, particularly for low-income and lone-parent families. Northern Ireland, Scotland and Wales were all to introduce their own strategies based on the same key aims. Plans were laid in England to expand services including more out-of-school places and guaranteeing a part-time place in early education for all three and four-year old children by 2004 (DEE Press Release, 26 January 2001). The strategy will be delivered through local-based Early Years Development and Childcare Partnerships (EYCDP) who will audit provision, assess demand, coordinate services and provide easily accessible information to all parents. According to the government the strategy has worked well in England with the creation of half a million more places for children and EYCDPs delivering their plans (DEE Press Release, 27 February 2001; DEE, 2000a). There are also other measures aimed specifically at children living in disadvantaged areas (discussed later).

Maternity, paternity and parental leave

In line with the aim to promote equality and choice, Labour also improved parental leave provision by reversing the opt-out of the Maastricht Treaty inherited from the Conservatives. Parents now have the right to three months' unpaid parental leave which can be taken anytime up to the child's fifth birthday and the right to leave for urgent family reasons. Other improvements include the extension of maternity leave from 14 to 26 weeks, a stepped rise in maternity pay up to £100 per week, entitlement to maternity pay for parents who are adopting children, and for the first time the introduction of two weeks' paid paternity leave for fathers (all to be implemented in 2003) (CYPU, 2001, p. 4). Effectively, this means mothers can take up to a year off around birth, though not all of this time will be paid. Through the government's *Work–Life Balance Campaign*, employers are being encouraged, but not directed, to produce best practice in the area of family-friendly employment practices (DEE, 2000).

This expansion in childcare provision and improvements in parental leave should make it easier for parents to reconcile work and childcare responsibilities, but problems remain; childcare services are highly fragmented, expensive and have poorly paid and poorly trained staff. Estimates show that while the gap in provision is closing, there is still only one registered place for every seven children in England under eight years old and there has been a substantial fall in the numbers of childminders (Daycare Trust, 2001). There are also concerns about whether children's needs and development in the early years are better served by parental care, whether childcare services will be of a sufficiently high quality and whether parents can activate a real choice to stay at home or to take up work. Moreover, further improvements in family-friendly employment practices have been hindered by opposition from representatives of British Industry (who objected to part-time working rights for mothers returning after birth), and from the government's own concerns to keep the costs of employment legislation down to preserve business competitiveness in a global economy.

Overall the policies above denote a commitment by the state to share the burden of parenting, but more importantly Labour have also embarked on a mission to end child poverty and they have made a longer-term commitment to tackle the social exclusion experienced by poorer families. These are now discussed.

Support for poor families with children

Support for poorer families with children goes beyond just alleviating financial poverty; rather policies aim to tackle multiple aspects of an individual's life that can lead to social exclusion. The concept of social exclusion is a contested one (Burchardt *et al.*, 1999) and it is not easy to make a distinction between it and poverty. At a basic level, poverty could simply refer to an inadequate level of income. Social exclusion on the other hand could be viewed as a 'shorthand label' where people or areas suffer from a combination of linked problems such as low incomes, unemployment, poor housing, high crime environments and racism (FPSC, 2000, p. 2). Social exclusion therefore describes more than just financial poverty by suggesting a combination of numerous coexistent problems which can often be related to living in particular areas and which prevent people from engaging in the normal activities of society. The key elements of policies supporting poor families are therefore to minimise the risks of some aspects of social exclusion, such as alleviating financial poverty through improved social security benefits for children, but also by promoting independence through employment, through neighbourhood regeneration and through specific programmes aimed at poor families to provide general health and welfare support in a mixed economy of care. The next section will cover some but not all of the strategies beginning with financial support for poor families, welfare-to-work strategies and targeted support for children.

Income Support and Working Families' Tax Credit

Financial support measures aimed specifically at poor families have included uprating the main subsistence benefit, Income Support (IS). While this is welcome, the increases in IS are not likely to be high enough to meet the needs of parents and children in full (FPSC, 2000, p. 10). This exemplifies that the government's major strategy on poverty is to encourage people back into work, 'giving people a hand up not a handout'. Top-up benefits to low-income working families have therefore been improved to make work pay. Thus, Family Credit (FC) was replaced with the more generous Working Families' Tax Credit (WFTC) in October 1999 (Disabled Persons' Tax Credit (DPCT) was also introduced on similar lines to replace Disability Working Allowance.) The government estimated that it will boost the incomes of 1.4 million low-income working families with children, about half a million more families than under FC (HM Treasury, 1999).

Childcare Tax Credit

As part of the strategy to make work pay, provisions for paying for formal childcare within WFTC (and Disabled Persons' Tax Credit: DPTC) was made more generous with the introduction of the Childcare Tax Credit (replacing the childcare disregard in Family Credit). The Childcare Tax Credit has been uprated twice in line with criticisms that the costs of childcare still operate as a significant barrier to taking up paid work, particularly for lone-parent families. Parents can receive 70 per cent of a fixed upper limit of £135 a week for one child and £200 for two or more, but they still have to fund 30 per cent of the actual costs and the credit is only available for registered formal care and not informal care provided by family and friends (the most commonly used childcare). In 2003 these measures will be replaced by payments for children and adults separately in two new credits, the Child Tax Credit and the Working Tax Credit for *working* adults only (whether they have children or not). Table 1.1 describes the current system and the reforms for 2003.

Child Tax Credit

The Child Tax Credit represents one single credit within which all benefits/tax credits *for children* will be subsumed, apart from Child Benefit, which will continue to be paid separately. Thus Child Tax Credit will contain the Children's Tax credits, and the children's allowances in Income Support and Working Families' and Disabled Persons' Tax Credit. This will be different from the current distinction between non-working and working families where the former are only eligible for Income Support and the latter for Working Families' or Disabled Persons' Tax Credit. Under the revised scheme all families with children will be eligible for the Child Tax Credit. The amount paid will vary depending upon income level (and number of children), requiring that employment status will have a bearing on the level of the credit. The latest figures show that the value of the Child Tax Credit and Child Benefit added together will be £26.50 per week for the first child in families with incomes of less that £50,000 a year and double that (£54.25) for families earning less than £13,000 per year (HM Treasury, 2002).

Working Tax Credit

The Working Tax credit is an adult-only credit and will be paid to all employed adults on low earnings whether they have children or not, the amount being higher for those with children. It replaces the adult allowances available in Working Families' and Disabled Persons' Tax credits and extends financial support to working households without children. The Treasury states that this credit will provide a guaranteed income of £237 per week for a family with one child and one earner working full-time on the minimum wage (HM Treasury, 2002).

Whilst the Child Tax Credit and Working Tax Credit appear separate from Income Support/Job Seekers' Allowance, they will nevertheless have an effect. In 2003, non-working families in receipt of Income Support or Job Seekers' Allowance will receive a personal adult payment under these benefits and child payments under the Child Tax Credit. Previously, all adult and child allowances would have been paid together within Income Support/Job Seekers' Allowance. For working families, they will receive Working Tax Credit for the adults and Child Tax Credit for the children (See table 1.1). In respect of childcare costs, the Childcare Tax Credit is likely to come under Working Tax Credit, but it will be paid to the main carer in the family and not necessarily to the person claiming Working Tax Credit.

The ultimate aims of these new credits are twofold. First to relieve child and family poverty, and second the Working Tax Credit (like its predecessor Working Families' and Disabled Persons' Tax Credits) also aims to increase work incentives and to make work pay. Another important element of the changes is the reorganisation of government departments to reflect their new responsibilities. The Inland Revenue is now responsible for delivering Child Benefit and all the Tax Credits, and the Department of Work and Pensions (previously the Department of Social Security) is concentrating on promoting work as the best route out of poverty for those people making

Table 1.1 Main financial support packages for families with children by family work status.

Current provision (2001)	Future provision (2003)
All families	
Child Benefit	Child Benefit
Low/middle-income working families	
Children's Tax Credit	Child Tax Credit (children only) *
Working Families' Tax Credit (or DPTC)	Working Tax Credit (adults only)
Childcare Tax Credit	Childcare Tax Credit (for childcare costs)
Non-working low-income families	
Income Support/Job Seekers' Allowance	Child Tax Credit (children only)
	Income Support/Job Seekers' Allowance (adults only)

* Variable amounts depending on numbers of children and whether parents are in work.

claims for Income Support/Job Seekers' Allowance. The aims of the reforms overall are to provide a continuing stream of income for families with children, irrespective of whether the adults in the family are in work, and which can be relied on by families who move into work; to pay support for children to the main carer, in line with Child Benefit; to remove the stigma attached to claiming the traditional forms of support for the poorest families, by creating one system of income-related support for all families with children; and to enable families to access financial support from one system, even as their income rises or circumstances change (IR, 2001, p. 13).

These reforms have much to commend them, not least the removal of stigma associated with claiming benefits, the promotion of children to receive financial support in their own right, and the payment of Child Tax Credit to the main carer, normally the mother, which should help provide maximum benefit to children. Potentially the reforms also provide women with an independent income, a factor identified by Bell in Chapter 9 as affording women some protection against domestic violence.

The government also insists that the reforms will simplify and streamline income-related support for families. It is not easy to see how this is achieved, as Table 1.1 shows the numbers of benefits/credits for the poorest *non-working families* increases from two to three under the reforms; Child Benefit, Child Tax Credit, and Income Support/Job Seekers' Allowance. Furthermore, the split of responsibility between the Inland Revenue for tax credits and the Department of Work and Pensions to provide Income Support/Job Seekers' Allowance to non-working adults makes the system appear more complex. It remains to be seen whether it will be as complex in reality when people start making claims.

Welfare-to-work

As stated, the government believes the best route out of poverty is through employment. The developments of the New Deal programmes are specifically designed to remove people from dependence on social security benefits into work. Alongside the changes to the tax and benefit system they make up the welfare-to-work strategy. Five groups of people are targeted by different and tailored New Deal programmes: lone parents, young people, the long-term unemployed, disabled people, the partners of the unemployed, and unemployed people aged over 50. The common theme across the New Deal programmes is the provision of a personal advisor who gives practical advice and support on local vacancies, job applications and CVs. In the case of lone parents information is provided on childcare places, benefits, calculations of in-work income and help with claiming child maintenance. While initially participation in the New Deal was voluntary for lone parents, they are now required to attend 'work-focused' interviews when their youngest child reaches school age. Failure to do so may result in benefit deductions (Gray, 2001). Unlike the long-term unemployed, lone parents are not required to actively seek employment. They may be supported financially to take up training and are free to do unpaid voluntary work. Even so, only 9 per cent of lone parents who participated in the New Deal took up training in January 2000 (Rake, 2001). Significant barriers to lone-parents' employment still remain, including access to high-quality, flexible and affordable childcare that fits in with working and school hours (Backett-Milburn *et al.*, 2001; Childcare Commission, 2001; La Valle *et al.*, 2000; Finch and Gloyer, 2000). Moreover, since the majority of lone parents are women, they are at greater risk of ending up in low-paid, low-skilled part-time work. Rake (2001) argues this raises questions about whether the New Deal should as its first step enhance skills rather than employment.

Targeted support for poor/disadvantaged children

In March 2001, another important document in relation to families with children was published. *Tomorrow's Future: Building a strategy for Children and Young People* (CYPU, 2001) provides a detailed description of all the initiatives directed at children and young people aged between 0–19 years and presents the government's plans for the future. This is the government's response to a report by the Social Exclusion Unit, *Report of the Policy Action Team 12: Young People National Strategy for Neighbourhood Renewal* (SEU, March 2000) which stated that new structures were needed to ensure new and improved arrangements for children's issues across government. In July 2000, a Cabinet Committee for Children and Young People was set up together with a new Children and Young People's Unit launched in November 2000. These structures appeared two years after the Supporting Families document was published, representing a move away from focusing on families *per se* and on children specifically, including promoting children's rights. The approach of the Children and Young People's Unit (CYPU) is to recognise:

> that we should have high expectations for every child and should work to ensure that provision for children and young people is designed to give every one of them an equal opportunity to develop. (CYPU, 2001, p. 1)

The intention of policy is to deal with and to prevent the effects of social exclusion, as well as to address poverty. Thus it states that improvements in financial packages for families are to be married with investments in services for children (CYPU, 2001, p. 4). Two broad strategies are identified, one aimed at *all* children through improvements in education (literacy and numeracy hours) and health services (through the NHS plan), and a second strategy as targeted support for vulnerable/poor children or children living in disadvantaged areas. This section will discuss major initiatives under the latter strategy, though it must be noted that some of these pre-date the arrival of the CYPU.

Early years childcare and education

Targeted measures for poor/disadvantaged children have been developed in the form of childcare and educational support and in that regard relate to the national childcare strategy. The nationwide programme of Sure Start was the first of these initiatives which aimed to provide better access to family support, health, early education and childcare services for children aged 0–3. The intention is to provide 'pathways out of poverty' to ensure these children are 'ready to thrive' when they start school. Building on Sure Start programmes are two other major initiatives, the development of Early Excellence Centres and, latterly, Neighbourhood Nurseries. Both of these aim to provide local integrated early education and childcare services as well as family support for children under five years of age living in disadvantaged areas (DEE, Press release, 26 January and 27 February 2001). The distinction between these initiatives is not clear, with many Neighbourhood Nurseries being encouraged to apply for Early Excellence Centre status and with many of the Early Excellence Centres and proposed Neighbourhood Nurseries linked to Sure Start programmes. The key element they have in common, however, is their reliance on partnerships as the delivery mechanism.

Targeted support for older children

As well as Sure Start for children under five years of age, there is also Sure Start Plus – a programme of support aimed specifically at teenage mothers to help them stay in education and training. Sure Start Plus forms one arm of the Teenage Pregnancy Strategy which aims to halt the cycle of social exclusion experienced by teenage mothers which is then thought to be replicated in later life among their children. The other arm of the strategy is prevention through better sex and relationship education as well as improving youth contraception services. The UK has the highest rate of teenage pregnancy in Europe and the government has set a target of halving the rate of teenage pregnancy among the under-18s in England by 2010. There are numerous other educational initiatives targeted at older children at risk of social exclusion. These include Educational Maintenance Allowances to help 15–16-year-olds continue their education; Pupil Learning Credits for the most challenged schools to improve in-school support and out-of-school activities; Playing for Success programmes to establish out-of-school study centres in football clubs and other sport venues (aimed at 10–14-year-olds to improve numeracy, literacy and ICT skills); and the Summer Activities for 16-year-olds Programme involving outdoor adventure and team-building for those children who are about to leave school but are disengaged and have no sense of future direction. More general support is also offered to all children between the ages of 13–19 through the Connexions Service.

Initiatives for young people who are looked after are also addressed through the *Quality Protects* programme which, as described in the Introduction was launched in 1998 to raise standards by specifying eight objectives. Targets are linked to the objectives which are to be met by joint-working between health, education and social services. Funding follows the successful achievement of the specified targets, measured through internal auditing processes and the completion by practitioners of forms and records. Some of the implications for practice with children and young people who are looked after are discussed by Wilson and Sinclair in Chapter 11.

Connexions Service

The Connexions Service offers general advice, guidance and support to help young people achieve their full potential by helping them to participate in work and learning, thus facilitating a 'successful' transition to adulthood. It is a central plank of the government's approach to dealing with truancy and exclusion among young people aged 13–19. It is a service provided through personal advisors, drop-in centres or by telephone or the Internet. Twelve Connexions Services have begun providing full services in April 2001, and by 2004 the service should be available to all young people in England. The mechanisms for delivery again involve local partnerships between local authorities' education, social and youth services and schools, employers, health authorities, police authorities, youth offending teams, the voluntary sector organisations and young people themselves. The government expects these partnerships to contain the full range of providers in order to meet the targets set for reduction in crime, teenage rates of pregnancy and drug abuse. There are also specific initiatives to support looked-after children in local authority care under the Quality Protects programme which was implemented in 1999, and which again involves 'cross-agency' working. One of the key differences between financial support packages and children's services is that government directly provides the former and a mix of organisations from the 'voluntary, community, faith and statutory sectors' provides the latter, mostly through partnerships.

Implications for social work practice

Despite the plethora of initiatives contained within Labour's family policy described above, it is possible to fit them into overlapping themes which ultimately aim to address and to prevent social exclusion. These are: eradicating child poverty, reducing barriers to paid work for low-income families, making work pay and reconciling work and family life. The various initiatives also operate at different levels – national, local authority and neighborhood level. Generally, financial support is provided at the national level, but strategies related to social exclusion cross all three levels. Social workers must learn how families interact with these initiatives across the various levels in order to have a holistic sense of how families are positioned in relation to complex service provision. So, it follows that learning what services might be available locally is not a simple task. The National Family and Parenting Institute (a voluntary organisation set up by government to promote parenting issues) has recognised the difficulties and has set out to map family services cross England and Wales for the first time. Preliminary results show that lack of access to stable funding resources, and an absence of strategic planning and information about services, were inhibiting service development (Henricson *et al.*, 2001). This raises important questions about the reliance on partnerships as the delivery mechanisms for many of the family support programmes, as well as the capacity of social workers already overstretched with statutory responsibilities to engage with the new initiatives. In particular, practitioners may have a major role to play in the battle against child poverty (by helping tackle the issue of non-take-up of benefits for example) and, in this respect, they need to have up-to-date knowledge of benefits and entitlements, advocacy skills, and time to take up and pursue individual cases. Knowledge of the communities they work within is also important. Practitioners from all agencies are struggling to keep abreast of the facilities in their area to help families, especially as a number of the projects and initiatives are short-lived because of their dependence on time-limited funding. At the same time, they need to be assessing need in the communities they work within in order to inform the direction of local service development. The decision-making process in relation to service-level agreements between local authorities and the voluntary sector, for example, has to be informed by detailed knowledge of the strengths and weaknesses of particular agencies in a locality, and the nature of relationships between them. Social Service Departments have a key role here.

In the government's welfare reform plans there is an assumption that most families have a latent capacity to help themselves out of poverty/social exclusion through employment as long as the right incentives are in place. The aim of promoting work as the main route out of poverty has a number of implications for social work practice. Local authority Social Service Departments have the task of registering and monitoring child minders and day nurseries. As day-care facilities proliferate, this task will require additional time and funding, and has important training implications for health, education and social care providers. Another implication may be that, where families face the dual burden of care and employment involving both long hours and increased stress, children's needs are not met adequately. Lone parents in particular and other families facing multiple stress factors such as relationship difficulties may face greater problems in meeting children's needs. Work commitments could make it more difficult for parents to be present and available to their children, for example after school, placing additional pressure on schools, social workers and the police. However, the role of social work is not considered an important strand of support for some of these families. The funding of numerous new initiatives rather than mainstream statutory practice is having an impact on recruitment and practice in social work and the allied professions. What is now glamorous and attractive – and supported by policies which applaud community building and social inclusion through employment – is work in the voluntary and community sectors and work in relation to initiatives which have received substantial funding and counselling in the private sector. While social work has a tradition in community work, even here, as Jordan (2000) points out, expanding developments are not closely tied in to the social work profession. Sure Start, for example, is seen as being staffed by health visitors, whilst the New Deal and the Connexions Service have personal advisers. The impact on where social workers will be based and on their roles and practice in these new initiatives is yet to be seen. What does seem evident is that their work load will increase.

There are other implications of the government's family policy for practitioners in the helping professions. Traditionally, much of the work with families has been with mothers and, increasingly, with children. The encouragement for women to seek employment, taken alongside efforts to enhance the role of fathers, for example by an entitlement to paternity leave, should require that fathers are more frequently included in the work with families in difficulty. Models for working with men and couples are being progressed, for example in the field of domestic violence, and practitioners need to develop their skills and confidence in working with men. Later chapters in this book by Miller and Bentovim and by McCluskey present formats for assessing families and family relationships and for working with couples.

As well as developing skills in working with men, the policy of maintaining children at home wherever possible also requires that practitioners include the wider family network in their work. This requires a change in their concept of family, so that diversity and cultural difference is addressed, and the strengths of the wider family in meeting children's needs are built upon. The involvement of aunts, uncles and grandparents in family group conferences provide a good example of one method of successfully including the wider family in the decision-making process. The use of kinship networks in foster care (Broad *et al.*, 2001) provides another.

So, while some of the implications of New Labour for social workers seem quite clear, as discussed above, overall there is a lack of clarity about their role and functions. The need to address statutory requirements – especially in the field of child protection work – continues, and arguably increases and becomes more complex, although provision and support for social workers in mainstream social service agencies now has a low national profile. Political debate about improving public services focuses largely upon health and education, with social work receiving little mention. Further, the new social care framework for children and families has potential to be dominated by health and privatised services – with the role of social work within that becoming increasingly marginalized and defined as care management. One implication for practice emerging from this agenda is that inter-agency working – especially across health, education and social services – must develop and improve. Certainly ways of working together on projects relating to, for example, school inclusion schemes and domestic violence projects are being piloted and developed across voluntary and statutory services. Bell's account of inter-agency projects relating to domestic violence in Chapter 9 provides a good example. In the field of health, similarly the need for practitioners to work together and across professional and geographical boundaries is clearly recognised. Health visitors play a key role in the community in preventative work in Early Years and Sure Start projects, and are increasingly working with social workers in parenting programmes, often jointly funded by health and social services. As professional roles become increasingly blurred, joint training is being developed at both pre and post qualification levels, and the need for clear procedures is addressed in *Working Together* (DoH, 2000).

A further impact of New Labour policy on social work has been to increase regulation and enforcement through the drive to modernise social services. As described in the Introduction, *Quality Protects* (DoH, 1998) lays out a number of outcomes which local authorities are required to meet, such as to decrease the numbers of looked-after children and to ensure children's views are listened to. However, the outcomes to be measured – such as an increased number of adoptions – are not necessarily consistent with good practice in individual cases. The risk is that social workers' professional judgment is compromised by pressure to meet performance indicators. Another concern is that the requirement to fill in forms, such as the looking-after children materials, takes time and might mean that essential direct work with clients has to be given up (see Bell, 1999). Jordan (2000) has suggested a further consequence of these tasks of surveillance and quality control is to further segregate the tasks of management from the tasks of the fieldwork practitioners. It seems somewhat ironic that the policy towards inclusiveness – to user-friendliness and empowering users by collecting their views on services – is not reflected in a similar policy of inclusiveness and value towards the staff who deliver the services.

References

Backett-Milburn, K., Cunningham-Burley, S., and Kemmer, D. (2001) *Caring and Providing: Lone and Partnered Working Mothers in Scotland*. London: Family Policy Studies Centre.

Bagilhole, B and Byrne, P (2000) 'From Hard to Soft Law and from Equality to Reconciliation in the United Kingdom' in Hantrais, L. (2000) *Gendered Policies In Europe: Reconciling Employment and Family Life*. Macmillan: London.

Bell, M. (1999) 'The Looking After Children Materials: a critical analysis of their use in practice', *Adoption and Fostering*, 22.4, pp. 15–24.

Bradshaw, J. (ed.) (2001) *Poverty: The Outcomes for Children*. London: Family Policy Studies Centre.

Bradshaw, J. (2000) 'Prospects for Poverty in Britain in the First Twenty-Five Years of the Next Century', *Sociology*, vol. 34(1), February, pp. 53–70.

Bradshaw, J. (2002) personal correspondence.

Bradshaw, J., and Stimson, C. (1997) *Using Child Benefit in the Family Budget*. London: The Stationary Office.

Brewer, M., Clark, T. and Goodman, A. (2002) *The Government's Child Poverty Target: How much Progress Has Been Made?* London: Institute for Fiscal Studies.

Broad, B., Hayes, R. and Rustforth, C. (2001) *Kith and Kin: Kinship Care for Vulnerable Young People*. York: Joseph Rowntree Foundation.

Burchardt, T., Le Grand, J. and Piachaud, D. (1999) 'Social Exclusion in Britain in 1991–1995', *Social Policy and Administration*, vol. 33(3), pp. 227–44.

Burden, T., Cooper, C. and Petrie, S. (2000) *'Modernising' Social Policy: Unravelling New Labour's Welfare Reforms*. Aldershot: Ashgate.

Callender, C. (2000) *The Barriers to Childcare Provision*, DEE Research Report RR231. Nottingham: DfEE Publications.

Childcare Commission Report (2001) *Looking to the Future for Children and Families*. London: Kids' Clubs Network.

Children and Young People's Unit (2001) *Tomorrow's Future: Building a Strategy for Children and Young People*. London: CYPU.

Coote, E., Harman, H. and Hewitt, P. (1990) *The Family Way: A New Approach to Policy Making*. London: Institute of Public Policy Research.

Daniel, P. and Ivatts, J. (1998) *Children and Social Policy*. Houndmills: Macmillan–Palgrave.

Daycare Trust (1999) 'Childcare Gaps', Briefing Paper 1 in *Childcare Now, The Next Steps* series. London: Daycare Trust.

— (2001) 'All Our Futures: Putting Childcare at the Centre of Every Neighbourhood', Issue 1 of *Thinking Big: Childcare for All* policy series. London: Daycare Trust.

Department for Education and Employment (DEE) (1998) *Meeting the Childcare Challenge: Green Paper*. London: HMSO.

— (2000) *Changing Patterns in a Changing World: A Discussion Document*. Suffolk: Prolog.

— (2000a) *A Survey of Early Years Development and Childcare Partnerships*. Nottingham: DEE Publications.

— Press Release 26 January and 27 February 2001.

Department of Health (DoH) (1995) *Child Protection: Messages from Research*. London: HMSO.

— (1998) *Quarterly Protests: Framework for Action*. London: HMSO.

— (2000) *Working Together to Safeguard and Promote the Welfare of Children*. London: HMSO.

— (2001) *Framework for the Assessment of Children in Need and their Families*. London: HMSO.

Department for Work and Pensions (DWP) (2002) *Households Below Average Income 1994/5–2000/01*. Leeds: Corporate Document Services.

Dex, S. (ed.) (1999) *Families and the Labour Market: Trends Pressures and Policies*. London: Family Policy Studies Centre.

Family Policy Studies Centre (1999) *Supporting Families*, Family Briefing paper II, London: FPSC.

Family Policy Studies Centre (2000) *Family Poverty and Social Exclusion*, Family Briefing Paper 15. London: FPSC.

Finch, H. and Gloyer, M. (2000) *Lone Parents and Childcare: A Further Look at Evaluation Data on the New Deal for Lone Parents*. DSS Research Report no. 68. London: Corporate Document Services.

Fox-Harding, L. (1996) *Family, State and Social Policy*. London: Macmillan–Palgrave.
— (2000) *Supporting Families/Controlling Families? – Towards a Characterisation of New Labour's 'Family Policy'*, Working Paper no. 21, ESRC Seminar Series, 'Postmodern Kinship', University of Leeds: Centre for Research on Family, Kinship and Childhood.
Gray, A. (2001) '"Making Work Pay" – Devising the Best strategy for Lone Parents in Britain', *Journal of Social Policy*, vol 30(2), pp. 189–208.
Harker L. (2000) 'The Provision of Childcare: The Shifting Public/Private Boundaries', *New Economy*, vol. 7(3) September pp. 172–5.
Henricson, C., Katz, I., Mesie, J., Sandison, M. and Tunstill, J. (2001) *National Mapping of Family Services in England and Wales – a Consultation Document*. London, National Family and Parenting Institute.
HM Treasury (1999) *Supporting Children Through the Tax and Benefit System*, no. 5 in the Tax and Benefit Modernisation series.
— (2000) *Tackling Poverty and Making Work Pay*, no. 6 in the Tax and Benefit Modernisation series.
— (2001) *Budget, March 2001*, http://www.hm-treasury.gov.uk/budget2001/index.html
— (2002) *Budget, April 2002*, http://www.hm-treasury.gov.uk
Home Office (1998) *Supporting Families: A Consultation Document*. London: The Stationary Office. Also available on the web: http://www.homeoffice.gov.uk/acu/sfpages.pdf
— (1998) *Supporting Families: Summary of Responses to the Consultation document*, London: The Stationary Office. Also available on the web: http://www.homeoffice.gov.uk/cpd/fmpu/sfamres.htm
Inland Revenue (2001) *New Tax Credits: Supporting Families, Making Work Pay and Tackling Poverty*, Available at: http://www.inlandrevenue.gov.uk/consult_new/new_tax_credits.pdf
Jordan, W. (2000) *Social Work and the Third Way*. London: Sage.
Land, H. (1999a) 'New Labour New Families?', in H. Dean, and R. Woods (eds), *Social Policy Review* no. 11, Luton: SPA.
— (1999b) 'The Changing World of Work and Families', in S. Watson and L. Doyal (eds), *Engendering Social Policy*. Milton Keynes: Open University Press.
La Valle, I., Finch, S., Nove, A. and Lewin, C. (2000) *Parents' Demand for Childcare*, DfEE Research Report no. 176. Nottingham: DfEE Publications.
Lister, R. (1996) 'Back to the Family: Family Policies and Politics under the Major Government', in H. Jones, and J. Millar (eds), *The Politics of the Family*. Aldershot: Avebury.
McRae, S. (ed.) (1999) *Changing Britain: Families and Households in the 1990s*. Oxford: Oxford University Press.
Murray, C. (1990) *The Emerging British Underclass*. London: Institute of Economic Affairs.
Rake, K. (2001) 'Gender and New Labour's Social Policies', *Journal of Social Policy*, vol. 30(2), pp 209–32.
Twomey, B. (2002) 'Women in the Labour Market: Results from the Spring 2001 Labour Force' Survey, *Labour Market Trends*, vol. 110(3) March.

2

Families, Social Change and Diversity

Nick Frost and Brid Featherstone

This chapter, alongside the previous one by Christine Skinner, aims to provide a wider context for the remainder of the book. Skinner has already outlined the current policy context in which social workers are operating, and we situate these developments in some competing theoretical explanations about the 'changes' occurring in contemporary UK households. We also aim to complement the policy perspective by locating developments in the context of family and demographic change.

Theoretical frameworks for understanding 'families' today

Although concern about the state of the 'family' is not new, the 1990s witnessed increasingly bitter exchanges among cultural commentators, academics and policy-makers about the extent and the desirability of the changes occurring. While debates were particularly contentious in the United States (Stacey, 1999), in the UK, also, considerable anxiety was expressed particularly about the growth in divorce and lone-mother families and the allegedly deleterious consequences for children (Featherstone, 1997). Here we explore three contemporary approaches to understanding what is happening and what should be done about it, and which appear to be influential to varying degrees within the policy context ushered in by the 'New' Labour government. These approaches are: communitarianism, risk theories and feminist theories

A shared responsibility? Communitarianism

It is beyond the scope of this chapter to explore in detail the differing approaches to communitarian thinking (see Driver and Martell, 1997). The

most eminent communitarian is Etzioni (1993, 1993a), an American soci-
ologist who has achieved considerable influence in this country through his
links with Demos, a think-tank associated with New Labour. While his
book, *The Spirit of Community* is wide-ranging in scope, it is the chapter on
the family which has attracted widespread attention in the UK (Frazer,
1999). This chapter was reprinted by Demos as a pamphlet entitled 'The
Parenting Deficit' (1993a).

Etzioni argues that there is a 'parenting deficit' in contemporary Western
society caused by the overinvestment of both mothers and fathers in paid
work and the growth in divorce. As a result of these social developments,
Etzioni suggests that children are not being effectively parented, leading to
their involvement in delinquency, substance misuse and poor educational
attainment. He argues that children need two committed involved parents
because childcare and education are highly labour-intensive and demanding.
Divorce, in particular, is problematic because it can lead not only to the loss
of one parent, but also to instability in terms of 'new' partners being
introduced. Changes in parenting partners lead to deep disruption for
children.

Etzioni does not, however, see the communitarian family necessarily as a
traditional family. He objects to the growth in the number of lone parents
on the basis that the difficult job of raising children requires three people
rather than two. He is clear that he does not want women out of the workforce; his objective is to decry parental overinvestment in paid work by both
genders. In terms of policy implications he advocates the active exploration
of, for example, the introduction of waiting periods before marriage, counselling programmes pre-marriage, and the discouragement of easy divorce
through the use of waiting periods. All parents have a responsibility, including economically, towards their children whether they live with them or not
and he outlines a range of measures to ensure this responsibility is enforced.

To summarise, Etzioni is not suggesting that mothers stay at home – but
that parents should make active choices in favour of their children and
against overinvestment in work. In promoting the active involvement of
both parents in family life he suggests raising children requires two parents,
rather than a family where one parent, usually the father, is effectively
absent. Etzioni's arguments therefore cannot be characterised as strictly
traditional although they are explicitly moralising in tone.

Etzioni's influence in the UK is important on a symbolic level as he speaks
to a widespread concern that, since the 1960s, the balance between rights
and responsibilities has become dangerously skewed with the pursuit of
individual rights taking precedence over wider responsibilities – particularly
towards children. His impact on government policy was vividly illustrated in
a broadcast by Home Office Minister, Paul Boateng (14 May 1999), who
seemed to be quoting directly from Etzioni when accounting for the high
rate of teenage pregnancy in the UK This he linked directly to the influence
of the 1960s and the pursuit of rights over responsibilities. While he did
stop short of endorsing marriage as the only acceptable arrangement within

which children should be raised, he nevertheless made it clear that it was the arrangement preferred by him.

Overall, Labour have taken up Etzioni selectively and their overriding concern to tackle poverty and social exclusion has led to some tensions in their agenda. Their policies prioritising paid work for parents, for example, run contrary to Etzioni's reservations about parental overinvestment in such paid work. In this respect it may be that given the problem of persistence identified above, New Labour policies of moving families out of benefits and into paid work are helpful (Hill and Jenkins, 1999). Moreover, the effect of tax and benefit changes under the Labour government has been to increase the incomes of the poorest more than those of the better off and of households with children more than others with up to 9 out of 10 children living in households where income has gone up, and by 2002 the proportion of children in poverty will probably fall by 6 percentage points.

The development of the national childcare strategy and the benefit changes described in the previous chapter are aimed at supporting both parents in family and work responsibilities. Also of relevance are a raft of developments such as the national minimum wage, the part-time work directive, and extensions to maternity and paternity leave allowances. New Labour has not fundamentally changed the availability of divorce, continuing the emphasis of the previous administration in relation to contact and financial arrangements. This continues a legislative trend of reinforcing the importance of first families with all the implications this has for post-divorce parenting and subsequent families (see Smart and Neale, 1999). Later chapters in this book explore some of the practice implications of such policies.

Overall, then, the communitarian influence on New Labour is not straightforward. Etzioni's work does speak to a strand within New Labour which sees behaviour as a key causal factor in the genesis of social problems. This links a range of social problems, for example criminality in children as a result of their parents' behaviour, leading to initiatives such as Parenting Orders for parents of children who offend. An interesting byproduct is some increased attention paid to the role of fathers in children's development and welfare, as demonstrated by the government discussion paper *Supporting Families: A Consultation Document* (Home Office, 1998). Indeed the government has encouraged and made resources available to projects aimed at working with fathers, a point to which we will return.

Frazer (1999) notes that *Supporting Families* and, indeed, Tony Blair's speeches display ambivalence about the traditional family. As Skinner has noted in the previous chapter, *Supporting Families* takes a pragmatic approach to families in recognising that there is considerable diversity. It also explicitly sets itself against preaching or moralising about families. However, the document also clearly sees children's welfare as being best safeguarded within a structure comprising married parents residing together looking after dependent children.

Embracing the future? The risk theorists

Other sociologists, notably Beck and Beck-Gernsheim (1995) and Giddens (1992) are more explicitly theoretical than Etzioni. Their approach differs particularly in terms of the desirability of what is happening. Beck and Beck-Gernsheim (1995) relate contemporary developments to the rise of the female biography. They argue that a general property of contemporary society is the process of individualisation, a key aspect being that it is a process open to women. According to Beck Beck-Gernsheim (1995), individualisation refers to the requirement that individuals produce their own biographies in the absence of fixed traditional or obligatory norms and within a context of new ways if thinking which are continually subject to change:

> Individualization means that men and women are released from the gender roles prescribed by industrial society for life in the nuclear family. At the same time, and this aggravates the situation, they find themselves forced under pain of material disadvantage, to build up *a life of their own* by way of the labour market, training and mobility, and if need be to pursue this life at the cost of their commitments to family, relations and friends. (Beck and Beck-Gernsheim, 1995, p. 6, emphasis in original)

One model, containing both restriction and freedom by another which seems more modern and attractive but which contains another balance of freedom and restriction, is thus replaced by another:

> That it is better adapted to the challenges of our times is shown by the fact that hardly anyone wants to go back to the 'good old days', however nerve wracking things may be for one self. There are of course a fair number of men who want to turn the clocks back, but not for themselves, only *for the women*. (*ibid.*, p. 7 emphasis in original)

Giddens (1992) argues that the world is undergoing profound transformation. He writes of the emergence of the pure relationship and confluent love. The pure relationship refers to relationships entered into for their own sake and for what can be gained by each person from a relationship with each other, continuing only while both parties achieve satisfaction. Confluent love is a contingent emotion lacking the forever quality associated with romantic love. He welcomes the changes, in which women are seen as central. Women have redefined themselves and destabilised the meanings attached to 'woman', 'wife' and 'mother'. In turn, this redefinition has a profound impact upon men as they negotiate and renegotiate their identities. Giddens notes that there are particular difficulties for men in constructing a new narrative of the self in the light of the above changes.

Ferguson (2001) has used Gidden's work to argue that new opportunities for women and children are opened up in what he calls a post-traditional society. They are able to seek freedom from traditional constraints including most importantly, experiences of sexual violence. He argues that these opportunities alter their relationship to expert systems such as social work in positive ways by enabling them to articulate their needs and seek help. Others such as Scourfield (2001) are less optimistic about the ability of social work to deliver the help required, arguing that women continue to be policed by social work systems because the systems are dominated by narrow concerns with risk, a point to which we will return.

Whilst accepting Gidden's analysis as persuasive, feminists such as Smart and Neale (1999) highlight some problems. They argue that Giddens does not fully explore the implications of differential access to lifestyles, work and the ways in which the pure relationship is mediated by religion, ethnicity and wealth. They point out that they are not implying that only the wealthy, white, secular communities in full-time employment might access the pure relationship. It may be the poor, urban unemployed white sectors who are less enmeshed in property concerns and for whom marriage might entail financial impoverishment who incline more towards this model. Their point is that, by neglecting difference, Giddens suggests that confluent love and the pure relationship is available to all men and women who are able to free themselves from the constraints of romantic love and patriarchal power (*ibid.*, p. 12).

Furthermore, they argue that Gidden's formulation of the pure relationship ignores the importance of children, particularly for mothers. The presence of children means that mothers feel less able to leave relationships which are unsatisfactory, especially in situations of domestic violence. Bell further develops these issues in a later chapter of this book. Smart and Neale recognise that while Giddens does not ignore the existence of children, what little he has to say about them sits poorly with his ideas about the reflexive self. Children are depicted as burdens, as a source of strain and as lacking agency and a voice. Further, his emphasis on people constructing new lives suggests his ignorance of the trend towards ongoing parenting after divorce, meaning a 'clean break' is rare.

In recent more policy-oriented work, Giddens (1998) begins to ground his analysis. Whilst clearly setting out why a return to 'the traditional family' is implausible and arguing against the right, he postulates that 'the notion that a proliferation of family forms is both desirable and unproblematic simply is not convincing' (1998, p. 92). In particular he notes research indicating that children raised by one parent do not do as well as children raised by both. Batchelor considers this issue in a later chapter. Like Etzioni he acknowledges that this may be partially attributable to economic factors; however, he argues that inadequate parental attention and lack of social ties are equally culpable and considers what political strategies might be effective in producing his ideal state of the family:

First and most fundamentally we must start from the principle of equality between the sexes, from which there can be no going back. There is only one story to tell about the family today and that is of democracy. The family is becoming democratised, in ways which track processes of public democracy; and such democratisation suggests how family life might combine individual choice and social solidarity. (Batchelor, 1999, p. 93)

His more concrete proposal is that family policy should be guided by the protection and care of children. At the same time, no attempt should be made to make divorce harder in order to tie people together in a commitment to the child/children:

> Marriage and parenthood have always been thought of as tied together, but in the detraditionalized family, where having a child is an altogether different decision from the past, the two are becoming disentangled ... Contractual commitment to a child could thus be separated from marriage, and made by each parent as a binding matter of law, with unmarried and married fathers having the same rights and the same obligations. Both sexes would have to recognize that sexual encounters carry the chance of life-time responsibilities, including protection from physical abuse. In combination with other cultural changes promoting a more positive view of fatherhood, such a restructuring of parenthood would undermine the very idea of the 'single parent'. (1999, pp. 95–6)

Equally, children should have responsibilities to their parents; for example, support them in old age. Such obligations could be meshed with lifelong parenting contracts. Unfortunately, Giddens does not explore the concrete issues which might arise in the implementation of such arrangements and space does not permit us to do so here.

To summarise, whilst Giddens and Etzioni differ particularly in terms of the desirability of what is happening, both appear united by a belief that ongoing involvement of two parents in children's lives is the best means of safeguarding their welfare. Some practice implications of this are considered further in Chapter 6 which considers work with divorcing parents. Both Etzioni and Giddens see a role for government in encouraging that involvement, they both explicitly reject any arguments which relate children's outcomes to poverty alone, and they both see parenting as a key factor in facilitating children's welfare.

The family and women: feminists and feminisms

Clearly there is not one single feminist approach to the family. The heterogeneity of women as a group, the diversity of family forms and women's varied experiences within families ensures this (Jagger and Wright, 1999). In the 1970s and 1980s conceptual and theoretically informed debate flourished as to the role of the family as a key site of gender oppression and of gendered inequalities. However, the influence of post-modernism and post-structuralism led to a rejection of the idea that there was only one site of women's oppression and there was also a rejection of the idea that the family could signify in the same way for all women. Later feminist theorists directed their attention to other issues (Smart and Neale, 1999). Empirical work continued but this work was not located within broader debates or changes.

In exploring feminist positions today we identify two approaches; the pragmatic and the critical. The Women's Unit located in the Cabinet Office appears to provide space within the policy arena for pragmatic feminists to operate. The issues highlighted by the Unit include the disparity between men's and women's incomes, the work/life balance, education and opportunities issues for girls, domestic violence and women, and drugs (www.womens-unit.gov.uk). As discussed, many of these issues such as the work/life balance and domestic violence are being tackled by cross departmental strategies.

Some feminists, such as Adrienne Burgess, are actively involved in developments by this government since 1997 in relation to fathers and fathering. As director of Fathers Direct, a new organisation supported by this government, she champions the agenda set out in her book *Fatherhood Reclaimed* (1996) in which she argues for a reevaluation of fathers' roles and for the importance of supporting their active involvement in families. She argues against what she sees as a dominant feminist tendency to represent fathers as risks. Bell looks at the issue of working with fathers in domestic violence situations later in this book.

Feminists involved in the policy-making arena do not, of course, hold uniform views. One set of tensions, explored in the previous chapter by Skinner, revolves around when mothers should be encouraged to go back to work after the birth of a baby. Other feminists are particularly critical of current legislative trends. Smart and Neale (1999) argue that the measures contained in legislation such as the Children Act, the Child Support Act and the Family Law Act (all legislation introduced by the Conservatives but continued under Labour) have the following implicit aims:

- to prioritise first families;
- to discourage clean breaks on divorce;
- to prioritise parenthood over spousal obligations;
- to prioritise biological parenthood and descent;
- to challenge the popular understanding of divorce as a solution to private problems; and
- to identify divorce as a social problem. (1999, p. 176)

They argue against any simple assumption of fathers as a resource and point out the risks they can pose to women and children. And they argue against policies which, in focusing on the welfare of children, fail to recognise the power inequalities women can face in families, issues which practitioners need to address and which are discussed in the Practice part of this book. Smart and Neale believe policies should aim to facilitate flexibility in family life rather than shape it in a particular form as government should not presume that certain outcomes are more desirable than others. This view is increasingly a minority view as is apparent from the review of approaches such as Etzioni and Giddens.

More critical views are also to be found in the consultation paper produced by the Lord Chancellor's Department (1999) on domestic violence and child contact. Here feminists such as Humphreys working in the areas of domestic violence have argued for reform of the Children Act because of their concern that the presumption of contact for fathers exposes women and children to danger from violent men. Whilst the law on contact has not been changed as feminists wished, magistrates and judges are advised to take allegations of violence seriously when considering contact arrangements.

The views of more critical feminists seem less in tune with a policy agenda which, although not coherent, veers more towards the encouragement of two-parent involvement in families and particularly the active involvement of birth fathers.

In this chapter we have discussed three perspectives on the current state of the family, and demonstrated how such contested views impact upon how we think about the family in the social world. These regularly spill over into the popular imagination – usually when there is a 'moral panic' about teenage parents, 'home alone' children or 'spiralling' divorce rates, for example. We now wish to move on to examine some of the empirical data which underpins discussions about the family.

Household structure in the UK today

This section brings together a range of material, mainly collated from official statistics. Statistics should not be read as a straightforward reflection of social realities; the statistics themselves are contested and can be 'read' in different ways. All statistics utilise categories, which socially construct the realities they purport to merely describe. For example, British official statistics construct social class in a particular way (social classes I to IV) by reference to the occupation of the father. This is, however, merely one way of assigning class. For example, a Marxist would stress the relationship of the person to the means of production, or their role in the workforce. There is also an obvious feminist objection to a definition that privileges the father's occupation as a way of assigning social class.

Moreover, it is difficult for statistics to grasp the real complexity of people's lives and how they are actually lived. Throughout their life-course people will occupy a number of categories, such as being single, married, divorced and/or cohabiting, at different times in their lives. Many move in and out of categories as the research on lone mothers demonstrates (Phoenix, 1996). Official statistics are merely a snapshot of a given moment in time and are not equipped to grasp the complexity and fluidity of our lives.

Finally, as stated, it is important to bear in mind that people with differing and conflicting perspectives can read the same statistics in quite different ways. The Family Policy Studies Centre (2000) research on family demographics exemplifies this. Whilst the publication of this research encouraged headlines such as 'Are we turning into a nation of loners?' (W. Woodward, *Guardian*, 27 March 2000) referring to the growth in single-person living, the research actually indicated four-fifths of dependent children still live in a family with two parents and nine out of ten of those parents are married. The statistics to follow provide a useful starting point for our debates.

Household formations

The government collects a range of information that allows us to examine changes in households, and these data can help inform and influence policy. Firstly, we examine the structure of households. Table 2.1 demonstrates the distribution of household types and changes in household structures in Great Britain since 1961 (the figures are presented as percentages of the total number of households).

One noteworthy pattern is the increase in the percentage of one-person households. Some of these are pensioner households – an increase that can be largely explained by extended life expectancy, particularly amongst women. The increase in single-person households under pension age may be explained by the fact that there has been a decline in the rate of marriage,

Table 2.1 Distribution of household types and structures, Great Britain

	1961	1971	1981	1991	1998–9
Type of household as a percentage of total					
One person	11	18	22	27	29
Two or more unrelated adults	5	4	5	3	2
One-family households					
Couple					
No children	26	27	26	28	30
1–2 dependent children	30	26	25	20	19
3 or more dependent children	8	9	6	5	4
Non-dependent children only	10	8	8	8	6
Lone parents					
Dependent children	2	3	5	6	7
Non-dependent children only	4	4	4	4	3
Multifamily households	3	1	1	1	1
All households (millions)	16.3	18.6	20.2	22.4	-

Source: *Social Trends*, 30 (2000).

a postponement of the age of first marriage and an increase in people living alone following separation or divorce since 1961.

The trend in postponing the birth of a first child also helps to explain the increase in the number of couples living in a household without children, and therefore, also, the decline in the proportion with one or two children. It should be noted that the trend towards later childbirth for women is an uneven one and that there is an association between the postponement of the birth of a first child and the mother possessing a higher educational qualification (ONS, 2000, p. 11).

The percentage of households with three or more children has halved since 1961, perhaps reflecting women's improved control of their own fertility. It can be noted than in 1961, 48 per cent of all households were couples with children (dependent and non-dependent), but that this declined to 29 per cent of all households by 1998–99 (ONS, 2000). The dominant view of the household as being made up of parents and dependent children is, therefore, no longer the majority experience of British households. This has implications in relation to how we think about policy initiatives.

It can also be seen that the sum of these trends is an increase in the number of households in Great Britain over the period. This remains the case even allowing for population growth. At the beginning of the twentieth century the average household size was about 4.6 people; by 1998–99 this had declined to 2.4 people (*Social Trends*, 30, 2000, p. 34). Thus we have seen more households of smaller average size developing over recent decades.

In terms of household formation, the number of first marriages peaked in 1970 at about 390 000; by 1995 it had just about halved to 192 000, and by 1997 had declined to 175 000. The rate of remarriage increased steadily from 1961, and by 1995 made up about two-fifths of the total of all marriages. Whilst first marriage is declining in frequency, a significant number of people are electing to remarry (*Ibid.*). It follows that the frequency of remarriage reflects previous divorces. The number of divorces more than doubled between 1961 and 1995. By 1997 the number of divorces per annum was only slightly less than the number of marriages – about 175 000. This is an uneven trend due to legal chances – such as the Divorce Reform Act 1969, which came into force in 1971 – contributing to increases in divorce and subsequent remarriages in the early 1970s (*Ibid.*, p. 50).

Lone-parent households with dependent children increased from 2 per cent of the total in 1961, to 7 per cent of the total by 1998–99. Again here there is a danger of statistics masking complex social realities. Whilst births outside marriage rose steadily throughout the 1970s, 80s and 90s, reaching about 38 per cent of all live births in 1998, the vast majority of births outside marriage are jointly registered, leaving the percentage of all live births solely registered at only about 8 per cent of all live births. Ford and Millar make a valuable point that the 'statistics on single, never married women are misleading' (1997, p. 2), and argue that:

the number of couples living together without marriage is rising. Women who separate from a cohabiting relationship usually appear in the statistics as single, but they are really separated. (1997, p. 2)

Secondly, 'the number of 'shotgun weddings' following a pregnancy outside marriage has declined. These marriages had a very high rate of breakdown and so these women would subsequently turn up in the statistics as divorced lone mothers. Today a pregnancy to a single woman most often leads to cohabitation, and so these women now turn up in the statistics as single lone mothers. (Ford and Millar, 1997, p. 2).

There are significant differences within household structure, also in terms of different ethnic groups, as outlined in Table 2.2, also derived from *Social Trends*.

It is important that social workers and policy-makers understand cultural differences in the way that households are constructed. Table 2.2 illustrates that South Asian (Indian, Pakistani and Bangladeshi) persons are less likely to live in single-person households, reflecting the younger age structure of these populations and probably differing attitudinal factors. South Asian households are more likely to be couple households and there is a considerable contrast with those in the Black (African Caribbean and African) population. In 1999, 24 per cent of all black households were single-parent households which differs from the Pakistani/Bangladeshi community where

Table 2.2 Ethnic group of head of household, by type of household, GB, Spring 1999

	White	Black	Indian	Pakistani/ Bangladeshi	Other groups	All
Household types as a percentage of the whole						
One person	29	30	14	7	25	28
Two or more unrelated adults	3	6	8	3		
One-family households						
Couple						
No children	29	10	18	9	13	28
Dependent children	23	21	42	56	33	24
Non-dependent children only	7	3	8	7		7
Lone parents						
Dependent children	6	24	5	8	13	7
Non-dependent children only	3	5	4			3
Multifamily households			7	10		1
All households (millions)	22.2	0.4	0.3	0.2	0.2	23.7

Source: *Social Trends*, 30 (2000).

under 10 per cent of households are lone-parent household and over 55 per cent are couple households with dependent children.

The only ethnic groups where there are enough multifamily households to register in the statistics are Indian (7 per cent of all households) and Pakistani/Bangladeshi where 10 per cent of all households are in the multi-household category. A number of qualitative studies such as Beison *et al.* (1998) and *Exploring Parenthood* (1997) illuminate the social, cultural and attitudinal factors which underpin these statistical differences.

To summarise when one examines household structures within the general population we find that people live in a diverse range of household types, the range and distribution of such types changes over time and there are significant variations in relation to ethnicity. However, when we consider what is happening to the living arrangements experienced by the majority of children this picture is more uniform as we have previously indicated. According to the Family Policy Studies Centre (2002) analysis of current trends, 80 per cent of dependent children still live with two parents and 90 per cent of those parents are married. More than 8 in 10 fathers live with all their biological children and more than 7 in 10 are doing so within their first family. Another study of almost 3000 young people exploring their experiences of family life and child maltreatment found that seven in ten had spent their whole childhood with both birth parents (Cawson, Wattam, Brooker and Kelly 2000). One-fifth had spent at least part of their childhood in a single-parent family and 13 per cent lived at some point in a reconstituted family. The implications for practice of such changing family patterns are explored in subsequent chapters.

These general trends contrast starkly with the living arrangements of those children currently the subject of child protection inquiries. In a study commissioned by the Department of Health to look at fathers in families Ryan (2000) makes some important observations about the demographic composition about the composition of households when the first inquiry in child protection practice took place: 38 per cent of children were living with both birth parents, 31 per cent lived with a lone mother and 28 per cent in reconstituted families.

In this section we have explored the statistical evidence relating to diversity in household structure. We now move on to another central dimension of diversity which relates to the socio-economic conditions of the households in which children live.

Social inequalities and poverty

Through data provided by the Office of National Statistics (ONS) it is now possible to explore this topic using official statistics. The publication in the year 2000 of their report on *Social Inequalities* made available a range of data previously unobtainable under Conservative administrations. This further illustrates our previous comments on how official data is socially constructed.

This report demonstrates the extent of poverty and inequality in Great Britain at the end of the twentieth century. However, due to ongoing reforms referred to by Skinner in the previous chapter, much of the data in this chapter may become outdated and readers are advised to consult subsequent editions of the *Social Inequalities* report. Utilising a definition of poverty as less than 60 per cent of median income, excluding housing costs approximately 3.2 million children were living in poverty during 1997–98 (ONS, 2000). For those within an ethnic-minority household matters are even bleaker _ in 1997–98, 'individuals in households headed by people from the Black, Indian, Pakistani or Bangladeshi groups were particularly likely to be in the poorest section of income distribution' (*ibid.*, p. 42). Nearly two-thirds of Pakistani and Bangladeshi people live in low-income households.

The experience of poverty is related to overall inequalities of wealth. In 1996, 1 per cent of the population owned 20 per cent of the total wealth. Additionally the wealthiest 50 per cent of the population owned 93 per cent of total wealth, leaving just 7 per cent for the remaining 50 per cent. Lone-parent families are disproportionately represented among those who are poor. According to the ONS, in 1997–98, 'just under 2 in 5 individuals in lone parent families were on incomes of less than 60 per cent of median income. After adjusting for household costs this figure rose to just over 3 in 5' (ONS, 2000, p. 49).

As already stated these statistics tend to take a 'snapshot' approach to poverty and social inequality. Hill and Jenkins (1999), using data from the Household Panel Survey, have looked at the persistence of poverty over time. They point out that children are more likely than others in the population to suffer the impact of persistent poverty:

> Almost three quarters (71 per cent) of the total poverty experienced by pre-schoolers was chronic, compared to three fifths (60 per cent) for all children and just over one half (56 per cent) for the population as a whole. (Hill and Jenkins, 1999)

In considering children's' welfare overall some sobering findings emerge in relation to the impact of poverty and inequality. The infant mortality rate (defined as death of children under the age of one) is less than twice as high in the unskilled social group compared to the professional group when the years 1995–97 are aggregated (ONS, 2000, p. 17). The actual rates for this period were 8 per 1000 for the unskilled group compared to 4 per 1000 for the professional group. The *Report on Social Inequalities* also examined child death rates. The death rate in social classes IV/V was 28 per 100 000 compared to 19 per 100 000 for social classes I and II (ONS, 2000, p. 19). This obliges us to acknowledge that children's welfare and the harm they may suffer is not just a matter of concentrating on parents' actions/inactions. This is important in a climate where the focus of social workers is about engaging with the needs of children and their families, an issue which is explored further in Iwaniec's chapter later in this book.

There is ample evidence that social workers encounter the poorest families and children. Again, looking at those who are represented within child protection statistics, 57 per cent of those lacked a wage earner (Ryan, 2000) and, as noted earlier, almost a third were in lone-mother families.

To summarise, the above statistics are important in obliging us to consider the following:

- There is considerable diversity within the general population in terms of household structure.
- Whilst the majority of children continue to live in a two-parent family a significant minority do not and there is evidence that there will continue to be changes when one considers trends in the divorce rate.
- There is a serious problem in terms of children's poverty and this is correlated with other dimensions of difference – ethnicity and lone parenthood.

The implications of this chapter for practitioners

Context

We argue that the wider social context has a considerable impact on social work practice. This is often masked by the way that social work practice is constructed – in the form of the individual 'case'. Inevitably we have to respond to each individual service user as unique, with their own individual characteristics. However, underpinning the individual referral of each family are social factors which will have an impact on the way that caseloads are constructed. Thus to take an obvious example – if there is a national increase in poverty then the number of poor 'individual cases' will increase. The social worker is then confronted by the consequences of wider social developments. Later chapters in this book explore some of the resultant practice issues.

Change

As we have seen, social workers need to constantly address the consequences of diversity and change. In constructing a genogram of a particular family, as suggested by Batchelor later in this book, we confront a particular manifestation of that change and diversity. Furthermore, it appears that families who come to the attention of child protection agencies are likely to exhibit considerable diversity in structure. One consequence is that children may have a range of actual or potential attachment figures in the lives, including fathers and father figures. The importance of considering attachment as a framework within which to work is spelled out in Herd's chapter later in this book, as is the theoretical framework underpinning the DoH Assessment framework.

As Giddens has suggested, the risk of not engaging positively with change is to fall back into a form of nostalgia about how things 'used to be'. Diversity is therefore to be welcomed and engaged with – with differing household forms, and with new ways of organising lives and roles. In particular we should note the freedoms such changes have brought to women and children seeking to escape sexual violence. However, we should also recognise that such changes are complex in their causes and consequences. Moreover, it is unlikely that workers will operate in a policy context which actively endorses forms of diversity, although the context will differ in terms of whether such diversity is condemned or embraced.

Furthermore, the ability of social workers to actively encourage and support those who are seeking to live in different ways is an ongoing issue. For example, there is some evidence from the work that one of us has been involved with (mothers of children who have been sexually abused) that they are neither actively supported nor hindered but often neglected in terms of the offering of ongoing support to cope with the many needs they may have (see Davies, Colclough and Featherstone, in press).

Influencing debates

Media views and public perceptions of social workers are often negative, and sometimes social workers are selected as scapegoats when wider social forces have negative impacts. However, the debates about the family suggest that social workers are also in the forefront of social change. Giddens, for example, has been influenced by therapeutic literature about how families work. Social work has been at the forefront of recognising the impact of sexual abuse (Campbell, 1988), and was influential in proposing anti-discrimatory ways of working – long before the Lawrence Inquiry. Thus social work as a profession, or as a social movement, has been a force for change, a social force for progressive thought which makes a real difference in the social world. In particular, social workers have ongoing and live knowledge about the impact of family change upon individual children and have the capacity to contribute to such centrally placed debates as those described here.

References

Beck, U. and Beck-Gernsheim, E. (1995) *The Normal Chaos of Love.* Cambridge: Polity Press.
Beishon, S., Madood, T., Virdee, S. (1998) *Ethnic Minority Families.* London: Policy Studies Institute.
Boateng, P. (1999) *Today Programme,* Radio 4, 14 May.
Burgess, A. (1996) *Fatherhood Reclaimed.* London: n. p.
Campbell, B. (1988) *Unofficial Secrets.* London: Virago.

Cawson, P., Wattam, C., Brooker, S. and Kelly, G. (2000) *Facing the Facts: The Prevalence of Child Maltreatment in the United Kingdom*. London: NSPCC.

Davies, L., Colclough, L. and Featherstone, B. (forthcomig) *Listening to Mothers of Sexually Abused Children*.

Department for Education and Employment (1998) *Meeting the Childcare Challenge*. London: TSO.

Department of Health (1995) *Child Protection – Messages From Research*. London: HMSO.

Exploring Parenthood (1997) *Moyenda: Black Families Talking – family survival strategies*. London: Exploring Families.

Etzioni, A. (1993) *The Parenting Deficit*. London: Demos

Family Policy Studies Centre (2000) *Family Change: Guide to the Issues, Family Briefing Paper 12*. London: Family Policy Studies Centre.

Featherstone, B. (1997) 'Introduction: crisis in the Western family' in Hollway, W. and Featherstone, B. (eds) *Mothering and Ambivalence*. London: Routledge.

Ferguson, H. (2000) 'Social Work, Individualization and Life Politics', *British Journal of Social Work*, vol. 31, pp. 41–55.

Ford, R., Millar, J. (1997) 'Private Lives and Public Responses: lone parenthood and future policy' *Foundations*, July.

Frazer, E. (1999) 'Unpicking political communitarianism: A critique of the communitanian family' in Jagger, G. and Wright, C. (eds) *Changing Family Values*. London: Routledge.

Giddens, A. (1992) *The Transformation of Intimacy: Sexuality, Love and Eroticism in modem societies*. Cambridge: Polity Press.

Giddens, A. (1998) *The Third Way: The Renewal of Social Democracy*. Cambridge: Polity Press.

Giddens, A. (1999) The Reith Lectures: 'Family', http://www.bbc.co.uk.

Giddens, A. (2001) *The Third Way and its Critics*. Cambridge: Polity Press.

Gregg, P., Harkness, S., Machin, S. (I 999) 'Child poverty and its consequences', *Findings*, March, York: Joseph Rowntree Foundation.

Hill, M. and Jenkins, S. (1999) *Poverty Among British Children*, Working Paper 99–23, University of Essex.

Home Office (1998) *Supporting Families*. London: Stationery Office.

Joseph Rowntree Foundation (1999) *Monitoring Poverty*.

MacLeod, M. (2000) Opening Address, Centre for Care, Values and Welfare, Leeds, 12 May.

Office of National Statistics (2000) *Social Inequalities,*. London: Stationery Office.

Office of National Statistics (2000) *Social Trends*. London: Stationery Office.

Phoenix, A. (1996) 'Social constructions of lone motherhood: a case of competing discourses' in Silva, E. (ed.) *Good Enough Mothering: Feminist Perspectives on Lone Motherhood*. London: Routledge.

Ryan, M. (2000) *Working with Fathers*. Oxford: Radcliffe Medical Press.

Smart, C. and Neale, B. (1999) *Family Fragments?* Cambridge: Polity Press.

Scourfield, J. (200 1) 'Constructing Women in Child Protection Work', *Child and Family Social Work*, 6, 1, pp. 77–89.

Stacey, J. (1999) 'Virtual social science and the politics of family values in the United States', in Jagger, G. and Wright, C. (eds) *Changing Family Values*. London: Routledge.

The Lord Chancellor's Department (1999) *Report by the Advisory Board on Family Law: Children Act Sub Committee*. The Women's Unit: Working Women at the heart of Government, http/www.womens-unit.gov.uk

Utting, D. *et al.* (1993) *Crime and the Family*. London: FPSC.

Woodward, W. (2000) 'Are we turning into a nation of loners?', *Guardian*, 27 March.

PART II

Theoretical and Practice Approaches to Working with Families

3

Assessing Families:
The Family Assessment of Family Competence, Strengths and Difficulties

Liza Bingley Miller and
Arnon Bentovim

Introduction

The *Framework for the Assessment of Children in Need and their Families* (DoH, 2000a) (the Assessment Framework) emphasises the importance of systematic and comprehensive assessments of children and their families as a basis for effective planning and provision for children in need. Parenting capacity and family history and family functioning are seen to form major elements of the context in which a child's developmental needs are responded to. It is therefore important to have an effective way of assessing family life and relationships and their contribution to meeting the needs of children.

The Family Assessment: Assessment of Family Competence, Strengths and Difficulties (The Family Assessment) was commissioned by the Department of Health to accompany the Assessment Framework as an aid for social workers who need to assess families, especially when undertaking core assessments where family relationship difficulties are a significant part of the reason why an assessment is being made. The Family Assessment is designed for use by any professional whose work involves making family assessments. It aims to enable practitioners to make a systematic, multidimensional, comprehensive and evidence-based assessment of family functioning and provides guidance on skills and methods for working directly with whole families during the assessment process. It is built on a model of family functioning which suggests that, while there are an infinite number of ways in which families relate, and bring up children, there are common tasks and aspects of family life to consider when trying to understand how children's needs are responded to within their families.

In this chapter we aim to introduce the reader to The Family Assessment model and to suggest how it can assist in assessing how family strengths and difficulties and competence contribute to the way families respond to the needs of children. We first look briefly at the family within the wider social context and some of the social and economic factors which need to be considered as an integral part of making a family assessment. We then outline the model of family functioning on which this assessment is structured. We briefly describe the skills and methods for working with families during the assessment process, then outline the Recording Form which forms the central instrument for making a systematic family assessment and for sharing the assessment with the family. We conclude with a discussion of some of the advantages and disadvantages of this approach to family assessment and its contribution to the Assessment Framework.

The Family Assessment draws on family therapy literature and is based on a specific model of family functioning developed from both research (see Bentovim and Bingley Miller, 2001) and practice developed at the Great Ormond Street Hospital for Children, London. The model underpins the skills and methods used in working with whole families during the assessment process taking into account the different ways in which family relationships and family life impact upon how children's needs are responded to.

The family as a system

This model looks at the family from a systemic perspective, that is as a set of interrelating individuals and relationships which all affect, and are affected, by each other. The family system provides the context within which some of the needs of individual members may (or may not) be met. One function of the family system is to undertake family tasks, including those related to meeting the needs of the children.

The family system is located within the wider social systems of the extended family, the local community and the society in which the family lives. Family tasks are affected by the social context in which they live. This includes the cultural norms within a society about what is expected of families and the position of children, both of which change over time and may vary depending on families different cultural and ethnic backgrounds. The balance between public and private responsibility for the care of children also differs from country to country with considerable variations in the provision for supporting the family, for example through the provision of childcare facilities and financial support which inevitably has an impact on family life and relationships.

The model of family functioning presented here is built upon the assumption that families have a number of tasks or functions they are generally

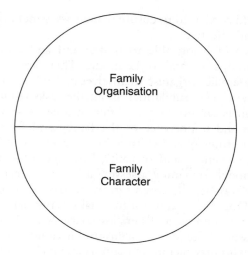

Figure 3.1 The family assessment dimensions of family functioning

expected to carry out, the most visible and well-accepted of which is bringing up children. It focuses in particular on the tasks and characteristics of family life and relationships which directly relate to how the needs of children can be best met and identifies two key dimensions of family life – family organisation and family character (Figure 3.1). The family organisation dimension focuses on family adaptability and parenting as the key functions or tasks of the family. The family character dimension identifies some features of family life, such as family communication and family alliances, which affect how a family carries out these tasks. We suggest these are best understood in the context of family history which informs how families are created and maintained.

The model also identifies a range of family strengths for each aspect of the two dimensions which help the family to undertake the necessary tasks and the difficulties which can impede their capacity to do so. This provides a framework for assessing the relationship between the problems which bring a family into the assessment process and the strengths and difficulties they may have in the dimensions of family organisation and family character. It also allows the practitioner to explore how the family is adapting to the changing life-cycle stages and how this is contributing to the children's development and well-being.

Assessing families and the wider context

Before we move into more detail about the family organisation and family character dimensions and their contribution to making systematic family assessments, it is important to establish some of the 'filters' of knowledge and awareness through which this, and we would argue any, model of family functioning should be viewed to ensure that an assessment is informed, anti-discriminatory and effective.

The importance of being able to understand and capture the unique nature of each family is central to the model. There are an infinite number of ways in which families organise themselves and relate to one another, so that while there are many similarities about the tasks families are expected to carry out, families can do them in different ways. The ways in which we perceive the role and importance of the family and family behaviours is influenced by our ethnicity and cultural heritage as well as by other aspects of diversity such as gender and sexuality, language, religious affiliation or disability. Any model for family assessment must respect and value such differences in the ways that children's growth, development and well-being can be secured. Oppression and institutional discrimination is experienced by a wide range of children and families (Barn *et al.* 1997; DoH, 1998; Morris, 1998). Issues of gender, sexuality and disability can pose challenges for practitioners who may feel more comfortable making assessments based on their own experiences, norms or values. It is therefore a core responsibility of any professional assessing families where there are differences of ethnicity, culture or class from their own to ensure they know enough about those differences to make an informed assessment. In some cultures, for example, members of the extended family may play a crucial role in everyday family life, including caring for the children (Hylton, 1997). Families with a disabled child will adapt and change the way their organise their lives in response to the specific needs relating to the child's impairment, and we have to be sensitive to the differences in the experience of disabled children and their families (Murray and Penman, 1996; Oliver, 1999).

The role of poverty, unemployment, poor housing, and inadequate educational, health and leisure facilities are other factors which present disabling barriers to families trying to meet their children's needs. In making family assessments we need to take into account how social conditions can affect parenting and family functioning and children's well-being (Acheson, 1998; Bebbington and Miles, 1989). We know, for example, that poverty can impact upon a family and it is a factor that can interact with gender. Poverty is also a factor in the increased incidence of physical abuse and neglect (Iwaniec, 1996). Women who are lone parents are likely to be more financially disadvantaged than men bringing up children on their own (Bradshaw, 1990). Economic dependence is often a key factor in preventing women who are the victims of domestic violence from leaving their partners, and we know that families where domestic violence exists are potentially abusive to children (Ashworth and Erooga, 1999; Cleaver, 1999).

To be empowering, the assessment process needs to recognise that many families regularly encounter disadvantage and discrimination and to value their ability to survive and counter a social system which can be undermining (Dutt and Box, 1998; Owusa-Bempah and Hewitt, 1999). In making a family assessment, then, all the dimensions of the model have to be viewed through the 'filter' of such a knowledge base if the strengths and difficulties of families are to be accurately perceived and assessed as the basis for useful planning with the family for future involvement.

All children, however, require their parents or carers to respond to their fundamental care needs including basic care, warmth, stimulation and guidance, boundaries and stability. These needs provide a common base-line for assessing parenting, family functioning and the development and well-being of all children and families.

The Family Assessment model of family functioning

The Family Assessment takes a systematic multidimensional approach to observing, describing and assessing family functioning. So assessments are made by a process of systematically collecting, describing and analysing information and observations about the different components of the two key dimensions of family organisation and family character, as well as about other aspects of family life. These components are also rated on a continuum of family strengths and difficulties on *family competence scales* which help to identify areas of difficulty which families might need help with and family strengths on which to build.

Family organisation dimension

How families are organised is central to how well children's needs are met. This dimension includes the performance of a number of tasks and operations which are common to all families as part of organising everyday life, and important in bringing up children. So, for example, though families may have different ways of doing things, decision-making and conflict resolution will be common to all. While there is an enormous range of parenting styles all children need stimulation, emotional warmth and encouragement if their development is to be promoted.

The pack allows for each of the different areas of family organisation and family character to be explored in detail. The descriptions of family strengths and difficulties in each area are based on research with a whole range of families (Bentovim and Bingley Miller, 2001; Kinston *et al.*, 1987) and form the basis of the *family competence scales* which are also briefly discussed in this chapter.

Family organisation is broken down into the two components of *family adaptability* and *parenting* (Figure 3.2), both of which are central to the well-being of all family members, including the children.

Family adaptability
This consists of a number of elements – organisational adaptability, problem-solving and decision-making, conflict resolution and relationships

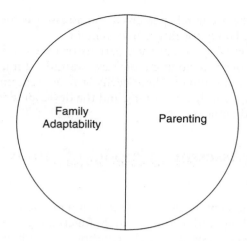

Figure 3.2   Components of the family organisation dimension of the family
assessment

with the wider family and community. A family's capacity to make decisions
and solve problems and conflicts significantly affects how well they can
adapt to changing life-cycle stages and circumstances and how well the
needs of individual family members are responded to.

Organisational adaptability is concerned with how flexible a family is
about roles, management of family tasks, arrangements and responsibilities,
and how far the family is able to adapt to the changing ages and stages of
development of the children and how they respond to and manage stress as
it arises at different parts of the family life-cycle. Different tasks have to be
negotiated with each stage and new difficulties with family relationships may
be a signal that a family is having difficulty in managing or completing a
stage in their family life-cycle or in moving on to the next stage.

It is useful to explore a range of aspects of the tasks of *decision-making*
and *problem-solving* including the participants, the process and implementation. There may be cultural variations in who is expected to be involved in
decision-making and taking responsibility for particular problems. The ways
in which family members think about gender as well as access to resources
outside the family (such as income, social support) may also affect the relative power of partners in decision-making.

Managing and *resolving conflict* refers to the ability of the family to
acknowledge and cope with the inevitable differences that occur between
members. Managing conflict is an important part of any family's life and it
is a major strength when conflicts are acknowledged and mostly resolved.

The help a family has available to them partly depends on *relationships
with the wider family and community* and any helping agencies. The focus
here is particularly on how far the family members' relationships with the
wider family and the community enhance their capacity to meet the needs
of family members or add to family difficulties.

Parenting

In assessing family organisation we are also interested in how families care for, guide and manage children and we want to assess the quality of care offered by parents in several respects. Parenting focuses specifically on parenting tasks and consists of promoting development – stimulation, emotional warmth and encouragement, the nature of attachments, as well as the guidance, care and management of the children.

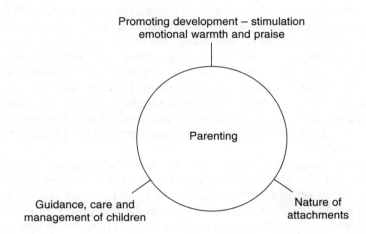

Figure 3.3   Elements of the parenting component of family organisation

Children need stimulation, encouragement and praise to promote their development and to build self-esteem, self-confidence and competence, and so it is important to assess how far the parents seem to be able to contribute to meeting these needs and what support, intervention or resources they might need to increase their capacity to do so.

The nature of *attachments* in families form an important basis for children's well-being. All children need secure attachments to significant carers to give them a sense of safety and security as individuals. We need to assess the care-giving and care-seeking relationship between parents or carers and children, including how children's attachment needs are met and how separations, losses and reunions are responded to. Differences in family structures, networks and communities and in patterns of who provides care for the children will affect who are likely to become significant attachment figures for children (Thomas, 1995). The wider context of a particular family's pattern of attachments needs to be integrated into assessment work with the family (Social Services Inspectorate and Surrey County Council 1995). Cultural differences may affect the pattern of attachments in a family; for some ethnic minority groups it may be important to understand a family's particular experience of separation, loss and sometimes trauma – through migration and asylum-seeking for example

We also need to find out about the *guidance, care and management of the children*, which involves exploring how parents care for the children and ensure that they are protected, how they guide and set boundaries for their behaviour and whether they have realistic expectations of them. Here, also, attention must be given to different emphases occurring in different cultures and ethnic minority groups about the guidance, care and management of children. For example, parents and children may experience a difference in values between their own culture and that reflected in schools which can produce particular parenting problems. Part of the work may be assessing whether a family needs support in negotiating with schools (Grant, 1996). Different children will also have varying needs for guidance and protection. For instance, parents of children with learning disabilities have the challenge of trying to ensure their child has the guidance and boundaries which allow them to reach their full potential while adjusting their expectations to take the child's impairment into account (Joseph Rowntree Foundation, 1999).

Factors related to gender can also influence how the guidance, care and management of children is handled in families. There may be gender differences in the premises on which guidance and boundaries are set and the expectations parents have for girls and boys. Gender and power differences may also contribute to conflicts between parents about how children should be handled, and norms about gender, authority and responsibility may contribute to the roles each parent plays in the care and/or abuse of children (Goldner, 1990).

Family character dimension

Family character are those features of family life which make up the pattern of typical ways the family go about their lives together. If the tasks identified in the previous dimension of family organisation are central to meeting the needs of children, the dimension of family character can be seen as providing the context for how those tasks are carried out. The different characteristics identified in this dimension all contribute to the ways families organise themselves and respond to the challenges posed by the evolving needs of family members or changing circumstances.

All the components of family character give each family its own characteristic style or 'thumb print'. Again, a range of strengths and difficulties can be identified for each component which affect how a family manages the tasks and challenges they inevitably face and how they approach resolving any problems they encounter.

Few of the tasks identified in the family organisation dimension can be effectively carried out without being able to communicate adequately. How people in the family talk to and listen to each other is at the centre of *family communication* as well as the non-verbal interchange between family members, such as tone of voice, pace, eye contact and body gestures. Family communication affects all areas of family life and impacts on children's development. For instance, we know that communication with children is an important factor for their later education. Children who are spoken and read to from an early age develop their verbal skills faster and learn to read earlier (Sinclair, 1998). Research on gender differences in communicating style suggests that women tend to give more emphasis to intimacy, connectedness and finding similarities, and men to independence, hierarchy and finding solutions. Such differences may inform how men and women communicate in families (Tannen, 1990).

Looking at the 'filters' or particular circumstances a practitioner takes into account when making an assessment – in families with deaf adults or children, or with family members who have visual or speech impairments for example – talking may not be the main means of communication with other family members and assessment work should be adapted accordingly.

When undertaking family assessments there are various elements of family communication which it is useful to explore, starting with the *expression and reception of messages*.

Looking at the expression of messages (the way family members communicate *to* other family members), clarity of expression is crucial for communication of meaning and for information to be exchanged effectively. For example, when families communicate in ways which are ambiguous or contradictory it becomes more difficult to resolve difficulties together.

Sending messages is one thing but effective family communication is also dependent upon the *reception of messages* and how far messages are acknowledged, listened to and appropriately responded to by family members.

Involvement and continuity are also important aspects of communication. Being able to focus on a topic, develop it and move it on is important if a family is to be able communicate effectively – this can be observed in a family with reasonable strengths. When continuity is interrupted or fragmented then it is difficult, for example, for families to make decisions or resolve conflicts effectively.

The practitioner should be able to rate how effectively the family communicates. In a family with reasonable strengths the family would be likely to ensure that everyone can participate in conversation, that no-one dominates and that family members are usually be able to communicate effectively. In a family where there are moderate strengths and difficulties, there may be strengths in that some members of the family can participate effectively, but one or more may dominate while others are not easily able to participate. With serious difficulties any domination, withdrawal or exclusion may be marked and severe.

The emotional life of the family

The emotional life of the family (Figure 3.4) is a complex area, involving both the inner emotional experience of family members and the observable expression of feelings in the family as a whole. It is therefore difficult to assess and yet it significantly colours the way in which family life is experienced by family members. Here, also, cultural norms need to be considered.

In this component of family character the focus is on how it might feel to be in the family and how feelings are conveyed between family members. Are relationships supportive, valuing and appreciative? Are people emotionally involved with each other? How do family members express and respond to feelings? What is the overall atmosphere or feel of the family?

The *expression and reception of feelings* is central to the emotional life of the family. How feelings are expressed and responded to affects the inner emotional experience of individuals and the internal map and expectations they build up of the relationships they have. It is often possible to observe an overall pattern in the *nature of relationships* in a family which helps to understand how family members expect to be treated by each other. These patterns can be largely beneficial or may pose difficulties for the individuals concerned and the emotional growth and development of children.

The level of *emotional involvement* of family members also affects the emotional well-being of everyone in the family. Family members who are reasonably well-attuned and empathic towards one another will have strengths to call upon. Where there are moderate strengths and difficulties some family members may be engaged with and empathic towards other family members, but there may also be evidence of significant emotional under or overinvolvement between others. For example, alternatively some members may be overresponsive or intrusive towards others who respond by defending themselves in a range of ways which restrict their self-expression.

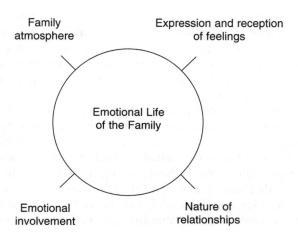

Figure 3.4   Elements of the emotional life of the family component of family character

The *emotional atmosphere* in a family is a more general aspect of the emotional life of the family and concerns the overall 'feel' of the family when they are all together. It is also an aspect of families likely to permeate the whole of family life for both children and adults. Family atmosphere, although a rather intangible idea, is something which is well-recognised by people working with families and has been reliably rated in research studies (Bentovim and Bingley Miller, 2001; Kinston *et al.*, 1987).

Family alliances

In making a family assessment, family alliances – that is the important groupings or subsystems in the family – are important to understand (Figure 3.5). We can see families as being made up of several teams each of which has a set of relationships. Where there are two adults they are a team as a couple but they also form a team as parents in which they may operate differently. The siblings are another grouping, as are the parents together with the children and the family as a whole.

It is useful to assess how well each of these teams work together to see whether there are particular relationships which would benefit from focused work. If there are two adults in the family who are partners, the nature of their couple relationship affects how they contribute to meeting each other's emotional and sexual needs as adults. The quality of the *couple relationship* affects all the other relationships in the family. Cultural differences influence expectations about what needs should be met in the couple relationship. For example, in some cultures companionship, affection and warmth may more often be provided by other relationships in a person's network of family or friends rather than in the couple relationship.

The *parental relationship* – the relationship between the adults in their

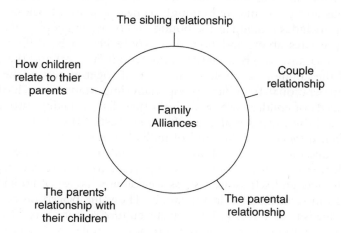

Figure 3.5 Elements of the family alliances component of family character

role as parents – is an important factor in how successfully they carry out the
tasks of parenting. Parenting includes the nurturing and socialisation of the
children which involves the adults cooperating over care-giving in response
to care-seeking by the children, providing stimulation, encouragement and
praise and the general guidance, care and management of the children. The
degree to which parents can cooperate effectively affects the quality of
parenting the children are likely to receive which in turn impacts upon their
well-being.

The *relationship parents have with their children* is an important factor in
how far the adults can understand and take appropriate action towards
meeting the particular needs of each child. *How the children relate to their
parents* also influences the scope for developing a strong and positive and
adaptable relationship between parents and children. In *sibling relationships*
children can be a source of strength, support and friendship to one another,
or the relationship between them may add to difficulties a child already has.
There is an opportunity in sibling relationship to develop a range of skills
such as sharing, communicating clearly, negotiating, conflict resolution and
care-seeking and care-giving. It is also an arena in which imbalances in
power can be encountered and where unresolved difficulties in other relationships may be acted out. We therefore need to be sensitive to the possibilities of sibling abuse. Sibling relationships have the potential to be the
source of considerable interpersonal pain and difficulty and influence how
an individual comes to view themselves and their capacity to relate to their
peers.

Family identity

In family identity (Figure 3.6) we explore the boundaries in the family to
find out how far individuals are able to be separate enough to be
autonomous and yet connected enough to have a sense of belonging as a
family. This includes looking at the boundaries between people – what each
person appreciates about and how they would like to be different from
others in the family, who is close to whom, who is far apart and the boundary round the family as a whole – the sense of togetherness in the family.
The intergenerational boundary is especially important when looking at
how the needs of children are met within their family, taking into account
life stages and the wider social and cultural context of the family.

Individual autonomy at the level of individual functioning is concerned
with the boundaries that contribute to each family member's sense of identity and degree of individuation. It is important to explore the degree of
self-assertiveness and self-awareness, as well as how issues of individuation
and separation were handled in the family. The value placed on autonomy
and individualism in a Western European culture is not shared by others
from different cultural backgrounds where, for example, the balance may be
more towards familial interdependence and bringing up children to take a

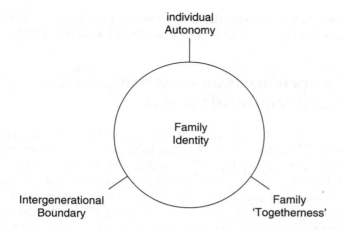

Figure 3.6 Elements of the family identity component of family character

role as a dependable family member in an extended family system. When children encounter different values in the social context outside the family this can lead to difficulties within family relationships and may be a useful focus for work with the family (Dosanjh and Ghuman, 1998).

Family togetherness is about whether family members are reasonably close – so we are looking at the separateness and connectedness of the family as a whole. The degree to which a family has a sense of cohesion and belonging together and the level of involvement of family members can have an important impact for their sense of identity as a family and as individuals.

It is also important to explore the ways in which *intergenerational boundaries* are drawn. Looking again at ways of rating strengths and difficulties, an important strength for managing life-cycle changes is when parents mostly act as parents and children as children. Where there are moderate strengths and difficulties, there will be some areas where there is clarity and appropriate flexibility about intergenerational boundaries, and others where there is significant ambiguity and confusion about the roles of parents and children. Alternatively, one parent may be much more able to keep in role as a parent in a way which is appropriate to the ages and stages of development, while the other is inappropriately rigid or seriously blurs or disrupts the boundary. It is concerning where, for example, the boundary between parents and children is overly rigid or where children have to 'parent' or emotionally care for their own parents to the extent of not receiving the parenting they need and the parents not taking up their role as parents with accompanying appropriately parental behaviour.

A situation involving intergenerational boundaries which requires careful assessment is when children have a parent with a physical or mental illness or impairment who needs care. It is a difficult task to define what is a reasonable level of care for a young carer to take on, and at what point the parent's need for care cuts across the child or young person's own needs and development (Aldridge and Becker, 1999; Blyth and Waddell, 1999).

Family Competence Scales: assessing family strengths and family difficulties

A key principle of the Family Assessment is to give equal importance to the assessment of family strengths as to charting their difficulties. Many existing models of assessment and methods for working with families tend towards a deficit model, whereas the one developed here focuses on family strengths as a central factor in planning future work or action with a family. For example, in the section on the nature of relationships you, as the practitioner, are invited to explore whether the relationships are 'supportive, valuing and appreciative' rather than 'lacking in support, undermining and unappreciative'. A qualitative picture of both strengths and difficulties is therefore built up over the assessment.

Most families have the capacity to organise themselves in such a way as to meet the needs of children well enough and to cope with the stresses of family life. We would define this capacity as 'family competence'. The family competence scales provide a quantitative way of assessing the family strengths and difficulties in each element of the components of family organisation and family character. They are based on a continuum of descriptors, ranging from how a family with 'reasonable strengths' in the particular area concerned might interact through a family with 'moderate strengths and difficulties' to one with 'considerable difficulties'. The scale is deliberately constructed to identify 'reasonable' rather then 'optimal' strengths in an attempt to identify the features which are likely to be good enough to contribute to the family being able to meet a child's needs. The ratings can also be used to assess whether there have been changes over time when you are working with a family. The scale shown in Figure 3.7 is an example of how 'managing and resolving conflict' which is one element of family adaptability is represented in a family competence scale.

The context of family history

In addition to exploring the current problem and how it relates to family organisation and family character, family history can provide a crucial context. We all bring past experience of families, relationships and significant family events which affect how we react and respond to our current families (Bentovim and Kinston, 1991; Glaser *et al.*, 1984; McCluskey and Miller, 1985). We are also influenced by the values, beliefs and culture of our extended family. The wider historical, social and political context in which we grow up has an inevitable impact on our parents and ourselves as

Component of family organisation	Reasonable strengths	Moderate strengths and difficulties	Considerable difficulties
Family Adaptability Managing and resolving conflict	Conflicts acknowledged and resolved despite occasional inappropriate reactions	Conflicts sometimes handled reasonably, other conflicts disrupt family task completion, family becomes caught up in conflicts at times	Conflicts frequent or continuous, futile arguments or major withdrawal of family member(s)
Tick appropriate level			

Figure 3.7

children, particularly if it has involved disadvantage, discrimination or experiences of separation, loss or trauma.

For example, significantly painful experiences in childhood which have been difficult to resolve can mean we feel strongly that we want to bring up our own children differently. We may seek to create the opposite in our own families or to erase our childhood. We may be able to do things differently by choosing partners who are different, or we may replicate the experiences or their like, even choosing a partner with whom we repeat the same pattern of interacting. Traumatic events can be so powerful as to organise the way individuals relate so that the family become a 'trauma-organised' family system (Bentovim and Davenport, 1992). For example, the impact of traumatic experiences may result in family members being silenced on emotional issues generally or, alternatively, a particular emotional issue related to the trauma may become a central focus in a family.

The Family Assessment has a section on family history which seeks to explore with adults (and sometimes older children) in the family how significant past experiences may be affecting how they understand and respond to current family relationships and difficulties and therefore have an impact on current family functioning.

Skills and methods for working with families during the assessment process

One major component of The Family Assessment is therefore to provide practitioners with a systematic evidence-based approach to making assessments. The Family Assessment also explores a range of methods for getting to know families and including them in the assessment in ways which are open and transparent, which promote the building of a working partnership and which enable the practitioner to collect the necessary information. Different interviewing tools provide ways of exploring family life and relationships. Most of the methods involve seeing the family together, with the exception of the family history interview where the parents or adults might be seen without the children either together or separately.

The Family Assessment Interview Schedules

The 'methods for promoting family interaction' section in the Family Assessment pack contains interview schedules with questions and family tasks which may be useful in assessment work with families. As with the rest of the Family Assessment, these point the practitioner towards exploring family strengths as well as difficulties. The semi-structured interview schedules cover each of the components of family organisation and family character, and also 'mapping the current identified problems, concerns and difficulties' and family history. Although each schedule comprises a structured set of questions, they are intended to be used flexibly and by negotiation with the family. This means that the practitioner regularly explains to the family why it is being suggested that they talk about a particular aspect of experience and then feeds back and discusses their observations about how the family responds.

The Family Assessment Family Tasks Schedule

Another way of exploring an area of family organisation or family character is to set a *Family Task*. In the Family Assessment a range of family tasks are suggested which families can be asked to do together. Some are activity-based and others involve talking together, appropriate to the different ages of the children. The purpose is to provide opportunities for the family to interact together in a more natural way without interruption, for professional observation, and give the family and practitioner an opportunity to reflect on how they carried out the task. The family tasks fall into four main categories:

- *Family activities*, for example building a tower from bricks together, or planning an outing together.
- *Thoughts about the family*, for example discussing everyone's likes and dislikes, or who is like whom in the family.
- *Family experiences*, for example special events in the family and how they are celebrated, when the children were babies, or how the children were given their names.
- *Significant issues for the family*, for example what have been the best and the worst times for the family, or why particular separations occurred.

Some criteria for choosing tasks include:

- *Wanting to gather information about a particular element of family functioning*: each task links in with the family organisation and family character elements, providing opportunities for collecting information about the same area from two different sources.
- *The ages of the children*: the tasks often help young children to participate and become actively involved.
- *Putting the family at ease*.
- *Changing the pace*: replacing part of the interview with a task to give the family a rest from talking.

The Family Assessment gives guidance about setting tasks and ways of exploring with the family at the end of the task how they relate together based on the immediate and 'live' example of interaction which a family task provides.

The Family Assessment Recording Form

The Recording Form forms the focus for making a systematic, structured assessment through the stages of observation, description and analysis (Figure 3.8). It enables the practitioner to gather referral and initial information and information on the current identified problems, the two dimensions of family organisation and family character and relevant aspects of family history. The form aims to build up a descriptive and transparent language which is accessible to the family to describe areas of family life which are relevant to making a family assessment. Each section is carefully structured to help the practitioner systematically describe, assess and rate each aspect of family organisation and family character and to map out the other areas covered. Each section has prompts derived from the interview

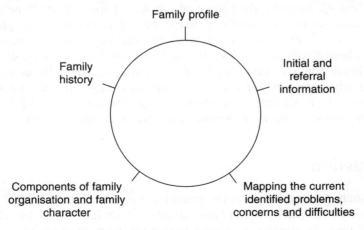

Figure 3.8 Elements of the family assessment recording form

schedules as a guide to the areas it may be helpful to explore, and a list of relevant family tasks is provided. In this way a profile of family strengths and difficulties is built up through the assessment process.

The *Family Profile* at the end of the Recording Form pulls together and summaries the information gathered into an evidence-based family assessment which includes the plans for intervention. It includes a summary of the family and the assessor's view of the main problems, a qualitative and quantitative profile of family strengths and difficulties in family organisation and family character. An assessment of the impact on the children's well-being and development is made. Important indicators of the potential for working successfully are whether the family are able to take responsibility to achieve change, whether supportive wider family members who are not involved could be included, and the need to work on any significant important unresolved past experiences which are getting in the way. Families also record their views. Finally, the outcomes needed to increase the likelihood of the needs of the child or young person concerned being appropriately met are identified.

The Appendix provides an example of a completed Family Profile on the Bradshaw family, comprising Gina, in her early 30s, Frank, in his late 20s, and their children Ben, aged five, and Annie who is three months old. The family's Health Visitor was concerned about Gina's immediate rejection of Ben when he was born. Their relationship has never been easy, and since Annie's birth the situation has seriously deteriorated. The arguments between Gina and Ben have increased significantly and the level of tension is high. The Health Visitor has never met Frank and does not know his view of the current circumstances. The Health Visitor has referred the family to Social Services, with Gina's consent, because she believes Ben is at increasing risk of significant harm. Details of the original family have been changed to ensure confidentiality.

Following conducting a family meeting using both interview schedules and family tasks, the practitioner struggles to understand the pattern of family interaction that she observes. In talking to the couple about their family history, however, the couple talk about experiences which help them all to make more sense of the pattern and the implications for planning future work. Frank was brought up as the middle of three brothers in a family where conflict led to his older and favourite brother being sent away when Frank was six years old. Frank then took on the role of reducing conflict whenever possible and protecting his younger brother to avoid a repetition of this disaster. Gina spoke for the first time about having been sexually abused by an uncle between the ages of six and ten years old.

Discussion

The Family Assessment assists the practitioner in making a systematic, multi-dimensional and comprehensive assessment of family functioning on which to base planning for support, resources, therapeutic work or other interventions to increase the likelihood that the needs of the children in the family are appropriately responded to. The assessment is evidence-based because it is built on careful observation, description and analysis and checking out the practitioner's assessment with the family. The focus on strengths as well as difficulties helps the practitioner to plan for building on strengths and reducing difficulties. The language and methods used promote sharing and building up the assessment with the family throughout the assessment process.

Our early experience of using this model suggests that families respond well to its open, transparent and accessible nature Working partnerships have been made with a range of families who enjoyed both the interview schedules and the family tasks and the completion of the recording form, and used them as basis for talking with workers about themselves as a family.

Practitioners have reported finding the model effective in enhancing their assessment skills and ensuring that they make a comprehensive assessment, addressing many of the areas contained in a core assessment, which they can back up with observations. They value the encouragement to use their skills as reflective practitioners and to employ a range of approaches when working with families during the assessment process. They particularly appreciate the focus on strengths and note that significant new information has emerged and they have found it a useful way of discussing their assessment with families. It is also likely that practitioners will find The Family Assessment useful for court proceedings because of the detailed and specific evidence supporting their recommendations and the greater confidence will give professionals using it.

At the same time, it is important that families are not led to believe that this process will be a gateway to resources. Workers need to be very clear with families about the purpose and nature of the assessment and the areas covered so that they are as well-placed as possible to make informed choices about their involvement. Equally, practitioners must avoid raising false expectations.

Implementing the use of the Family Assessment has implications for organisations. Practitioners require training in its use and supervision to maintain their skills the instruments. In the early stages practitioners should undertake assessments in pairs. Planning, setting up and conducting the necessary family meetings may be time-consuming depending on the purpose of the assessment, especially while practitioners are becoming familiar with the Family Assessment approach, although the outcomes are usually worth the investment and have benefits beyond the assessment process. While the information about the type and level of need for children and their families is directly relevant to the Assessment Framework it does not cover all aspects of the social and environmental context in which the family lives – so additional assessment work may be required. Also, the recording form will need to be integrated with other agency recording procedures.

Finally, the family assessment has yet to be fully evaluated in its current form, though it is based on well-researched instruments, but current indications from professionals using it in a range of agencies are that it can provide a useful and effective aid to making systematic and evidence-based assessments which can be used to plan for responding to the needs of children in need and their families.

Appendix: The Family Assessment family profile

Family name: Bradshaw

Current identified problem(s), concerns or difficulties in the family

Current problems: family members' views	*Current problems: assessor's views*
Ben, at five years old, is perceived as a child whose behaviour is difficult to manage, particularly his frequently aggressive behaviour towards three-month-old Annie. His mother, Gina Bradshaw, sees Ben as defiant – a bad child who invites punishment. On the other hand, his father, Frank Bradshaw, perceives him as 'just a child'. Frank feels excluded from the relationship between Gina and Annie. Gina is determined to protect Annie from Ben's aggression which she has complained about to her health visitor.	The assessors see Gina as over-protective of Annie which contributes to Ben's feeling of being displaced by his sister. This is demonstrated by his oppositional, jealous behaviour which Gina perceives as evidence of Ben being an aggressive child, justifying her angry, rejecting attitude towards him. Frank attempts to defuse the conflict and is far more supportive of Ben and feels somewhat excluded from contact with Annie. At the same time he also attempts to defuse conflicts between himself and Gina. Inevitably, his emotional support for Ben maintains Ben's defiance of his mother, and this means that Frank, as Ben's father, has to continue in his attempts to defuse conflicts between them. However, this action inevitably maintains them.

Profile of family competence, strengths and difficulties

5 = reasonable strengths — 4 — 3 = moderate strengths and difficulties — 2 — 1 = considerable difficulties

Family adaptability (family organisation dimension)	**Level of family competence** (place rating score in each box)	
Narrative summary of strengths and difficulties In ensuring that Annie's needs are accommodated in a highly protective fashion, Ben's needs as a five year old are not well-responded to. He is kept at arm's length by Gina, and is distanced. His response is to be angry and distancing and he shows jealousy towards Annie. His father tries hard to compensate and to adapt more appropriately. He sees him as a normal child, and tries to respond to him more appropriately. Difficulties in decision-making are evident in many areas. Frank attempts to adapt to Gina's negative views and decisions concerning Ben and Annie so there is no process of decision-making. There are failures to reach decisions and so mixed messages are given to Ben about decisions. Ben makes arbitrary decisions and grabs objects from Annie, but he	Organisational adaptability	3
	Decision-making & problem solving	3

responds to his father who makes more appropriate decisions independently of Gina.

Conflicts are not adequately resolved, and remain unsolved between the parents. Frank attempts to rescue Ben from increasing conflicts between his mother and himself over his attitude towards the baby, and his generally defiant and oppositional behaviour. Frank's attempt to avoid conflict with Gina, and to support Ben means that conflicts are generally unresolved.

We have little information about current links with family and community, but there is a suggestion that Gina has distanced herself from her own family, particularly her father. The fact that the health visitor made the referral gives an indication that there may be reasonable links with the community. It is not possible to give this a score.

Managing and resolving conflict	3
Relationships – family/community	
Overall level: family adaptability	3

Parenting (family organisation dimension)	Level of family competence (place rating score in each box)
Narrative summary of strengths and difficulties	
This is an area again where Ben has a very different quality of parenting from each of his parents with his father being empathic, responsive, praising and supportive to Ben, whilst his mother is critical and demanding and perceives him in a negative light.	Promoting development stimulation, emotional warmth — 3
There seems to be a positive, secure attachment between Ben and his father which they demonstrate by warmth and closeness, but the attachment between Ben and his mother seems aversive. Ben attempts to control his mother, and feels rejected because of her focus on the baby.	Nature of attachments — 3
Again Ben is presented with a very different set of messages from each of his parents. His father uses appropriate means to control Ben, helping him in the appropriate direction, whilst his mother is angry, punitive, smacks, shouts and creates an aversive atmosphere.	Guidance, care and management of children — 2
	Overall level: Parenting — 3

Family communication (family organisation dimension)	Level of family competence (place rating score in each box)	
Narrative summary of strengths and difficulties		
Each of the parents has considerable strengths in making their needs known, and in expressing messages. But the mother's messages to Ben are sharp and critical, as are Ben's towards Annie. Gina's communications with the baby seem warm, but there is an exclusion of Frank as Annie's father. Gina and Frank often express opposite views without apparently recognising or acknowledging the fact.	Expression of messages	3
Frank shows considerable skills in listening to help him avoid conflict and to bridge the gap between statements that he has made which may have been contradicted by Gina. He and Ben listen intently, and Ben hears his father and vice versa. Gina listens with considerable difficulties to Frank, to Ben, and only has ears for Annie.	Reception of messages	3
The family participates and communicates a good deal, but Gina is central in the family, seeking others to agree with her views, Frank and Ben have to comply which results in conflict, particularly on Ben's part, and Frank withdraws from Gina.	Involvement	3
There are periods of reasonable continuity, but topics are not sustained and remain undeveloped because of the demand for agreement and compliance with Gina's views. Differences are not acknowledged or resolved. This frustration results in mother's negative views of him being reinforced.	Continuity	3
	Overall level: family communication	3

Emotional life of the family (family organisation dimension)	Level of family competence (place rating score in each box)	
Narrative summary of strengths and difficulties		
Gina expresses her feelings clearly and forcefully, even though they are negative towards Ben. Although distressed at her negative perception, Frank does not express what could be highly negative feelings which might provoke conflict. He attempts to avoid conflict between them, and gives covert warmth and support to Ben. This undermines mother's attempt to take control. Ben's behaviour towards the baby tends to be negative.	Expression and reception of feelings	3
Gina's relationship with Ben is characterised by sharpness and criticism. There is a much more supportive relationship between Ben and his father even though this can negate Gina. Frank is basically supportive of Gina emotionally, despite showing some points of disagreement, but this is not expressed and is avoided. There is less of a relation-	Nature of relationships	3

ship between Frank and the baby.

There is a good deal of closeness shown in Frank's close tracking of Gina's feelings, thoughts and attitudes to which he accommodates. He becomes involved with Ben to buffer Gina's negativity towards him, which perpetuates the negative involvement between Ben and his mother, reflected in her sharpness rejection towards him. Gina is particularly focused on the care of Annie with whom she is closely involved.

Emotional involvement	3

The pleasant atmosphere created by Frank's genial acceptance of Gina's opposing statements is perturbed by the angry, uncomfortable atmosphere which replaces it when Ben shows his feelings of lack of emotional support by attacking Annie. This in turn provokes Gina's anger and a distressing atmosphere which Frank tries to rescue.

Family atmosphere	3
Overall level : Emotional life of the family	3

Family alliances (family organisation dimension)	Level of family competence (place rating score in each box)

Narrative summary of strengths and difficulties

There appears to be considerable support on Frank's part given the way he attempts to accommodate Gina's views. This reflects his determination to maintain the strength of their relationship despite the negative relationship between Gina and Ben.

Couple partnership	3

The couple do not relate to Ben in a collaborative way. They act without reference to one another and perceive Ben quite differently and this leads to potential conflict between them as parents. Frank then has to defuse the situation, given his considerable listening skills and desire to avoid conflict.

Parental partnership	3

There is support and encouragement of Ben, accompanied by some unsupportive and harmful attitudes. Ben may be being used by the couple as a focus for their own conflict which they avoid expressing directly. This results in their giving Ben very different messages, and the parent/child relationship shows signs of strain and conflict.

Parent–child relationship	3

Ben's response to his parents is to be close and warm with his father and to listen and accept his control and discipline. He is in considerable conflict with his mother, rejecting her attempts to communicate with him, or her attempts to control him.

Child–parent relationship	3

Ben shows a degree of jealousy and rivalry towards Annie at least partially as a result of his mother's protective and attentive approach towards Annie in contrast to her treatment of him.

Sibling relationship	3
Overall level: Family alliances	3

Family identity (family organisation dimension)	Level of family competence (place rating score in each box)	
Narrative summary of strengths and difficulties		
There seem to be particular strengths in Ben's assertiveness and self-awareness. Through the support he is given by his father, his sense of autonomy is maintained. However, Frank's support of Ben does undermine his mother's authority. Gina also shows considerable strengths in assertiveness, though some of her messages are highly negative. Frank is less strongly assertive of his views because of his desire to maintain family togetherness.	Individual autonomy	3
There is a good deal of family togetherness here despite rejection and negativity between Ben and his mother. Frank's desire for conflict to be avoided is also a sign of his desire to maintain family togetherness.	Family 'togetherness'	3
Strengths in some areas, with some clear parent/child distinctions, though the arguments between Gina and Ben are somewhat sibling-like. Gina tends to come down to Ben's level, and Ben is given authority through his father's support, and Frank fails to deal with issues between himself and Gina through avoidance of conflict.	Intergenerational boundary	3
	Overall level: family identity	3

Estimate the overall level of strength and difficulty in this family	Overall level for this family	3

Impact of current family strengths and difficulties on the children

How are current family strengths and difficulties affecting the children's development and well-being?	*Are the parents aware of the family difficulties and do they take relevant responsibility for the impact on the children*
There are elements of good care in this family. Annie is protected, perhaps over-protected as her father is not allowed to be sufficiently involved with her. There are concerns about the quality of care given to Ben. Although there is a good deal of emotional support from his father, this has the effect of increasing his sense of anger and frustration with his mother's protection of Annie and rejection of	During the earlier interview there appeared to be only limited responsibility taken for the attitudes, particularly on Gina's part who saw Ben as bad. Frank seems to have more insight, and is attempting both to reduce Gina's sense of frustration and conflict, as well as to give Ben adequate support. Once the family history was shared these responses became much more understandable and

himself. Gina perceives Ben as bad, ungrateful, and deserving punishment, smacking and rejection. There is therefore risk of harm to Ben with the possibility of emotional or physical abuse with associated conduct difficulties and behavioural problems. His positive relationship with his father does have some buffering effects but is also currently maintaining difficulties.

pathways to more appropriate responsibilities seem to be laid open.

Family context and history

What resources in the present family and strengths from the family history can be built on to help deal with difficulties?

Significant issues from the family history to be addressed

The two major strengths that come through from the family history is Frank's determination that there should not be the degree of rejection or oppositional behaviour which he evidently experienced in his own family when his brother was sent to live with another family member. This led him to become determined to attempt to try to reduce the conflict between himself and Gina, and to compensate Ben for the difficulties between Gina and Ben. Gina is determined that Annie should not be abused in the way that she was, and is determined that Annie should be protected, including from both Frank and Ben. She was able to see that because of Ben being a male she has never been able to be emotionally close to him in the way that she evidently is with Annie. It is to be hoped that these family strengths can be built on which will help to avoid unnecessary rejection of Ben and distance between Frank and Annie.

What needs to be addressed is the distinction between Frank and Gina now, their current circumstances and the issues from their history that they are preoccupied with. Ben and Frank have a different identity to the uncle who abused Gina. The fact that Gina has now begun to reveal aspects of her own history may mean that she can process these abusive experiences so as to be able to become free from their shadow and relate to Ben and to Frank in a way which sees them as they really are. Frank needs to be able to find other strategies to deal with conflict other than trying to avoid it and agree with everything Gina says. His fear is that conflict will lead to destruction, rejection and breakdown. Gina will need to be helped to be able to distinguish between those men who are safe and supportive and those who can be dangerous. Frank will need to be able to manage conflict more successfully with Gina so that Ben can be helped not to hit out at Annie, or be locked into a perpetual conflict with his mother which is supported by his father.

Comments by family members

This space is for family members to record their view of the strengths and difficulties in their family and what impact they think these have on the children's development and wellbeing, and their comments on the assessment in this recording form. Continue on further sheet if required.

[Because this family profile is based on a family created for the purposes of the training video, we do not have this section completed by a family.]

Objectives for meeting the needs of the child/young person

Outline goals for future work, identifying any specific objectives for changes in family functioning, and indicate how these objectives can be achieved and your assessment of the likelihood of achieving changes.

Goals for future work would therefore be:

To assist each of the parents to deal with the anxieties and fears for their own family which have arisen from their families of origin. Gina in particular is likely to respond to and benefit from individual counselling for the abuse she experienced. Frank and Gina may also benefit from some work together as a couple to integrate the new information and build on their strengths to find new ways of managing differences between them.

For the parents to be able to settle conflicts directly between themselves, rather than avoiding them and diverting them through Ben instead.

To help Ben and Annie to relate in a more appropriate sibling way so that Ben develops an attachment with her in which he can share things with her and respond to her with gentleness.

For Frank to understand that his emotional support in compensation for Ben's oppositional behaviour only maintains it, and for Gina to learn that rejecting, angry responses will only reinforce a child's negative, oppositional behaviour. Other parenting strategies for caring for Ben need to be developed.

To help develop more appropriate ways of discipline and management, and for the parents to agree and share these approaches so that Ben is faced with a consistent message about his behaviour.

Changes would be recognised through a change in overall family strengths and difficulties, with the parents being able to communicate with equality of expression, listening and acknowledgement. Improvements in the continuity of conversations involving Ben without Ben differentiating in his communication between father and mother also need to be made. Both parents also need to respond equally to Annie, with a greater sense of trust and collaboration between them in relating to Annie, and to Ben. Ben to show more collaborative behaviour and less oppositional negative behaviour and to be equally involved with both his parents.

References

Acheson, D. (1998) *Independent Inquiry into Inequalities in Heath*. London: The Stationery Office.

Aldridge, A. and Becker, S. (1999) 'Children as Carers: The Impact of Parental Illness on Children's Caring Roles', *Journal of Family Therapy*, vol. 21, pp. 303–20.

Ashworth, A. and Erooga, M. (1999) 'Child Protection and Domestic Violence: Pointers for Practitioners', (ed.) the Violence Against Children Study Group, *Children, Child Abuse and Child Protection*. Chichester: Wiley.

Bebbington, A. and Miles, J. (1989) 'The Background of Children Who Enter Local Authority Care', *British Journal of Social Work*, vol. 19, pp. 5 349–68.

Barn, R., Sinclair, R. and Ferdinand, D. (1997) *Acting on Principle, an Examination of Race and Ethnicity in Social Services Provision for Children and Families*. London: BAAF.

Bentovim, A. and Bingley Miller, L. (2001) *The Family Assessment: Assessment of Family Competence, Strengths and Difficulties*. Brighton: Pavilion Publishers.

Bentovim, A. and Davenport, M. (1992) 'Resolving the Trauma-Organised System of Sexual Abuse by Confronting the Abuser', *Journal of Family Therapy*, vol. 14, pp. 29–50.

Bentovim, A., Kinston, W. (1991) 'Focal Family Therapy: Joining Systems Theory with Psychodynamic Understanding', in A. S. Gurman and D. P. Kniskern (eds), *Handbook of Family Therapy*, Vol. II. New York: Brunner/Mazel.

Blyth, E. and Waddell, A. (1999) 'Young Carers – the Contradictions of Being a Young Carer', in (ed.) the Violence Against Children Study Group, *Children, Child Abuse and Child Protection*. Chichester: Wiley.

Bradshaw, J. (1990) *Child Poverty and Deprivation in the UK*. London: NCB.

Butt, J. and Box, C. (1998) *Family Centred. A Study of the Use of Family Centres by Black Families*. London: REU.

Cleaver, H., Unell, I. and Aldgate, J. (1999) *Children's Needs – Parenting Capacity: the Impact of Parental Mental Illness, Problem Alcohol and Drug Use, and Domestic Violence on Children's Development*. London: The Stationery Office.

Dutt, R. and Phillips, M. (1996) 'Report of the National Commission of Enquiry into the Prevention of Child Abuse', vol. 2 *Background Papers*. London: The Stationery Office.

Department of Health (1998) *Removing Barriers for Disabled Children*. London: Department of Health.

Department of Health, the Department of Education and Employment and the Home Office (2000a) *Framework for the Assessment of Children in Need and Their Families*.

Department of Health (2000b) *Framework for the Assessment of Children in Need and Their Families: Practice Guidance*. London: The Stationery Office.

Dosanjh, J. S. and Ghuman, P. A. S. (1998) 'Child Rearing Practices in Two Generations of Punjabi Parents: Development of Personality and Independence'. *Children and Society*, vol. 12, 25–37.

French, S. (1993) 'Can You See the Rainbow? The Roots of Denial', in V. Finkelstein (ed.) *Disabling Barriers and Enabling Environments*. London: Sage.

Glaser, D., Furniss, T. and Bingley, L. (1984) 'Focal Family Therapy: the Assessment Stage', *Journal of Family Therapy*, vol. 4, pp. 117–32.

Goldner, V., Penn, P., Sheinberg, M. and Walker, G. (1990) 'Love and Violence: Paradoxes of Volatile Attachments', *Family Process* 29, 343–64.

Grant, L. (1996) 'Parenting in Black Families', *The Parenting Forum Newsletter*, no. 5.

Hylton, C. (1997) 'Family survival strategies', *Exploring Parenthood*.

Iwaniec, D. (1996) *The Emotionally Abused and Neglected Child*. Chichester: Wiley.

Joseph Rowntree Foundation (1999) *Supporting Disabled Children and Their Families: A Summary of Research Findings*. York: Joseph Rowntree Foundation.

Kinston, W., Loader, P. and Bingley Miller, L. (1987) 'Quantifying the Clinical Assessment of Family Health', *Journal of Marital and Family Therapy*, vol. 13: pp 49–67.

McCluskey, U. and Bingley Miller, L. (1995) 'Theme-focused Family Therapy: The Inner Emotional World of the Family', *Journal of Family Therapy*, vol. 17, 411–34.

Morris, J. (1998) *Still missing? Volume 2: Disabled Children and the Children Act.* London: Barnardos.

Murray, P. and Penman, J. (1996) 'Let Our Children Be: A Collection of Stories', *Parents with Attitude.*

Oliver, M. (1999) *Understanding disability: from theory to practice.* London: Macmillan.

Owusu-Bempah, J. and Hewitt, D. (1999) 'Socio-Genealogical Connectedness, Attachment Theory and Child Care Practice', *Child and Family Social Work*, vol. 2, 199–207.

Social Services Inspectorate and Surrey County Council (1995) *Unaccompanied Asylum-Seeking Children: A Training Pack.* London: Department of Health.

Tannen, D. (1991) *You Just Don't Understand: Men and Women in Conversation.* London: Virago Press.

Sinclair, R. (1998) *The Education of Children in Need. Research into practice.* Dartington: NCB.

Thomas, L. (1995) *Multi-Cultural Aspects of Attachment.* Internet.

4

Using Extended attachment theory as an evidence-based guide when working with families

Dorothy Heard

Introduction

The title of this chapter immediately raises questions: why, and how, has attachment theory been extended; and in what way does one use a theory as a guide. Addressing each of these questions in turn divides the chapter into three sections. The first provides our reasons for extending attachment theory; the second describes the ways in which Bowlby and Ainsworth's work has been extended, and the third explores some of the ways in which the extended theory can be used in practice.

1   Reasons for extending Attachment Theory

The Bowlby/Ainsworth attachment theory, built on reliable empirical evidence, is of immense value. It has, over time, although not without meeting resistance, revolutionised the way in which the needs of children are regarded by authority figures. It has opened children's hospital wards to parents; it has produced reliable evidence showing the caring professions the untoward effects on the psychological and physical health of children when they have insecure relationships with their parents and those in a parental role.

Nevertheless it has not been developed far enough to give practitioners within the caring professions guidance when working with adult clients who are in parental or mentor roles or with adolescents and adults more interested in life with their peers than with their parents or those of that generation. Furthermore, attachment theory does not include ways to conceptualise the array of sexual relationships commonly seen, ranging from stable affectional relationships to those that are promiscuous, often violent, and in which sustained long-term affection is lacking; nor does the theory throw light on the confusion of feelings aroused in parents and their offspring when they begin to make romantic attachments and their parents split up to make new sexual relationships.

Attachment theory was extended (Heard, 1978, 1982; Heard and Lake, 1986, 1997) to (1) bring within the frame of attachment and caregiving the part that companionable and exploratory interest-sharing relationships with one's peers and affectional sexual relationships play in one's life; (2) give consideration to the large range of highly ingenious defensive strategies by which individuals maintain important relationships that are experienced as conflict and fear-ridden and are shown to be insecure; and (3) explain the powerful subjective effects on mood and sense of self that are evoked whenever non-verbal signals are exchanged though body language. For example, their body language leads some people to be described as: 'he is always winding me up'; or 'she is a lovely person to be with, she makes me feel great'; and 'whatever I do, he is always critical so I feel no good'.

We have included in the extension to attachment theory the effects on mood and sense of self awakened through body language because we focus on an aspect of Bowlby's attachment theory not commonly considered: his concept that instinctive behaviour is based on goal-corrected behavioural systems. Such systems are organised so that behaviour is adapted to meet a defined goal. He selected two for study, care-seeking and care-giving. Adopting the view that the behaviour of care-seeking and care-giving are goal-corrected shifts the main focus of the theory from security and insecurity to the subjective experience of approaching, reaching and failing to reach the goals of these two behavioural systems. This change of focus means that security for adults becomes a consequence of having had, regularly enough, the experience of reaching the goal of their care-seeking and care-giving systems, whilst insecurity is the opposite experience.

Subjective experience is an issue John Bowlby, for good reason, did not try to investigate until late in his life, although he was well aware of its significance. When he first thought out attachment theory there was no methodology to study subjective experience. The alternative strategy he and Mary Ainsworth adopted was to study aspects of relationships that could be objectively measured (such as changes in closeness and distance between people) and leave the study of our subjective experience until later. He did, however, lay foundations for the study of the inner subjective world in his use of the concept of internal working models (IWMs) and his thoughtful approach to the ways in which we process the mass of information that relentlessly bombards our senses (Bowlby, 1969/1982, 1988).

In the twenty-first century methodologies are, fortunately, being developed to study non-verbal language. Two leaders in this field, Daniel Stern and Colwyn Trevarthen, have demonstrated that the quality of non-verbal signals exchanged between adults and infants – the only means of communication between them before the development of speech – have crucial effects on the development of an infant's social and psychological capacities.

Methodologies for investigating the effects of interactional exchanges between adults, verbal and non-verbal, however, are still at an early stage. Dating from the time Freud observed the phenomena of transference and countertransference, psychoanalysts and others have recognised the emotive power of body language. Practitioners still need more understanding, based on reliable research evidence, if they are to find answers to questions about why non-verbal signals should have such powerful effects on one's sense of worth and competence.

In section 2 we first describe how Bowlby came to introduce care-seeking and care-giving. We then introduce the view that there exists a dynamic relationship between these two systems that safeguards both exploration and well-being. We describe how, by adding three systems which are organised on the same lines as care-seeking and care-giving, five goal-corrected behavioural systems can be seen to function in adults as one instinctive process to sustain well-being and exploration in regard to four relational activities: (1) sharing mutual interests with ones peers which includes 'playing' with them in the sense defined by Winnicott. From this activity friendships can arise, or in special instances (not discussed in this Chapter) affectional sexual relationships; (2) seeking care as defined by Bowlby from parental figures or help in developing psychological capacities; (3) giving Bowlbian care when it is seen as necessary, alternating with helping psychological development. The latter is usefully seen as educative, taking place during mentoring; (4) being able to look after oneself as far as is possible, including being able to defend oneself appropriately when attacked or being influenced to join in activities that in the long term will affect one's well-being. Reaching the goals of each of these activities sufficiently regularly safeguards the capacity of individuals to be exploratory and adaptive to environmental realities, whilst collaborating with others, with a sense of self-worth and well-being.

2 How has the Bowlby/Ainsworth Attachment Theory been extended?

The origins and major tenets of Attachment Theory

Bowlby (1982, pp. iv–v) faced the task of coming to an understanding about love and hate, anxiety and defence, and attachment and loss: the same issues that Freud had struggled with 60 years earlier.

Like Freud, Bowlby considered that these issues were concerned with instinctive behaviour. However, by the middle of the twentieth century Bowlby was able to use systems theory, and the concept of feedback taken from control theory to explain how instinctive behaviour is organised. He produced a model (Bowlby, 1982, 37–64) based on two complementary goal-corrected systems (care-giving and care-seeking) as an alternative to Freud's models; and looked to the new discipline of ethology for a method-ology to explore and investigate this model. He introduced Mary Ainsworth to the methodology ethologists were then in the process of evolving. She used it ingeniously and very productively to construct the reliable Strange Situation Test (Ainsworth *et al.* 1978), the findings of which support the concept that the degree of security shown by infants at one year of age to their mother depends upon how sensitively and rapidly their mothers have responded to care-seeking since their birth. The theory was further devel-oped by Mary Main through the use of the Adult Attachment Interview (Main and Goldwyn, 1989; Hesse, 1999). For further references to relevant research see the *Handbook of Attachment* (Cassidy and Shaver, 1999).

The characteristics of the goals of Bowlby's two goal corrected behavioural systems

Bowlby's theoretical model of instinctive behaviour is based on an explana-tion drawn from control theory: reaching a goal means that a match has been achieved between an inbuilt representation of what is required and what is obtained.

Bowlby's two instinctive systems are organised on lines similar to all our physiological systems. Physiologists can demonstrate, in precise biochemical terms, the ways in which when the goal of one physical system is satisfied, the outcome is associated with the activation of another system. These biochemical studies reveal that many systems act in this way, fitting together in an ordered and integrated manner. Between them they ensure that our nutritional needs are satisfied, our waste products removed, and that we can procreate and adapt (within finite limits) to changes on our physical envi-ronment. In this way our physical survival is safeguarded.

Physiological systems function mainly outside our awareness. They enter awareness as signs and symptoms when one or a group of systems fails to reach its goal. When all is well we have a sense of well-being.

Physiologists inform us about how we are organised to survive, without bringing in our social life or the feelings that go with reaching and not reaching goals appropriate to it. Sound evidence is emerging that shows ways in which reaching and not reaching Bowlby's two social goals affects our physiological systems. The more we learn how variations in our sense of self affect the smooth running of our physiological systems, the easier it will be to understand and manage stress-related disorders.

To return to Bowlby, he postulated that each of his two systems is activated by well-known specific signals and expressed through the behaviour of care-seeking and the complementary behaviour of care-giving. Care-seeking has a part to play throughout the lifespan of an individual (Bowlby, 1982; Heard and Lake, 1997); care-giving is not fully functional until early adult life.

Once care-seeking is activated, care-seekers seek to relate primarily to selected care-givers expecting a comforting and protective response to satisfy current bodily needs and reduce fear. In so doing the goal of the attachment system is met. The care-givers who are most effective in enabling the goal of care-seeking to be met are members of a small hierarchy of familiar protective care-givers, to whom one is attached (attachment figures).

When the goal of the care-seeking system is met, care-seeking behaviour is terminated. The attachment/care-seeking system then becomes quiescent but ready to be reactivated when a relevant signal is next perceived.

This description shows that the goals of the two systems are interpersonal in that a care-seeker requires a care-giver in order to reach the goal of care-seeking and vice versa. The striving to reach an absent care-giver, when care-givers cannot be found, shows that when care-seeking goals are not met the intensity of arousal of the system increases and the behaviour escalates. The state can often be reached when both seeker and carer are trying to find each other or influence each other to behave as each wants.

Bowlby and Ainsworth did not discuss, nor investigate, the care-giving system in the detail they gave to the care-seeking system. It is set out as being organised on the same principles and activated when attachment figures, actively involved in looking after specific children, perceive that they are not around when they might be expected. Attachment figures then start searching for them. Or if the infant or child is near by, they perceive care-seeking by recognising signs of physical distress or fear and move to protect, comfort and relieve distress. The goal of the care-giving system is reached when the care-seeker accepts and is satisfied by the care on offer; At that point the behaviour of caregiving ceases and the system becomes quiescent but capable of being reactivated when the relevant signals are next perceived. I will return to the care-giving system later.

Bowlby emphasised that physical and psychological capacities unfold gradually, according to a timetable that can, within narrow limits, be slowed down or speeded up. The processes of development ensure that the circumstances that activate attachment behaviour change in keeping with our developing competence in satisfying our own bodily and social needs, and the capacity for children and their attachment figures to develop what Bowlby has termed goal-corrected partnerships.

The latter is the product of radical developments of psychological capacities. It happens as children (around four years of age) are developing: a sense of the future, the ability to give care and the ability to see life from the point of view of another person. The latter has been explored in research on the theory of mind (Astington *et al.*, 1988) and discussed within the concept of mind mindedness (Meins, 1997), and reflective functioning (Fonagy, 1991).

The special emphasis we put on the development of the capacity to see life from the point of view of another person relates to development of empathy which I define in Section 3.

Internal working models (IWMs) and their function

Besides setting out a model for our instinctive behaviour, Bowlby also adapted the concept that we construct internal working models (IWMs) of our environment and of ourselves relating to people and to the rest of our environment. Bowlby's adaptation of this concept was built on a long tradition of its recognition to which philosophers, and psychologists (such as Piaget and Inhelder, 1948; Bartlett, 1932; and Craik, 1943) have contributed.

Bowlby considered that the main function of our IWM is to help us to plan our future lives through enabling us to rehearse the possible outcome of any particular plan. I return later to a further function for our IWMs. He considered that the most important IWMs are those of the relationships we have with other people, which in extended attachment theory are referred to as Internal Models of Experience in Relationships (IMERs). A special class of IMERs are those of relationships with the people to whom we are attached and to whom we instinctively turn – our attachment figures.

A working model of a relationship means that the model is not just a model of an attachment figure, or any other person, but is a model of oneself interacting with that other person. The model therefore includes: (1) the model one has of oneself as one feels, is affected by, thinks and behaves, when and after interacting in particular circumstances with a particular person; (2) the model one has of that person as they are feeling and thinking, and behaviour in relation to oneself and other people in their other relationships.

The essential features of extended Attachment Theory

The First Steps towards an Extension: the Concept of the Attachment Dynamic

The attachment dynamic was introduced by Heard (1978). It was conceptualised after comparing Ainsworth's research findings during the Strange Situation Test (Ainsworth *et al.*, 1978) with Winnicott's clinical anecdotal evidence describing 'play' (Winnicott, 1971); and seeing close likenesses between the two. Winnicott's clinical observations and Ainsworth's formal test both describe a pattern of relating between mother and child that suggests the operation of an interpersonal dynamic process that sustains exploration.

Ainsworth found in one year old infants that exploration of toys, or taking an interest in toys as though to find meaning in them, is either diminished or extinguished whenever the infant is left in a strange situation either with a friendly stranger or alone. She then found that the way the infant greeted the mother, when she returned after leaving the infant was highly significant. Following a brief interaction (sought by both mother and infant), securely attached children returned to exploration. Insecure children were different and could be reliably classified as avoidant, resistant/ambivalent, or disorganised.

According to Winnicott, play involves creativity and 'investing objects and phenomena from the external world with meaning and feeling of, and from dreams'. It involves doing things, through objects and people, that have meaning for the doer. Thus play has a tangible outcome; and can be distinguished from daydreaming and from the activity of fiddling with objects.

Winnicott considered that 'play' belongs to all ages and is creative in that new associations are formed between objects as they now appear and as they have been symbolised before. This solitary activity is exciting and satisfying, but also precarious. It is inhibited whenever too high a degree of physical excitement is around as may happen when strong emotions of fear, anxiety or anger are evoked or erotic feelings are engendered demanding a climax for their resolution. In the absence of these threats, Winnicott considered that play ends when a saturation point is reached.

Although he did not mention attachment, Winnicott was clear that the mothers of the children he watched could restore play by interacting in a specific way, referred to as 'holding the situation' (Winnicott, 1965, p. 49). He went further by saying that although an empathic adult can enter into a child's play, the child is unable to play when the adult takes on a managerial role. The rules and organisation that are part of recognised games can be looked on as attempts to forestall the frightening aspects of play.

Although Winnicott mentions extending his concepts into the field of cooperative social endeavours and family life, he does not develop this theme. In 1982 I went further in developing the concept of the attachment dynamic, proposing that the operation of the attachment dynamic determines whether:

- A family behaves as a more open system in which members are free to be exploratory and creative;
- Or as a more closed system in which the behaviour and thinking of family members is more inflexible and rigid (Heard, 1982).

The degree to which the family behaves as a more open system reflects the degree to which the attachment dynamic fulfils its function of restoring the capacity of family members to be exploratory. The crucial importance of empathic care-giving for this activity is underlined.

My 1982 paper was the first attempt to develop a more sophisticated model not only of the attachment dynamic, but also of parental behaviour that goes beyond care-giving as described by Bowlby. However, the concept of the family living within a more, or a less, open system was a description of a state and the outcome of that state. It was not a full enough explanation of what had brought family members to be in that state.

My understanding of the concept of the attachment dynamic remained 'stuck' until a colleague translated the psychoanalytic concept of ego strength into tangible acts that can be seen as personal and social competence appropriate to any age (Lake, 1985; Heard and Lake, 1986, 1997). Personal competence and incompetence are closely associated with reaching and not reaching goals, which in turn are associated with well-recognised feelings. Lake regarded personal competence as the ability to carry out tasks on one's own whereas social competence describes the ability to relate to others with understanding and empathy whilst sustaining a known task, requiring cooperation.

When we began to discuss the attachment dynamic, it became clear that the experience of ability to show social competence within the family circle was a central issue. We then began to develop the concept of the dynamics of attachment.

The third and fourth phase in the development of the attachment dynamic

The third phase of the evolution of the Attachment Dynamic is described in a paper (Heard and Lake, 1986), the fourth in a book *The Challenge of Attachment for Caregivers* (Heard and Lake, 1997). The difference between the two lies in the new evidence that we could use in the 1990s to support what we had originally said.

The most important new evidence was:

- The findings of Daniel Stern (Stern, 1985; Heard and Lake, 1997) on (1) cross-modal affect attunement, especially his findings that straightforward affect attunement (when mother reacts with pleasure to a baby moving towards a new level of development but in a different mode) was different from empathic attunement, which requires a cognitive input; (2) his demonstrations that mothers were able to regulate the emotional arousal of their infants through what he called 'purposeful misattunement'. This meant attuning to the feeling state of the infant but at a slightly higher or lower level of emotional arousal. The infant then attuned to the level used by the mother; and (3) his description of mother showing affects completely at variance with those shown by the baby and the baby ceasing to explore his or her environment.
- The studies of Colwyn Trevarthen (Trevarthen 1979, 1990, 2001; Heard and Lake, 1997) on primary and secondary intersubjectivity.
- The studies of MacLean (MacLean, 1990; Heard and Lake, 1997) on the evolution of patterns of instinctive social signals that define different kinds of relationships.

MacLean's findings showed that the rainbow lizard, whose offspring, once hatched, require no care-giving, and whose cognitive capacities are almost non-existent (therefore they are unable to envisage the state of another), communicates through inbuilt unchanging signals (whose neurological source he pinpointed). These signals define dominant and submissive hierarchical relationships (for humans this means master/slave and benign dictator/submissive subject relationships). He then found that primates (MacLean used the squirrel monkey) have signals that are associated with care-giving and care-seeking. Nevertheless they also use instinctive dominant and submissive patterns of communication similar to those used by the rainbow lizard and by human beings. In our book (Heard and Lake, 1997) we suggest that humans have evolved a stage further than other primates. This evolutionary step gives human beings the capacity to relate using a manner we call supportive and companionable, which is in accord with Trevarthen's descriptions of primary and secondary intersubjectivity and his more recent work (Trevarthen, 2001).

Human beings are, however, similar to other primates in that they also carry the evolutionary much older patterns of interactional behaviour shown in dominant/submissive forms of relating. We consider that the more recently evolved patterns of instinctive behaviour can be inhibited in definable circumstances, leading human beings to use two distinct interpersonal forms of relating: supportive and companionable and dominant/submissive. The former is associated in adults with the capacity to use empathy and exploration; the latter is associated at all ages with interactions that are defensive and fear-based.

Trevarthen's studies (2001) allow us to conclude that human infants, although born with very limited physical capacities, usually have from the beginning the capacities to relate to adults through the reciprocal exchange of enjoyable non-verbal signals, referred to as primary intersubjectivity. On the other hand, infants do not have the capacities: to manage high levels of emotional arousal; to cope with feelings of loneliness in the absence of familiar protective and comforting figures; and to look after others as well as oneself. These capacities unfold over years and are powerfully influenced by the quality of the social exchanges infants have with the adults who look after them.

The key features of extended Attachment Theory

In rethinking the concept of the attachment dynamic we added three other goal-corrected systems, two of which have interpersonal goals, to Bowlby's model of two instinctive complementary goal-corrected behavioural systems. The additions are:

- Two interpersonal goal-corrected partnerships – one for exploratory interest-sharing with one's peers and the other for affectional sexuality;
- A goal-corrected behavioural system for personal defence;
- Two other systems that function internally and not as goal-corrected

behavioural systems. They enlarge the function of IWMs beyond planning.

The system for exploratory interest-sharing with peers

We consider that the system for exploratory interest-sharing with peers is the social component of the exploratory system and therefore associated with mutual 'play'. Like the exploratory system (and also the system for care-giving), it is liable to be overridden by the activation of care-seeking behaviour.

A definition of peers is now suggested. Peers are people of broadly similar intelligence and the capacity to handle fear. They have similar competence in pursuit of the interests they share, and share a similar degree of stamina, defined as the capacity to stay with a demanding exploratory task despite discomfort and fatigue. Chronological age is not a prime consideration.

Major differences between exploratory interest-sharing with peers and Bowlby's complementary care-giving/care-seeking systems lie in:

- The kind of specific signals that activate the system. Activation follows reaching new levels of understanding in regard to an interest, or new achievements in an associated skill (Heard and Lake, 1997, p. 53).
- The goal is reached during interactions with interested peers who have become familiar and are trusted. The experience of reaching the goal is the same for all participants in the interaction. It is demonstrated in body language communicating pleasure that new levels of understanding and/or skill, in which others also have a stake, have been achieved. A good example is what happens on the football pitch when special skill results in an unexpected goal being scored.
- The goal of interest-sharing can be reached by members of a group as well as within a dyadic interaction.

Unlike the attachment system, which is functional from birth, the system for interest sharing with peers is not functional until just over the age of two years, except under very familiar secure conditions. It develops rapidly during childhood and adolescence. It is the system that we consider enables individuals move from the position of having parental figures as the most important in one's life, to regarding a peer in this light.

The system for affectional sexuality

We consider sexuality to be expressed through two systems: the system for affectional sexuality between peers and as an expression of the system for personal defence. Affectional sexuality can be regarded as an offshoot of the system for interest-sharing with peers boosted by the hormonal upsurge of adolescence and the attraction of 'chemistry between individuals'.

Passionate sexuality, not accompanied by long-term affection, is considered to be a form of defensive behaviour to relieve unbearable tension and loneliness (see Heard and Lake, 1997, for a fuller discussion),

The system for personal defence

The system for personal defence is active from birth. It includes all the instinctive knee-jerk reactions to danger evoked by fear. However, fear also activates attachment behaviour, and the relations between the two behaviours have been discussed (Bretherton and Ainsworth, 1974; Ainsworth *et al.*, 1978; and in Cassidy and Shaver, 1999). We consider the system for personal defence undergoes development in line with physical and psychological capacities. It is present in maturative and non-maturative forms.

The maturative form is present in situations in which individuals are able to find allies who share a common fear regarding a common enemy and are drawn to work together cooperatively for so long as this situation lasts,

The goal of non-maturative stage 1 defence is to reach a form of relating with feared attachment figures in which acceptance and approval can be experienced. When attachment bonds have withered, if ever made, non-maturative stage 2 defence is used. The goal then is to achieve pleasure and immediate relief from distress without concern for others.

Non-maturative forms of the system for personal defence give rise to many subtle and complex forms of behaviour, demonstrated in all reactions to loss that are labelled pathological. Psychological defensive capabilities and defensive behavioural strategies have as their goal the mitigation of pain, frustration, disappointment and sense of failure. Some strategies keep one in close contact with the parental figure, some lead to avoidance to maintain a comfortable distance from parental figures. Many strategies aim to influence parental figures to give some care that is less coercive or painful and more supportive and companionable. Affectionless sexuality and compulsive masturbatory activities can be considered as forms of defensive behaviour in which emotional overarousal or the sense of loneliness are relieved by the experience of orgasm.

The system for development and care-giving

From the first mention of the attachment dynamic, Heard considered care-giving to have an educative function. After further considering Trevarthen's findings and the views of attachment researchers, we now believe it more accurate to consider that the care-giving system, as described by Bowlby, represents one of two components of a parental system; the first component is care-giving as defined by Bowlby and provides protection, comfort and satisfaction of physical needs; the second promotes and sustains the development of the psychological capacities to be autonomous, exploratory and able to share mutual interests with one's peers. The care-giving component is active in a fragmentary way from early childhood. Until early adult life the development component is not fully mature and the system as a whole is not fully functional; a state exemplified by early teenage mothers who cannot look after their baby without high levels of support.

An individual whose parental system is sufficiently functional moves instinctively from one component of parenting to the other, and gives empathic responses to an infant, child or adult who is either seeking care in circumstances as defined by Bowlby, or seeking help to cope with some situation by their own efforts.

From Trevarthen's observations of primary and secondary intersubjectivity and widely recognised anecdotal evidence, no one is able to seek both components of parenting simultaneously. Seekers oscillate instinctively from seeking Bowlbian care-giving, to seeking help in developing their own interests after care-seeking needs have been satisfied.

The internalised supportive system and the personal supportive environment

The internalised supportive system and the personal supportive environment extend the function of IWMs beyond planning. The internal supportive system is made up of IWMs of an individual's relationships with attachment figures. These particular IWMs have the function of bringing instances of parental interactions into consciousness whenever attachment figures are not available. It becomes activated whenever attachment figures are unavailable and the care-seeking system has been activated either by external events or one's own physical state and feelings. Individuals are drawn back into how they were treated by that attachment figure, particularly if that figure was a primary parental figure.

Whenever attachment figures have evoked fear by their impatience, anger, unresponsiveness or absence, a fear-ridden defensive aspect of the relationship with these attachment figures is represented in the internal supportive system. This kind of representation renders the system dysfunctional in regard to these attachment figures, although relationships with other attachment figures may have contributed messages of approval conveyed through affect attunement as described by Stern and intersubjectivity as described by Trevarthen.

The internal supportive system can be a more pragmatic model for talking about Fairbairnian good and bad internal object relations and transference phenomena.

The system underlying the construction of a personal supportive environment

Associated with the internalised supportive system, although differing from it, is the system underlying the construction and maintenance of a personal supportive environment. This system guides one throughout the life-span to construct a style of life (Heard and Lake, 1997, p. 88) from memories of circumstances in which one experienced supportive and companionable interactions. When this highly personal environment cannot be maintained well enough and enjoyed, anecdotal evidence shows that feelings of depression about one's competence and worth commonly follows and with it the tendency to use dominant/submissive forms of relating.

The exploratory system

It is important to mention the exploratory system itself which fuels Winnicottean play and personal competence. It is not part of the dynamics of attachment and exploratory interest-sharing, but rather it is sustained through them. In terms of survival it is understandable that the capacity to explore should be overridden by the activation of the care-seeking system. Human beings cannot survive without having their needs for nurture and protection met and cannot engage in Winnicottean play whilst suffering high emotional arousal, fatigue or malaise. When their concerns are met, through experiencing a relationship in which a proper balance between the two components of the parenting system is maintained, the capacity for Winnicottean play re-emerges, personal competence is sustained and the internal supportive system functions more effectively.

3 Using extended Attachment Theory as an evidence-based guide when interacting in a professional role with a family

This final section describes how practitioners can use the theory as a guide when interacting with a family. Many practitioners, despite believing that the model described here is plausible, struggle to understand how it can be used as a guide when working with a family or a member of it.

Difficulties include firstly unfamiliarity with the concepts on which the extended theory is founded, second the fact that the evidence for the meaning of messages sent through non-verbal emotive signals is still under-developed and finally the emphasis we place on giving empathic responses to clients and how we envisage the task any practitioner undertakes when interacting with one or with several clients.

Empathy is a subject with a literature and several definitions. We define empathy as: (1) the ability to see another from his or her point of view, which includes the recognition of the non-verbal signals the other is sending; (2) appreciating the information contained in the non-verbal signals the other is sending that tell one (a) about the overall state of the other, (b) the feeling the other has about oneself, and (c) what is expected of oneself by the other; (3) being able to appreciate the differences between the situation the other is in and the situation one is in oneself; (4) treating the other as worthy of respect and attention without showing the fear and/or frustration that his or her non-verbal signals may have aroused.

There are suggestions in the literature that securely attached children, once old enough to see life from the point of view of another, show degrees of empathy. However, it is commonly known that a warm-hearted response, whether given by a child or an adult, is liable to be infiltrated by anxieties, especially fear engendered by defensive dominant and/or submissive modes of relating used by another person. This infiltration leaves the capacity to be empathic diminished and often overridden by defensive strategies.

Practitioners facing difficult families often find themselves at a loss over handling the situation presented by the family, and they can feel incompetent about not finding something likely to be helpful. In this state practitioners have to cope with their own defensive stategies; they can become silent and seem withdrawn and uncaring. Or, strategies are suggested that would lessen conflict or help someone face handling the difficulty about which he or she is complaining and protesting, only to find that both continue and that some family members become withdrawn or angry.

Long experience in working as a practitioner suggests that none (or very few) practitioners work effectively without having to experience and handle situations of this kind. When caught within emotions of one's own (although engendered by the way the family is relating to oneself as well as to each other), it is worth remembering that a carefully worded empathic comment directed to each family member is usually helpful.

Accurately empathic comments can release the capacity of family members to talk more constructively about the situation they are facing. When an sufficiently empathic comment does not come to mind, a statement that shows how seriously you, their practitioner, recognises their situation to be for them, and a request for more specific information (such as when it is worst, and who feels most/least affected) can demonstrate that you are concerned and interested and are prepared to learn, rather than to 'tell' them what the trouble is – even when this is exactly what they seem to be asking.

Practitioners can be helped to handle their own defensive modes of relating, many of which are used unconsciously, by asking them to engage in a personal therapeutic experience and/or by setting up the opportunity for regular supportive and companionable peer group consultations, especially those in which there is an opportunity for the practitioner to watch a video of her interactions with the client in company with an experienced and trusted consultant. This kind of training helps practitioners to recognise that they have a safe base from which to work, and keeps alive their capacity to be exploratory and empathic.

The empathic exploratory approach to forming a therapeutic relationship follows Bowlby's (1988, p. 138) view of what therapy is about. In essence it involves the practitioner helping clients to explore their own internalised representational models with a view to reappraising and restructuring the relevant IWMs in the light of new understanding and new experiences within the therapeutic relationship. Practitioners who relate to their clients in an empathic, anxiety-free and exploratory manner are modelling a way of relating to which most clients respond favourably. In this ambiance, members of a family can begin to talk about the beliefs which are embedded in their IWMs; they are more able through mutual Winnicottean 'play' to reappraise and restructure them, and they begin to feel better about themselves.

Apart from explaining why such emphasis is given to remaining exploratory, the theory I am describing needs to be seen not only as a process that is dynamic, interpersonal, goal-corrected and with a function, but also as a theoretical structure (made up of the five instinctive systems, plus the experience of reaching and not reaching their goals within (1) family relationships and (2) those outside the family) which is common to all human beings, and against which the personal narrative of each client can be matched.

Despite having this underlying common structure, pressures on the process the structure represents renders everyone's personal narrative a unique story. These pressures are exerted by the developmental changes the individual undergoes and by the quality and frequency of the interactions individuals have with (1) members of their family, (2) with their available peer group, (3) with authority figures outside the family and (4) with those with infants and children throughout the life-span.

For this reason it is not feasible to give examples of how to explore this structure by describing one family. The alternative I have adopted is to describe how to use the dynamic structure to guide assessment. Regular assessment on the lines described below enables changes in the behaviour, feelings and thoughts of family members to be noted regularly. The practitioner is able to observe progress and the final outcome.

When the process, that the common structure represents is functional, the goals of the two component systems (care-giving and development-promoting) the parents' own parental systems are being met. Parents are then able to manage family life so that everyone is related to in a sufficiently balanced way. This appears to be the context in which individuals of all ages seem to be most comfortable and productive, and can be adopted as a standard for effective parental care.

To achieve this balance parents attend to each member, keeping an eye on each member in turn, so that no one feels excluded or of no account. If this happens, as it undoubtedly will from time to time, the situation is discussed with empathy. Excesses of all kinds are regulated gently with a kind firmness and appropriate humour, and without curbing enjoyment of life. Sorrows, disappointments and losses are noted and handled with empathy. The causes for frustration and anger are enquired into and when they cannot be remedied there is empathic understanding of feelings that makes facing reality situations easier to bear; finally parents acknowledge their mistakes and do their best not to have rows in front of their children or row with them.

Parents who can reach the goals of the parental system understand the necessity to move between the need to give care as described by Bowlby, and to help their children fulfil their desires to grow up. They can recognise the complaint by children of being bored as their experience of an environment that is either not sufficiently stimulating or is confusing and over-stimulating. This list can sound an impossible task to achieve, but perfection is not required, only the level that Winnicott would have described as good enough.

In practice it is suggested that practitioners listen to all the family's contributions while noting the quality of the non-verbal communications exchanged between members. For example: who looks at whom, who is given most attention and least attention; what tones of voice, posture and 'looks' are used; do parents look at and address each other or does one parent act as spokesperson and claim the attention of the practitioner. The following chapter by McCluskey describes this process well.

Practitioners listen to what is said noting references to each of the four systems with interpersonal goals; omission of a reference is noted. The systems that may not be referred to by members of anxious defensive families are the system for exploratory interest-sharing with peers and the system for affectional sexuality. If no anecdotes about hobbies or interests emerge, the answers to a question about whether that member(s) has friends who are interesting and stimulating can bring a negative reply. The tone of the reply will carry messages such as 'what on earth are you suggesting'; 'No one interesting would be bothered with me'; or 'I have no time for hobbies but wish I had'. The third message is less defensive and despairing than the others.

Parents often behave as though parenting is based on the care-giving component only. Their care-giving can be adequate in many respects but protection from the attentions of hurtful family members or friends is often lacking, and scant attention is given to helping children manage their natural urges to grow up. These children when approaching adolescence tend to be at the mercy of the culture provided by their peers, who are often similarly deprived. As a consequence these youngsters often give little thought to the future or to managing money, relationships and possessions in relation to their future.

A pattern that should be listened for is the insecure and deprived parent who is in reality seeking care from his or her children, commonly from one particular child, Such parents commonly become angry and withdrawn, or angry and demanding when their expectations are not met.

When parents are alone, enquiries into how much they enjoy a sexual life will usually reveal an affectional relationship that may not be as good as wished for, or a marriage or partnership that is based on defensive modes of sexuality.

Practitioners are often treated by clients with defensive reserve, undue deference or veiled hostility. This means that while a practitioner is assessing how the process is functioning in the way the family relates to each other, the client is assessing how safe it is to relate to the practitioner without experiencing responses that were experienced in the past and still arouse fear. Their IWM of relating to parents may hold many examples of being put down by criticism or shaming; or of having to face hostile non-verbal messages that, for example, lead to over arousal, disorganisation and incompetence.

It is unnerving for practitioners who are not aware of feeling anything towards a client other than a desire to help, to be treated as though they were behaving in any of the ways described above, and they are often left feeling unrecognised and incompetent.

An explanation, that can be relied upon, is that something in the practitioner's physical appearance, posture, tone of voice or accent has reminded a family member of someone who has behaved as described above; the consequence being that the client's IWM of themselves within that relationship is awakened, leading the client to behave defensively. The 'someone' may not be an attachment figure but someone with whom the client was expected to interact (for example an older sibling, a member of the extended family, a childminder, a neighbour, or a school teacher) and from whose hurtful attentions the client was not protected by his or her parental figures.

Finally, families who come for help can be assumed to be insecure in regard to the difficulties they are facing and therefore to have some working models of being treated by their parental figures in unsupportive fear-evoking ways that activated defensive processes. It is therefore an important task for practitioners to work out, from the way they are themselves being treated, the kind of person(s) that has made the client so defensive. In this way a practitioner has access to some of the IWMs of each family member and can envisage the work that will be needed before these IWMs can be updated. Handling these defensive psychological mechanisms is therefore the prime task of all practitioners.

References

Ainsworth, M., Blehar, M., Waters, E. and Wall, S. (1978) *Patterns of Attachment: Assessed in the Strange Situation and at Home*. Hillsdale, NJ: Erlbaum.

Bretherton, I. and Ainsworth, M. D. S. (1974) 'Responses of One-Year-Olds to a Stranger in a Strange Situation', in M. Lewis and L. A. Rosenblum (eds), *The Origin of Fear*. New York: Wiley.

Bowlby, J. (1951) *Maternal Care and Mental Health*. Geneva: WHO; London: HMSO. Abridged version, *Child Care and the Growth of Love*, Harmondsworth: Penguin Books, 2nd edn 1965.

—— (1969) *Attachment and Loss*, Vol. 1: *Attachment*. New York: Basic Books; and London: Hogarth (2nd revised edn 1982).

—— (1988) 'On Knowing What You Are Not Supposed to Know and Feeling What You Are Not Supposed to Feel' in *A Secure Base*. London: Routledge.

Cassidy, J. and Shaver, P. R. (1999) *Handbook of Attachment*. New York and London: the Guilford Press.

Fairbairn, R. (1952) *Psychoanalytic Studies of the Personality*. London: Tavistock.

Fonagy, P. (1991) 'Thinking About Thinking: Some Clinical and Theoretical Considerations in the Treatment of a Borderline Patient', *International Journal of Psychoanalysis*, Vol. 72, pp. 639–56.

Heard, D. H. (1978) 'From Object Relations to Attachment Theory', *British Journal* of Medical Psychology, vol. 51, pp. 67–76.

—— (1982) 'Family Systems and the Attachment Dynamic', *Journal of Family Therapy*, vol. 4, pp. 99–116.

Heard, D. H. and Lake, B. (1986) 'The Attachment Dynamic in Adult Life', *British Journal of Psychiatry*, vol. 149, pp. 430–9.

—— (1997) *The Challenge of Attachment for Caregiving*. London: Routledge.

Hesse, E. (1999) 'The Adult Attachment Interview: Historical and Current Perspectives' in J. Cassidy and P. R. Shaver (eds), *The Handbook of Attachment: Theory, Research, and Clinical Applications*. New York and London: The Guilford Press.

Lake, B. (1985) 'Concept of Ego Strength in Psychotherapy', *British Journal of Psychiatry*, vol. 147, 471–78.

McCluskey, U. (2001)'A Theory of Caregiving in Adult Life: Developing and Measuring the Concept of Goal Corrected Affect Attunement', unpublished PhD thesis, University of York.

MacLean, P. D. (1990) *The Triune Brain in Evolution*. New York: Plenum Press.

Main, M. and Goldwyn, R. (1989) 'Adult Attachment Rating and Classification System', unpublished scoring manual, Department of Psychology, University of California, Berkeley.

Meins, E. (1997) *Security of Attachment and the Social Development of Cognition*. Hove: Psychology Press.

Schank, R. C. (1982) *Dynamic Memory*. Cambridge: Cambridge University Press.

Stern, D. (1985) *The Interpersonal World of the Infant*. New York: Basic Books.

Trevarthen, C. (1979) 'Communication and Co-operation in Early Infancy: A Description of Primary Subjectivity', in M. Bullova (ed.), *Before Speech: The Beginning of Interpersonal Communication*. New York: Cambridge University Press.

—— (1990) Editor's preface, 'Growth and Education of the Hemispheres', in C. Trevarthen (ed.), *Brain Circuits and Functions of the Mind*. Cambridge: Cambridge University Press.

—— (2001) 'Intrinsic Motives for Companionship and Understanding: Their Origin Development, and Significance for Infant Mental Health', *Infant Mental Health Journal*, vol. 22, pp. 95–131.

Winnicott, D. W. (1965) *The Maturational Processes and the Facilitating Environment*. London: Hogarth.

—— (1971) *Playing and Reality*. London: Tavistock.

5

Theme-Focused Family Therapy:
Working with the Dynamics of Emotional Abuse and Neglect within an Attachment and Systems Perspective

Una McCluskey*

Introduction

Theme-focused Family Therapy (TFFT) is a form of therapeutic intervention which addresses the emotional world of traumatised families. It does this by organising the family sessions around a central key theme which focuses on the affective experience of the family members. The work is to enable the family to discuss their emotions, the impact they have as individuals on one another, and the meaning they have for each other. The work requires listening to and exploring the meaning of the emotional, cognitive and non-verbal information that people pick up from one another, some-

I wish to acknowledge the contribution of Liza Bingley Miller, who contributed to the drafting of the sections on the family history and the current concerns and setting the parameters for the theme-focused work. She and I have worked together over many years with social workers applying this way of working within the context of social services departments. More recently we have taught TFFT on the York and Regions Post-Qualifying Child Care Partnership.

times unprocessed from one generation to the next. It is theme-focused because a 'theme', which captures present and past unresolved trauma, is used as a device for helping the family and the worker carry through a programme of work (McCluskey and Bingley Miller, 1995).

Theme-focused family therapy aims to provide families and their social workers with a framework for understanding the nature of emotional dynamics with particular reference to the way in which abuse, particularly emotional neglect, is carried forward transgenerationally and enacted in the present. The purpose is to help social workers and families to move beyond providing descriptions of events, and to move towards an understanding of interpersonal interaction in the here and now based on an appreciation of the meaning of past life events for both parents and their children. In order to understand the emotional dynamics of family life it is necessary to understand dyadic interaction in the context of a group and how the dyad and the group interact and affect one another. The main theoretical underpinnings of TFFT are attachment theory (essentially a formulation of dyadic interaction) and the theory of living human systems (a formulation of individual development in the context of a group).

This chapter will set out a method for engaging the family in change-directed work and provide the theoretical framework within which the work is embedded.

TFFT was originally based on an understanding of group process derived from the analytic model of object relations theory (Sutherland, 1971; Fairbairn, 1952). It was based on the principles set out by Fairbairn that individuals are primarily person-seeking and that they seek a relationship with a person with whom they can find support for their development.

TFFT was developed in the context of a residential family unit within a department of child and family psychiatry (Haldane, McCluskey and Peacey, 1981; McCluskey, 1987). The setting offered a containing environment both in terms of buildings and staff to facilitate the development and practice of exploratory work of this nature.

Over the late 1980s and 1990s this work was developed in conjunction with Liza Bingley Miller and adapted to fit the context of a busy crises-driven social services department (McCluskey and Bingley Miller, 1995). The theoretical foundation for the work was expanded to encompass the work on (1992) Focal Family Therapy (Bentovim and Kinston, 1991) and the work by Bentovim on 'Trauma-organised systems'.

This chapter will present TFFT as it has been further developed and extended to incorporate research into the dynamics of attachment in adult life (McCluskey, 2001). It will provide a framework for thinking about the actual processes that one is trying to address and change, and the skills required to conduct therapeutically-oriented family sessions, which are explicitly set up to address defensive and unconscious processes. I shall start by identifying the social policy and social work context for therapeutic interventions with families. This will be followed by a brief examination of the research and theoretical formulations which provide the basis for TFFT starting with a short account of attachment theory (Bowlby, 1969, 1973, 1980, 1988). I shall then look at the way that attachment theory has been extended by Heard and Lake (1997, 1998, 1999, 2000) beyond the two interpersonal goal-corrected systems – that of care-seeking and care-giving originally identified by Bowlby (1969). Finally, the reader will be introduced to the method of setting up TFFT and ideas for how to conduct the family sessions drawing on Systems-Centered® Group Psychotherapy (Agazarian, 1997). The chapter concludes with a short case study and suggestions for further research.

Social work as a context for therapeutic work with families

The context for working with the emotional dynamics of family life has been provided by government guidelines and policies, in particular the *Framework for the Assessment of Children in Need and their Families* (DoH, 2000) (the Assessment Framework). This and other initiatives (DoH, 1995, 1999) emphasise keeping families together or helping families to get back together following traumatic experiences and events. It points to a preventative role for social workers in working with families to reduce the stresses and difficulties they face, both from within and from outside the family. The Assessment Framework highlights the importance of parenting capacity, family functioning and family history, and their impact on the well-being, development and safety of the child.

We know from the literature and from practice the impact and lasting effect of experiences of separation, loss, abuse and neglect can have on children's well-being and development that it makes them vulnerable to mental health problems and affects the way they go on to parent. Social workers in children and families teams frequently work with families where abuse, neglect, losses and even trauma are significant features of both the present and past experience of family members.

We also know that resilience, competence and well-being are enhanced if as children we live in a supportive family environment where individual children's needs are responded to and where the family has the capacity to adapt to changing family life-cycle stages and cope with the challenges and stresses they encounter in everyday life (Brassard *et al.*, 1987, Burnett, 1993; Glaser, 1993; Glaser and Prior, 1997; Gibbons *et al.*, 1995; Iwaniec, 1995; Thoburn *et al.*, 2000). Demands on families have changed enormously over the past 20 years; social workers and other professionals see many families who live with the experience of stress and uncertainty resulting from the various forms of social disadvantage which are part of our current social context, in addition to the impact of discrimination which is directed against a range of minority groups.

Social workers have a pivotal role in working preventatively and developmentally with families where relationship problems are seriously affecting the capacity of the parents to respond to their children's needs effectively. The strength of social work has always been its capacity to locate personal experience within a social as well as relational context. However, the pressures of having to manage child protection concerns as a priority, the current focus on assessment and the heavy workloads social workers often have means that lengthy therapeutic interventions are handed on to other professionals. TFFT has been developed to provide a short-term, brief, focused method of engaging, assessing and working with families therapeutically which is accessible and can be used by social workers and other professionals.

Attachment Theory

Attachment Theory (Bowlby, 1969, 1973. 1980) describes the function of attachment behaviour (survival), the situations under which care-seeking behaviour is activated (fear, distress, illness and anxiety), the object of attachment behaviour (protection through proximity with a preferred care-giver) and the conditions under which attachment behaviour is assuaged. Care-seeking behaviours continue throughout the life-cycle and are activated under circumstances of fear, distress, illness and loss. Attachment theory is increasingly seen as a useful theory for social workers and other professional practitioners (Howe, 1997; Daniel, Wassell and Gilligan, 1999; Hindle, 1998).

The classification of individual attachment style is provided by the work of Mary Salter Ainsworth (Ainsworth *et al.*, 1978) who developed the method known as the Strange Situation test to classify infants' behaviour with their mothers on reunion following a brief separation. The infants' behaviour fell into two main groups: secure and insecure. The insecure group has been further classified into insecure avoidant, insecure ambivalent and disorganised. These classifications have been shown to be stable over time and persist into adulthood (see Cassidy and Shaver, 1999, for a full account of research into attachment behaviour and clinical implications; also Main, 1991, 1995). Summaries of research findings on the three types of infants (Campos, Barrett, Lamb, Goldsmith, and Stenberg, 1983) and research on the general population (Hazan and Shaver, 1987) confirm that the secure group account for about 60 per cent of the studied population.

Ainsworth (1967, 1978) was the first to make the connection between secure attachment to a care-giver and the way in which the care-giver responded to the infant's affective non-verbal signals. Clear communication of emotional content, both intra- and interpersonally, reliably predicts secure versus insecure attachment style (Ainsworth and Wittig, 1969; Ainsworth, Blehar, Waters, and Wall, 1978; Ainsworth, 1991; Fonagy *et al.*, 1995; Grossmann, Fremmer-Bombik, Rudolph and Grossmann, 1988; Grossmann and Grossmann, 1991a, 1991b; Grossmann, Grossmann, Spangler, Suess and Unzner, 1985; Main, 1991, 1995).

Tronick (1989), Tronick and Cohn (1989), Stern (1985), Kiersky and Beebe (1994) and Beebe and Lachmann (2002) have all observed and documented the behavioural strategies of infants to cope with intrusive and non-attuned behaviour on the part of their care-givers. Haft and Slade (1989) noticed the connection between adult care-giver security and the capacity to tune into and encompass without retaliation or dismissal a variety of emotional expression from infants and young children.

The major review of research by Alan Shore (1994) into early psychobiological development asserts the importance of affect and affect regulation in the development of a secure sense of self and the interdependence of affect regulation and relationship with others. Infants cannot regulate the level of emotional arousal that they experience; they need a sensitive and 'tuned-in' other to do this for them. Affect regulation is at the centre of any form of therapeutic work. All this research supports work with family members that helps them address and deal with their emotional states, the impact they have on each other, both verbally and non-verbally, and the way they support and encourage one another's general level of social and interpersonal competence.

The dynamics of attachment in adult life

Heard in Chapter 4 argues that in addition to the instinctive goal-corrected systems of care-seeking and care-giving, sexuality and companionable interest-sharing are the other major motivational forces that bring human beings together into relationship with one another (Heard and Lake, 1984, 1997). All instinctive systems are stimulated by signals (information) in the environment and are goal-corrected (that is, they shut down and cease to be active when they get the information or response they require from either inside or outside the boundaries of their system). When systems fail to reach their goal, the instinctive system for self-defence is aroused. When this happens the infant or adult resorts to self-regulation (in terms of dealing with the arousal of painful affect) as best they can.

The non-verbal behaviour which accompanies the pain of failures in care-giving has been clearly described by the researchers into infant development referred to earlier. This has been tracked in the context of adult therapeutic interventions by McCluskey (1999a, 2001) and McCluskey *et al.* (1999b) and provides support for the theoretical propositions contained within the concept of the attachment dynamic presented in Heard's chapter in this volume. In addition, McCluskey (2001) has developed the concept of goal-corrected empathic attunement and provided some research evidence that such an interactive process is an essential part of effective care-giving without which both care-giver and care-seeker resort to their respective systems for self-defence, thereby inhibiting the goal of any therapeutic work.

The above research into misattunement to affect and intrusiveness implies that in any therapeutic endeavour it will be crucial to work in a way that addresses the affective experience of all the participants so that each person feels accurately attuned to. In addition, the therapist or social worker must express empathy towards individuals and work in such a way as to promote the development of an empathic stance within individuals towards themselves and towards each other.

When working with a family one is working with the dynamics of a group. Affect attunement and empathy are communicated verbally and nonverbally, very often through facial expression. It is therefore through the face-to-face encounter in the dyad that authentic or inauthentic communication will be expressed and experienced in the family group; groups can be conceived as a web of transient dyadic relationships (see McCluskey, 2002). I will now present a more detailed account of this method of family work.

Theme-focused family therapy

Since the original publication on theme-focused work (McCluskey, 1987), it has become clearer that what a theme does is to capture the underlying unresolved affective issues as experienced in current interactions and as internalised from past relationships. It therefore follows that working in this way requires considerable empathic skill. The work itself is essentially about creating the conditions whereby family members can be empathically attuned to each other, and can make decisions based on what is genuinely in the children's best interests, even if that means separation and cessation of contact. Clearly, some children will be too young and therefore developmentally unable to contribute fully to this process.

Criteria for choosing families

The first issue that confronts a social worker thinking about undertaking this work is selection. Until one develops some confidence and competence in the work it is best to start with families who do not present with too many difficulties but who could clearly benefit from the work.

Families experiencing the following troubles may well be interested in working with a social worker, psychologist or other professionals using TFFT:

(a) families where the members are operating at survival level and who are not achieving their full potential in terms of their physical, intellectual, cognitive, social and interpersonal capacities;
(b) families where there is clear scapegoating;
(c) families where there is unresolved grief;
(d) families where there is motivation to change the experience they are having together;
(e) families who are having difficulties with authority, their own or others;

(f)　families experiencing depression, tension or anxiety;
(g)　families facing the premature death of a member;
(h)　families where there is a risk of a family member, especially a child, leaving the family;
(i)　families who are finding it hard to let a member leave and establish their own independent home base.

Contrary indicators include:

(a)　where there are suspicions of child sexual abuse or where there are current investigations into child abuse;
(b)　where family members are currently addicted to drugs and are unable to give the necessary commitment to the work;
(c)　where one or more family members are suffering from an acute psychotic episode;
(d)　where there is no motivation whatsoever to engage in change-related work.

Points to consider prior to undertaking therapeutic work are that if there are child protection aspects to the case, it is important to establish boundaries between child protection and therapeutic work. It is also worth remembering that therapeutic work must be offered in a way that can be refused. It needs to be a choice that the family can opt for if they so wish, and must not be coercive or a condition of other aspects of social service or court involvement.

Recruiting the family

While it is important that the family should not be coerced into relationship work, nevertheless they might need persuading that focusing on the past or meeting all together can and may be useful for them. The following are some suggestions for how to build on their interest and communicate to them what the work might actually involve, for example:

* focus on what is of most concern to the family, for example the child in trouble;
* suggest a family approach because usually difficulties in families affect everyone and are affected by everyone;
* validate the fact they are the experts when it comes to information and knowledge about their family;
* suggest one starts with the adults and then later meet with all the family members so that one hears everyone's current concerns;
* it is helpful in terms of recruitment to make time to see *all* the family members without exception; it is often the children who express the most motivation for the work, they often have an overdeveloped sense of

responsibility for the welfare of the family as a whole;
• negotiate a sequence and timetable for the work.

There are four stages of the work: (a) family history; (b) current concerns; (c) formulating the theme; and (d) work with the whole family on the theme.

Undertaking the family history

There are four main reasons for taking a history:

1 it provides a context for each individual in which they can locate their own experiences of care-seeking and care-giving, and its impact on current relationship patterns with their partner, their children, their peers and authority figures;
2 it engages the adults in the family in developing a working partnership with the social worker, which should help sustain the work with the whole family;
3 it enables the social worker and client to work towards identifying a theme which would embrace a more complex understanding of the pattern of family interaction;
4 it provides an opportunity for eliciting the care-giving system in the social worker.

Through the process of conducting the family history of the individual family members, each person gets a sense of the nature of the therapeutic work and whether it is something they would wish to pursue. A full account of the way in which to conduct the family history is provided in an earlier paper (McCluskey and Bingley Miller, 1995).

Current concerns interview

The main reasons for conducting the current concerns interview (CCI) can be summarised as follows:

(a) it confirms that the concerns of every member of the family are important;
(b) it gathers together matters of concern in the present that family members wish were different in some way;
(c) it establishes a shift from dyadic work (the family history-taking) to working with the family group;
(d) it establishes a pattern of communicating which is likely to facilitate undefended exploration of feelings and experiences of family members.

In addition, the process of undertaking the work establishes a pattern of communication which promotes the individuation of family members. This communication pattern enables family members to hear each other and reflect and respond in an exploratory way, which takes into account the impact of exchanges on other family members. Finally, it gives the family the experience of the worker taking responsibility for the structure and boundaries of the meetings, important aspects for creating the conditions of safety within which to explore.

Establishing and conducting the CCI

When arranging the current concerns interview, it is useful to negotiate the environment for working prior to the first meeting, especially if the meetings are to be held at the family's home. For example, it is important that chairs can be placed in a circle so that everyone can see and hear each other. It is also important that there is space in the middle for young children to use paper and pens so as to maximise their involvement and ensure they can hear what is being said and have a voice. The family need to know the time boundary for the meeting so that everyone knows when it is going to finish. In order to reduce distractions and noise one needs to negotiate to have the television turned off and for neighbours and friends not to be present during the period of the session.

The interview starts with introductions, first of oneself, and the time boundary is stated. The family is reminded of the purpose of the current concerns meeting which is for the worker to find out the current concerns or worries of each person in the family. They are reminded that it is part of the assessment process before meeting together to do the work that they all want to do. Ground rules are suggested for the way that both children and adults should talk with one another during the meeting so that each person is able to say what they want to say. It is emphasised that each person's view is important and that people speak for themselves. The introduction should end with some phrase such as, 'who'd like to start, what are the main concerns or worries for you at the moment?'

The theory that is being tested by this way of working is that affect attunement and empathy assuage care-seeking behaviour, reduce distress in the person and promote exploration. It is therefore important to keep working with each individual until you have a clear understanding of their concerns. This is likely to be achieved by ensuring they are not interrupted, talked over, dismissed, or have their sentences finished for them. Try and paraphrase what they have said in a way that captures the context and meaning of what is being said. Pick up any ambiguities or contradictions and seek to clarify them. Get as clear a view as possible of who is concerned about what and why. Tune into the feeling content and check out that you are picking it up accurately. Notice the non-verbal communication, for example the level of emotional arousal, tone and pitch of voice, eye contact, gestures, body position.

Help children to voice their concerns, making sure that if children have made drawings during the session that they get time to tell the family what the drawing is about. It is important not to interpret the child's drawing but to ask the family if they see a connection between the drawing and what is being discussed. In this way the adults and the older children begin to see and hear just how much the younger children are paying attention to the discussion, the sense they are making of it, and the way it is affecting them emotionally. End the session with a summary of each person's concerns and with the work done so far (family history and current concerns interview), remind the family about the next step which is the family sessions proper, and resolve any transport issues in relation to the work.

Creating a theme

The theme addresses a number of dimensions of family life and carries various functions in relation to the work. For example, it forms a focus and anchor point for the family sessions and is designed to engage and interest all the family members and be about a matter important to them as individuals. It has to relate to significant aspects of their experience as individuals and have emotional relevance for each person. It needs to link in with past unresolved issues and conflicts about such things as losses, separations, big changes, abuse, neglect or traumatic experiences where their impact is reducing the individual's capacity to cope or respond to the needs and challenges of the present.

In working towards a theme, the worker carefully records the salient information from the family assessment on the TFFT Profile Form 3(see case example later in this chapter). The profile lays out the information in columns across the page. The form is designed to enable the worker and their supervisor to see what connections there may be between past experiences and current experiences and happenings. The idea is to help in the process of identifying themes, which may have been carried through from one generation to the next. Each column is filled out for each family starting with the adults at the top and moving down through the older children and finishing with the youngest.

In relation to *significant past events from childhood*, the worker's task is to note in a few words the key salient events, relationships and circumstances for each individual, which were of emotional significance for the individual. The *current concerns and events* column records the current concerns for each individual, and so is recorded against their name in the same position horizontally across from their name. This column is also used to record significant events and experiences for the family in their past, that is experiences which they have in common (for example partners breaking up, parents leaving the family, new partners arriving, unemployment, children being accommodated or looked after, illness or moves).

In relation to *meanings*, here the worker reflects on and records the meanings the family members seem to give to their experience, especially those which link the past to the present. These are best captured in the words of family members as they will then be much more accessible to them and have more resonance. These might be: 'those close to you let you down', 'happiness turns to sadness', 'children cause you pain'. These meanings are likely to be informed by the inner working models of the experience of relationship with significant others (IMERs, see Heard, Chapter 2 this volume) and be the lens through which they view current relationships. They can affect the way individuals respond to certain situations.

In the column on *worker's hypotheses,* the worker and supervisor note their understanding or hypothesis about how the past experiences of family members may be impacting upon their ways of relating to those close to them in the their current family (and outside). These hypotheses contribute to the worker moving closer to identifying a theme. Later, when the therapeutic work commences they will be tested by the worker against what actually happens (particularly the pattern of interaction between family members in the sessions), and will either be confirmed or disconfirmed.

Under *current patterns of interaction* the worker records characteristic sequences of interaction which indicate how the family communicates, especially where it incorporates the current identified problem or concerns which have brought the family to the attention of the agency or resulted in family work being undertaken. These sequences show how the 'problem' is embedded in interaction and may well be supported and maintained by the ways family members respond to the perceived difficulty. Also changes in these sequences are often one of the best ways of assessing whether change has taken place during the process of the work.

Identifying possible themes

Here the worker and supervisor work to identify themes or issues which they know from the assessment process are likely to have live and direct emotional significance for each person in the family. They work carefully to check across the columns and down for each member of the family to reflect on how each theme might 'fit' for each person. Such themes might for example be: 'loss in the family and how people feel about it'; 'comings and going in the family and how people feel about them'. These themes can look at first glance broad and relatively unspecific. What the worker and supervisor need to be confident of is that they have a particular significance for each person and the reasons why this is so. For example, for mother it might be the early death of a parent and loss of job and self-esteem, for father it might be involuntary exile from his country of origin, for the teenage son it might be changes in family fortunes, for the four-year-old it might be the death of a pet. Knowing why the theme might have significance for each family member ensures that the worker is more likely to hold to the theme and use it confidently as an anchor for focusing and refocusing work in the family sessions.

Keep themes short and succinct such as, 'loss', 'fairness', 'being in this family'. The theme is then often developed into something which opens it up and carries a balance of both strength and difficulty, positive and negative – for example, 'fairness and unfairness in this family', or 'caring for and being cared for in this family'. Some themes are open already such as 'what it feels like to be in this family'.

Theme-focused family therapy sessions

The aim of the sessions is to enable family members to communicate with each other about how they relate to each other and their experience of their life together as a family. The idea is to help family members talk about these matters, especially those which have been hard or impossible to talk about, in a relatively safe and supportive environment. Family members are encouraged to express themselves clearly and to listen to each other. In short, therefore, the aims are:

1 to promote an open, attentive, empathic and reflective way of communicating so that family members can gain a greater understanding of each other's experience;
2 to promote a pattern of communicating which validates individual experience and supports individuation;
3 to promote a pattern of communicating where the voice of children can be heard so that their wishes and needs can be better understood and responded to;
4 to support choice.

In preparing for the theme-focused sessions it is useful to review the theme before going to the family meeting to remind oneself how the theme is grounded in the assessment, this helps the worker to be confident of its relevance. Start the work on time, either at the family's home or at the office and make sure the room is set up to create the best environment for work.

Conducting the first TFFT session

Once you have the family in the room, remind them of the ground rules for talking to one another established during the *current concerns interview.* State how long the meeting will take. Explain that you are responsible for keeping time and ensuring everyone is heard. Explain that, unlike the CCI, you will not be conducting the session and that they will not be taking it in turns to speak, but rather using the theme which you have been working on as a focus or central point for discussion. Explain that you will help them to keep to the theme and from time to time will draw their attention to the way they are going about this task so that they have access to the verbal and non-verbal information in the room. Remind them that you are going to meet for whatever the agreed number of sessions were to talk together using the theme to focus the meetings.

Explain that you have thought very carefully about all the different and important things they have talked about with you and that in deciding the theme you have chosen something which you think is important to every single member of the family. Then state the theme, putting it in a phrase such as 'From now until 10.30 we will discuss comings and goings in the family and how everyone feels about them'.

This work requires that one understands something about individual and group process and the defences against change and development based on early abuse and neglect. From what we know from group theoreticians such as Agazarian (1997, 2000, 2001) individual and group defences are similar in structure and function within the context of the phase of development of the system. In group terms, the first phase of development is flight (see Bion, 1961; Bennis and Shepard, 1957). Group behaviour in the flight phase is to create the identified patient (see Agazarian, 1997, p. 94). Communication patterns between individuals will be stereotypic, such as 'boys don't do that', 'children don't understand'.

Therefore having left the family with the task of talking about what is most important to them one is likely to be presented with the defences appropriate to any new or strange situation. Strange situations can either activate fear or curiosity. Fear in turn will activate the instinctive defences of flight and fight. Flight defences may be expressed in the form of children running out of the room or climbing up pipes and so on (playing about). Flight defences (a movement away from the present reality) may also take the form of making negative or positive predictions such as 'this is a waste of time' or 'this is going to be the best thing for the family'. They can also take the form of imputing thoughts and feelings to other people (called mind-reads), i.e. John is too young and doesn't understand what you are talking about.

It is important that the worker is not thrown off course by these comments and can work with the family members to explore what they are actually experiencing in the here and now.

Mind-reads of other people need to be checked instantly so that if one member of the family says another does not understand what is going on you encourage that person to check if that is true. If one does not do this one is promoting a climate in the group where what people *think* is going on inside other people is accepted *as if* it is in fact true. Readers may be familiar with Bowlby's (1988) paper 'On Knowing what you are Not Supposed To Know and Feeling what you are Not Supposed To Feel'. The main theme of that paper is the way in which children's experience is often discounted by adults leaving the children with a great deal of confusion and disorganization.

Checking mind-reads is done by asking the person with the mind-read to put it in the form of a question that the other person can answer with a yes or a no. For example: 'I think you have not understood what has been said, is that true?' The other person answers with a yes or a no if they are old enough, or in other ways if they are too young (see case example later in this chapter). One then asks the person who had the mind-read whether they believe the answer. What one does now is to encourage the person giving the answer to say what is true for them and make it clear that what is being imputed to them has much more to do with the other person than with them. Depending on the answer, that is whether they got a yes or no, one then asks the person who checked their mind-read what it is like to have ones assumptions about someone confirmed or disconfirmed in reality. In this way they bring their affect (their emotion) into the session to be worked with and attention is diverted away from their ideas about another person that are not based in reality.

Negative and positive predictions of what is going to come from the sessions also need to be checked in terms of (a) whether the person with the prediction believes they can tell the future, and (b) what is being predicted is actually happening this minute (see Agazarian, 1997, p. 149 and Agazarian, 2001, p. 42 for more detail on how to work with these defences).

The next defence against experiencing one's emotional experience in the here and now is likely to be tension. This may take the form of a headache, tense shoulders, stomach or back pain. Again one needs to check whether there is a known medical history and current treatment for this and whether the person needs to do or take something to alleviate the pain. The over-riding objective is to help family members access their competence in terms of self-care and care for others and to give them a choice as to whether they would rather have their tension or be open to having their emotional experience. If they say they would rather know what they were feeling then one can ask them to let the tension drain away and see what they are actually experiencing when they are not tense. The experience contained in the tension could be one of sadness or indeed frustration. One encourages individuals to make space for their experience – to make enough room inside to have their full experience without acting it out (in tension or outrage or whatever).

If as a worker one becomes anxious oneself one loses the capacity to work skillfully with what is taking place in the group and so fails to offer a safe environment for this type of exploration. With the defences mentioned above it is important to know how to undo them and to do so in a hierarchical order, starting with the social defenses, then moving to cognitive and then to somatic (see Agazarian, 1997, 2001; and Agazarian and Gantt, 2000, for a full explanation of these procedures). In this way the family learns the skills involved in moving from defensive to non-defensive communication.

As mentioned earlier, this process takes place with a group climate which itself is moving through the ordinary phases of group development (fight and flight, intimacy, and work (see Agazarian, 1997; Bennis and Shepherd, 1957; Bion, 1961). In the flight phase, the family is prone to producing an identified patient or a scapegoat in order to manage the uncomfortable emotions aroused by uncertainty. Communication patterns that target one person are a clear sign that someone is being actively scapegoated, and is important to intervene to interrupt this pattern. One thing a worker can do is to ask the family whether they have noticed the current pattern of communication which is that one person is currently the focus of all the conversation or attention. If they have noticed this, then ask them whether they think continuing with this pattern is likely to increase or decrease their capacity as individuals in the family to take in what each other are saying.

As individual family members become less defensive in their communications with each other, theoretically they begin to re-edit their internal working models of their experience of relationship (IMERs). This hypothesis needs to be checked against empirical evidence. The theoretical basis for this hypothesis has been presented in a recent article (McCluskey, 2002). It is a fact, however, that family members have reported improved relationship with each other following this type of intervention (McCluskey, 1987; McCluskey and Bingley Miller, 1995).

In addition to having a theoretical grasp of the work and some personal experience of a therapeutic process, there are a number of skills which the worker can use to facilitate the task. For example, many of the skills and techniques used in the current concerns interview continue to be relevant; such as managing interruptions, helping family members be clear and unambiguous in what they are saying, picking up on non-verbal communications, and carefully helping the family members put into words what they are communicating in other ways. Sometimes the whole family will be communicating about the theme in a way that is not obvious to them: the worker needs to be alert to the connection and present their observations to the family in a way they can think about and use – the intention being to keep the exploration going.

It is natural for a family or any member of a group to join on similarity (that is, to feel comfortable with what appears to be similar to themselves) and to separate on differences (to move away from, or to scapegoat what they perceive as different from themselves). When family members interrupt each other or express something different or oppositional to what is being discussed, ask if they can find some similarity with what the other person is saying and build on it.

Encourage the family to sub-group (join each other) around similarities so that conflict around differences in the group is held in subgroups and not in individuals. This will reduce scapegoating (that is, one member of the family being isolated and left on their own to carry the difference for the group). According to Agazarian (1997), the impulse to scapegoat is present in any group where a difference is perceived as too great to assimilate.

It is important to notice the children's behaviour and non-verbal communication and to ensure that there is space for them when they have something to contribute. It is also important to point out to the rest of the family if any of the children's behaviour changes (including heightened colouring or changes in muscle tone) in response to painful or difficult subjects being talked about in the family. This could be an indication that the child is constricting their emotion (through tension) rather than expressing and exploring their affective experience.

In families where there is a dominant versus submissive way of relating – that is, a clear hierarchy in terms of power which operates in terms of either dominating people or having them submit to you – the abuse of power is never far away. This type of relating to people is based on fear (see Heard and Lake, 1997). The arousal of the instinctive fear system will influence the functioning of the attachment dynamic mentioned earlier in this chapter. All five systems within the dynamic – care-seeking, care-giving, interest-sharing, sexuality and self defence – will be expressed in a way that is likely to be misattuned and unempathic towards the other person. The nature of this work is to change the communication pattern so that people experience a different way of relating to one another. The experience of something different carries its own momentum towards change.

It is often the case that when involved in therapeutic work directed at unconscious communication patterns, one can lose a sense of time. It is important therefore to remind the family about five minutes before the end of the session that they have just so much time left. Equally it is important to keep track of the number of sessions and to keep reminding the family where they are in the sequence of the work.

Case study

The following is a shortened case study presented to illustrate the method. While the family gave permission for material from their history and sessions to be used to illustrate the work, key aspects of their lives and circumstances as well as names and location have been changed to protect their anonymity. Given the wealth of material gleaned from working with this family on and off over a period of two years, only a snapshot of the process of the work can be described here. The Family Profile Form (FPF) shown in Figure 5.1 is used to capture some of the salient features.

As can be seen, a dominant theme running through this family is that of ineffective care-giving. Research (McCluskey, 1999, 2001; and McCluskey *et al.*, 1999) is demonstrating that effective care-giving in situations that arouse the dynamics of attachment is provided through the process of goal-corrected empathic attunement. In order to promote the exploration of affect and to sensitise individuals in the family to each other's affective experience the theme chosen was 'What it feels like to be a member of this family'. I shall present some of the detail from the first session, which illustrates the way that the family were able to use the theme to explore in an authentic way matters of important concern to them.

The family met for the first session without Tony (Dad) as he was in prison. Mum in the meantime had decided to use this experience to begin the process of separating from him. Having given the family the brief for the session and asked them whether they wished to put out a chair for dad or not, it began with an initial discussion about the room, the equipment, one-way mirror etc. This was followed by Monica leaving her seat and sitting on 'Dad's' chair, which drew comment from Patrick. He felt that Monica often treats him like his father used to do. He went on to say that Dad often called him and Danny imbeciles. I asked what this word meant. Monica intervened to say Danny would not understand what we were talking about. Patrick explained the problem Danny had. I suggested we ask Danny if he knew what it meant to talk about what it feels like to be a member of this family. Danny proceeded for the next five minutes to tell us very clearly what it felt like to be him. He explained he had a hole in his body; there were hairs on it; and as he grew older the hairs got bigger; the hole had been put there by somebody using a knife. Mother interjected and told him that he had been born like that. Danny persisted that a doctor had done it to him.

Monica then accused Mum of being too laid back about Danny's 'deformity', and said she should not let him go out to play when he was not covered up. Monica talked angrily about a time when this had happened and she was embarrassed in front of her friends. She insisted he frightened the other children. Danny made a grimace and said he felt like a 'hairy monster'. I pointed out to the family the expression on Danny's face as he said these words and drew their attention to the possible connection between Danny's feelings, his facial expression and what they had just been discussing. They were all (including Monica) visibly taken aback that he responded so immediately and that he felt like he said he did. It was news to them.

Monica then mentioned the first baby who was 'born dead'. Patrick mentioned how Monica had changed after Danny was born. He said he felt Monica liked being the baby. Monica got angry, Danny left his seat and went to sit with Patrick. Monica left her seat and went and sat on Danny's chair. Patrick asked her if she would like to be Danny. Monica again got agitated and angry. Patrick remembered the night Danny was born and brought in some of the material already referred to in the FPF. Patrick and Monica recalled Danny being born in a taxi. Mother interjected to say this was not true. Patrick said he remembered being pleased that the baby was a boy, as his father wanted a boy. He was pleased because he wanted a brother as well as a sister.

At this point, Monica left her seat and got very heated about Patrick having 'fits' and with Danny's deformity (note that Monica moves into action and into deflecting blame onto others as Patrick talks about his father's gender preference). She got very angry with her mother as if it were her fault. Mum said that Monica was acting just like her Dad and told us that her husband used to say to her that she could not have 'normal' children. All three children looked intently at their mother and

Names, ages and position in the family	Significant events in childhood for each family member	Current concerns and events in the family	Meanings given to the events by the individual	Worker's hypotheses	Current patterns of interaction
Tony, 35, father	Taken into care for neglect and abuse at age 7, followed by a series of placements in residential units and with foster carers.	His first child was born with a physical deformity and died shortly after birth. He spends a lot of time out of the family drinking with his mates. He accumulates debts wherever he has lived. He has recently been committed to prison.	Tony has few memories of his childhood. He sees the past as having little impact on the present. He holds his partner responsible for the different medical conditions of all three sons. He sees Monica as his only normal child.	He is likely to behave defensively in the area of care-seeking and care-giving in adult life and to be unable to sustain empathic care-giving for very long. As a result, likely to adopt a dominant/submissive form of relating.	Tony is aggressive towards his partner and when she seeks help with parenting he flies into a rage and accuses her of being unable to control the family. He accuses her of being unable to produce normal children.
Maureen, 35, mother	'I remember being taken to see my mother (in hospital) and being told I would never see her again'. The death of her mother was followed by a series of stays with relatives, culminating in being admitted to a Barnardo's residential unit when she was 9.	At her wits end with her daughter's behaviour. 'I can't control her, she takes no notice of me, nothing I do makes a difference … she is making the whole family miserable'.	Describes herself as having had a bleak miserable childhood following the death of her mother. One of the best times in her life was when she was first admitted to a children's unit run by Barnardo's. She has good memories of one particular member of staff who worked in the unit during her first year.	Her early history combined with her marital choice and subsequent life in an abusive and uncertain situation in spite of its stability over time, has impacted on her self worth and self-esteem and her capacity to provide continuous empathic care for her children.	She oscillates between being dominant and submissive in relation to her husband and her children. She often begins by saying no to Monica and then quickly gives in. children and family.
Patrick, 13, son and brother	Being with his mother the night Danny was born, rubbing her back. Grateful to dad for saving him one day	He sits at the top of the stairs waiting for his father to come in at night fearing he is going to be drunk and the	It is up to him to keep the peace between his mum and his dad. He sees Monica as like his dad.	He is hypervigilant in relation to the interaction between his mum and dad. Has limited capacity for empathic	Blames Monica. Distracts his father when he is having a row with his mother. He finds it difficult to go to sleep and

	when a piece of toast stuck in his throat and triggered a seizure. Scared when dad went white with shock and seemed more frightened than he was.	consequences of this for his mother. He is angry with Monica about her aggressive behaviour towards mum, himself and Danny.	attunement. In role of caregiver to both parents. His own care-seeking is ineffective. His care-giving is likely to be in the service of care-seeking.	calls to his mother to settle him. She is not prompt in responding.
Monica, 11, daughter and sister	Underperforming in relation to ability. Has no friends. Tends to concentrate on what is irritating her in the present, particularly the behaviour of her mother	There is nothing wrong with her behaviour. School is awful, everyone picks on her. Her dad is great. Her mother and brothers are 'weird' and brothers.	She sees her mother and her two brothers as 'imbeciles'.	Parental care-giving has been insufficiently responsive and empathic, leaving her in a position of unresolved care-seeking which is presented in aggressive form.	She talks loudly and makes a noisy racket when Mum, Patrick and Danny are talking. Accuses Patrick of 'being mental' during one of his seizures and insists he should be locked away'.
Danny, 4, son and brother	Born with a mild physical disability. He has had three moves of house in as many years.	Monica and mum shouting and Monica bossing him about.	Danny dislikes the noise and the fights at home. He too blames Monica.	The family is split in their perception of Danny's mild disability. Dad distances, Monica attacks, Mum and Patrick protect. Danny is left feeling 'weird'; his natural instinctive care-seeking unassuaged most of the time and his exploratory processes impeded.	Presents behaviourally and socially as more incompetent than he is. Puts on 'scary' faces

Figure 5.1 The family profile form

Patrick and Monica said they had not heard this before (there was a sense of them all taking in the reality of how they were seen by their father).

Monica got restless (note Monica's immediate restlessness) and wanted to know when the session finished. Mum: 'You want to leave now when this is the first time we have had an honest conversation with each other'. I reminded the family we would be finished in a few minutes. Danny started to tell me that Patrick had lost a finger (his finger had caught in a door when Monica was two years old – the finger had been stitched back on). Session ended with a reminder we would be meeting again in two days time.

Subsequent sessions maintained the same level of engagement with the members of the family working in depth at the connections between what was in the sessions, the affect being experienced by individuals and the behaviour being expressed.

Dad was later allowed back into the family by Mum and joined the family sessions. He was amazed at the level of the discussion and to hear that he had so much meaning for the family and that they wanted to see more of him and be more involved. During one of the sessions where dad was present, Patrick had a major seizure while recounting how he had stepped in between his mother and father to resolve an argument between them. Unusually Dad took care of him, and looked after him until he recovered. This event was enormously important for both Patrick and Tony. Subsequently Patrick made a link between his seizures and conflict between his parents. On the strength of this evidence, Tony and Maureen accepted help with their marital relationship and engaged in marital therapy with a consultant psychiatrist and myself. This work went on for over a year and was very successful. In terms of Patrick, it is worth reporting that the frequency of his seizures reduced considerably and he was completely free of them when followed up two years later.

The work described yielded considerable improvement in both Maureen and Tony's capacity for empathy. Improved responses to each other's care-seeking behaviour led to improved capacity to parent effectively. Tony took an interest in his children and spent more time with them. He stopped drinking, he turned down a job which would have taken him 200 miles away and got a job nearby. He went to metalwork classes and made a wonderful game for Danny. Maureen started to put boundaries on unwanted intrusion from her neighbours.

After five months of twice weekly family sessions, Maureen described the changes in the family as follows: (1) we talk to one another, (2) Tony is not drinking, (3) there is more money in the house, (4) I am better able to manage money, (5) no violent rows, (6) we enjoy the children. Follow up with this family two years later found that Patrick was enjoying an apprenticeship and doing well. Monica was succeeding at school. Danny was also doing well at school. Dad was not drinking, and had taken a less well-paid job locally in order to stay with his family. Maureen and Tony were paying for Monica to take riding lessons. There had been a couple of violent incidents in the locality – Maureen was attacked at knifepoint in the street. Tony and Maureen described this as quite unsettling and that whereas formerly it would have triggered an impulse to move they had coped by sitting down together as a family and talked about it like they had done when having family sessions.

It is often the case that even after a first session, family members will say this is the first time they have had an honest discussion with one another. The worker's job is to continue to give them the skills necessary to pursue their work together. What one is promoting is the full functioning of the attachment dynamic. If care-seeking is responded to empathically, other systems within the attachment dynamic, such as interest sharing, sexuality and self-defence will operate empathically in much the same way as the changes in the family interaction outlined above describe.

A further case example, drawn from a social services caseload, and an exploration of the type of supervision necessary to contain and promote this work appear in a previous paper (McCluskey and Bingley Miller, 1995). A paper on supervision by Dick Agass (2000) which deals directly with the containment necessary to support this work is highly recommended, as is a book by Yvonne Agazarian which deals with the process of a group session (Agazarian, 2001).

Conclusion

In this chapter I have drawn attention to the encouragement within government policy for social workers to undertake therapeutic work with families. I have briefly presented a theoretical framework (attachment theory), which makes sense of current family relationship patterns in terms of the experiences the adults have had of significant relationships during their formative years

Theme-focused family therapy has been presented as a way of working with families, which is grounded in attachment theory and an understanding of group behaviour and development. It provides the social worker or other professional working with the family with clear guidelines for how to engage the family, conduct a social history with empathy and compassion and introduce change in current patterns of behaviour. Skills were identified which might promote the therapeutic work with the family. In addition, the reader is referred to further reading on group process and defense modification and encouraged to seek supervision which will understand, contain and promote the nature of the task being undertaken It remains for a more detailed working out of the process of therapy during the family sessions. Such work would provide clearer guidelines on how to conduct the actual therapy sessions for those workers or clinicians who have not been trained in group or family therapy. Research is required to examine whether such a programme of intervention with a family is effective in changing their individual attachment status.

References

Agazarian, Y. M. (1997) *Systems-Centered Therapy for Groups.* New York: Guilford.
— (2001) *A Systems-Centered Approach to inpatient Group Psychotherapy.* London and Philadelphia: Jessica Kingsley.
Agazarian, Y. M. and Gantt, S. P. (2000) *An Autobiography of a Theory.* London and Philadelphia: Jessica Kingsley.
Agass, D. (2002) 'Containment, Supervision and Abuse', in U. McCluskey and C. A. Hooper (eds), *Psychodynamic Perspectives on Abuse: The Cost of Fear* (pp. 209–22). London: Jessica Kingsley.
Ainsworth, M. D. S. (1967) *Infancy in Uganda: Infant Care and the Growth of Love.* Baltimore: Johns Hopkins University Press.
— (1991) 'Attachments and Other Affectional Bonds Across the Life Cycle', in C. M. Parkes, J. Stevenson-Hinde and P. Marris (eds), *Attachment across the life cycle* (pp. 33–51). London and New York: Routledge.
Ainsworth, M. D. S. and Wittig, B. A. (1969) 'Attachment and the Exploratory Behaviour of One-Year-Olds in a Strange Situation', in B. M. Foss (ed.), *Determinants of Infant Behavior* (Vol. 4, pp. 113–36). London: Methuen.
Ainsworth, M. D. S., Blehar, M. C., Waters, E. and Wall, S. (1978) *Patterns of Attachment: A Psychological Study of the Strange Situation.* Hillsdale, N.J.: Erlbaum Associates.
Beebe, B. and Lachmann, F. M. (2002) *Infant Research and Adult Attachment: Co-Constructing Interactions.* London: The Analytic Press.
Bennis, W. G. and Shepard, H. A. (1957) 'A Theory of Group Development', *Human Relations*, vol. 9, pp. 415–37.
Bentovim, A. and Kinston, W. (1991) 'Focal Family Therapy Linking Systems and Psychodynamic Thinking', in A. Gurman and D. Kniskern (eds), *Handbook of Family Therapy*, Vol. 11. New York: Basic Books
Bentovim, A. (1992) *Trauma Organized Systems: Physical and Sexual Abuse in Families.* London, New York: Karnac.
Bion, W. R. (1961) *Experiences in Groups and Other Papers.* London and New York: Tavistock Publications and Basic Books
Bowlby, J. (1969) *Attachment and loss* (Vol. I). London: Hogarth Press.
— (1973) *Attachment and loss* (Vol. II). New York and London: Basic Books.
— (1980) *Attachment and loss* (Vol. III). New York and London: Basic Books.
— (1988) 'On Knowing what you are Not Supposed to Know and Feeling what you are Not Supposed to Feel', in *A Secure Base* (pp. 99–119). London: Routledge.
Brassard, M. R., Germain, R. and Hart, S. N. (1987) *Psychological Maltreatment of Children.* New York: Pergamon Press.
Burnett, (1993) 'The Psychological Abuse of Latency Age Children: A Survey', *Child Abuse and Neglect*, 17: 441–54.
Campos, J. J., Barrett, K. C., Lamb, M. E., Goldsmith, H. H. and Stenberg, C. (1983) 'Socioemotional development', in M. M. Haith and J. J. Campos (eds), *Handbook of child psychology* (Vol. 2. Infancy and psychobiology, pp. 783–915). New York: Wiley.
Cassidy, J. and Shaver, P. R. (1999) *The Handbook of Attachment: Theory Research and Clinical Applications.* New York, Guilford.
Daniel, B, Wassell, S. and Gilligan, R. (1999) *Child Development for Child Care and Protection Workers.* London and Philadelphia: Jessica Kingsley.
Department of Health (DoH) (1995) *Child Protection: Messages from research.* London: HMSO.
— (1999) *Working Together to Safeguard Children: A Guide to Inter-Agency Working to Safeguard and Promote the Welfare of Children.* London: HMSO.
— (2000) *Framework for the Assessment of Children in Need and their Families.* London: HMSO.

Fairbairn, W. R. D. (1952) *An Object Relations Theory of the Personality*. New York: Basic Books.

Fonagy, P., Steele, M., Steele, H., Leigh, T., Kennedy, R., Mattoon, G. and Target, M. (1995) 'Attachment in Adults: Clinical and Developmental Perspectives', in S. Goldberg, M. Roy and K. John (eds), *Attachment Theory: Social, Developmental and Clinical Perspectives* (pp. 233–79). London: The Analytic Press.

Gibbons, J., Gallagher, B., Bell, C. and Gordon, D. (1995) *Development after Physical Abuse in Early Childhood: A Follow Up Study of Children on Protection Registers*. London: HMSO.

Glaser, D. (1993) 'Emotional Abuse', in *Bailliere's Clinical Paediatrics*, vol. I, pp. 252–67.

Glaser, D. and Prior, V. (1997) 'Is the term child protection applicable to emotional abuse?' *Child Abuse Review*, vol. 6, pp. 315–29.

Grossmann, K. E. and Grossmann, K. (1991b) 'Attachment quality as an organizer of emotional and behavioural; responses in a longitudinal perspective', in C. M. Parkes, J. Stevenson-Hinde and P. Marris (eds), *Attachment Across The Life Cycle*, pp. 93–114. London and New York: Routledge.

Grossmann, K. and Grossmann, K. E. (1991a) 'Newborn behaviour, early parenting quality and later toddler-parent relationships in a group of German infants'. in J. Nugent, K., B. M. Lester and T. B. Brazelton (eds), *The Cultural Context of Infancy*, Vol. 2. Norwood, N.J.: Ablex.

Grossmann, K., Fremmer-Bombik, E., Rudolph, J. and Grossmann, K. E. (1988) 'Maternal attachment representations as related to child-mother attachment patterns and maternal sensitivity and acceptance of her infant', in R. A. Hinde and J. Stevenson-Hinde (eds), *Relations Within Families*. Oxford: Oxford University Press.

Grossmann, K., Grossmann, K. E., Spangler, G., Suess, G. and Unzner, L. (1985) 'Maternal sensitivity and newborns' orientation responses as related to quality of attachment in northern Germany', in I. Bretherton and E. Waters (eds), *Growing Points in Attachment Theory and Research. Monographs of the Society for Research in Child Development*, Vol. 50, pp. 233–78.

Haft, W. L. and Slade, A. (1989) 'Affect attunement and maternal attachment: a pilot study', *Infant Mental Health Journal*, vol. 10, pp. 157–71.

Haldane, J. D., McCluskey, U. and Peacey (1980) 'A Residential facility for families in Scotland: developments in prospect and retrospect', *International Journal of Family Psychiatry*, vol. 1, pp. 357–72.

Hazan, C. and Shaver, P. R. (1987) 'Romantic love conceptualized as an attachment process', *Journal of Personality and Social Psychology*, vol. 52, pp. 511–24.

Heard, D. (1982) 'Family systems and the attachment dynamic', *Journal of Family Therapy*, vol. 4, pp. 99–116.

Heard, D., and Lake, B. (1986) 'The attachment dynamic in adult life', *British Journal of Psychiatry*, vol. 149, pp. 430–39.

— — (1997) *The challenge of attachment for caregiving*. London: Routledge.

— — (1998) *Attachment theory, intimacy and ideals*. Paper presented at the Fifth John Bowlby Memorial Lecture, February, London, England.

— — (1999) *A conceptual extension of attachment theory: the attachment dynamic*. Paper presented at the First annual conference on the dynamics of attachment, March, York, England.

— — (2000). *The dynamics of attachment*. Paper presented at the International Attachment Seminar, June, London.

— — (2002) *The dynamics of attachment and exploratory collaboration*. Unpublished paper given to the Northern Attachment Seminar, University of York, 7 March.

Hindle, D. (1998) 'Loss, recovery and adoption: a child's perspective', *Journal of Social Work Practice*, vol. 12, pp. 17–26.

Howe, D. (1997) *Attachment Theory for Social Work Practice*. Houndmills, Basingstoke, Hampshire and London: Macmillan Press.

Iwaniec, D. (1995) *The emotionally abused and neglected child: Identification, assessment and intervention*. Chichester: Wiley.

Kiersky, S. and Beebe, B. (1994) 'The reconstruction of early nonverbal relatedness in the treatment of difficult patients: A special form of empathy', *Psychoanalytic Dialogues*, vol. 4, pp. 389–408. London and Philadelphia: Jessica Kingsley.

Main, M. (1991) 'Metacognitive knowledge, metacognitive monitoring, and singular (coherent). vs. multiple (incoherent). model of attachment: findings and directions for future research', in C. M. Parkes, J. Stevenson-Hinde and P. Marris (eds), *Attachment across the life cycle* (pp. 127–59). London: Routledge.

— (1995). 'Recent studies in attachment: overview, with selected implications for clinical work', in S. Goldberg, R. Muir and J. Kerr (eds), *Attachment theory; social, developmental and clinical perspectives* (pp. 407–474). London: The Analytic Press.

McCluskey, U. (1987) 'In Praise of Feeling, the Ethics of Intervention', in S. Walrond-Skinner, and D. Watson (eds), *The Ethics of Family Therapy*, (pp. 56–71). London: Routledge & Kegan Paul.

— (1999). *The Attachment Dynamic in Adult Psychotherapy: Evidence from Research*. Paper presented at conference The Attachment Dynamic from Childhood to Old Age, March, York, England.

— (2001) *A Theory of Care-Giving in Adult Life: developing and measuring the concept of goal-corrected empathic attunement*. Unpublished thesis. University of York, England

— (2002) 'The Dynamics of Attachment and Systems Centered Group Psychotherapy', *Group Dynamics*, vol. 6i, pp. 131–42.

McCluskey, U. and Bingley Miller (1995) 'Theme-focused family therapy; the inner emotional world of the family', *Journal of family Therapy*, vol. 17, pp. 411–34

McCluskey, U., Hooper, C. and Bingley Miller, L. (1999) 'Goal-corrected empathic attunement, developing and rating the concept', *Psychotherapy, Theory, Research, Training and Practice*, vol. 36, pp. 80–90.

McCluskey, U., Roger, D. and Nash, P. (1997) 'A Preliminary Study of the Role of Attunement in Adult Psychotherapy', *Human Relations*, vol. 50, pp. 1261–73.

Shannon, C. E. and Weaver, W. (1964) *The Mathematical Theory of Communication*. University of Illinois.

Stern, D. (1985) *The Interpersonal World of The Infant*. New York: Basic Books.

Sutherland, J. D. (1971) 'The individual's relationships in the group', in H. Walton (ed.) *Small Group Psychotherapy*. Harmondsworth: Penguin Books.

Thoburn, J., Wilding, J. and Watson, J. (2000) *Family Support in Cases of Emotional Maltreatment and Neglect*. London: The Stationery Office.

Tronick, E. (1989) 'Emotions and emotional communication in infants', *American Psychologist*, vol. 44, pp. 112–19.

Tronick, E. and Cohn, J. (1989) 'Infant Mother Face to Face Interaction: Age and Gender Differences in Coordination and Miscoordination', *Child Development*, vol. 59, pp. 85–92.

PART III

Working with Family
Groups in Difficulty

Part III

6

Working with Divorcing Partners

Christopher Clulow and Christopher Vincent

Divorce is a fact of life for families in the United Kingdom. While the marriage rate has been falling steadily over the past 20 years, it is predicted that just over four in ten of those who choose to tie the knot nowadays will see their marriage end in divorce. This outcome will affect 28 per cent of all children by their sixteenth birthday (FPSC, 2000). These figures do not include the increasing frequency with which cohabiting relationships are entered into and exited from, and which can have effects on family members that may be indistinguishable from those triggered by divorce. While this chapter addresses some implications of marriage ending, it is important to keep in mind other transient relationships that have not involved a formal legal commitment.

The fact of divorce is capable of generating concern at public and private levels. For some it represents an attack on institutions that are considered to be vital to the security of individuals and society as a whole. It threatens the well-being of children, incurs huge costs that may be carried by those who have no control over decisions taken and places in jeopardy justice, morality and a sense of fair play in relationships. For others, divorce is regarded as symptomatic of a changing relationship between women and men, a socio-economic environment that is radically different from even 50 years ago and a culture that is tolerant and accepting of doing something about, rather than putting up with, a restricting and sometimes destructive relationship-cum-institution.

However divorce is represented in the public debate, the prospect and actuality of this major life transition is likely, in the short term at least, to be a distressing private experience. The knowledge that so many people divorce does little to mitigate the pain of those going through it. The process, however much it is wanted, is likely to involve the grand passions associated with betrayal, injustice, rejection and loss. With the rupture of marriage – what is arguably the most significant attachment adults form with other adults – comes an experience that can resonate with previous experiences of loss, focusing the anxieties of a lifetime within a single process. These anxieties are highly infectious, affecting the 'greek chorus' of families, friends and anyone else sucked into the drama being played out before them.

The drama is likely to begin years before the legal ending of a marriage, and involve many different kinds of practitioners. Many relationship problems will first present themselves indirectly as physical symptoms, engaging the attention of doctors and other health workers. Some may come to the attention of social workers and mental health practitioners in the guise of concern about children, money worries or delinquent behaviour. These indirect communications may indicate a lack of recognition about or wish to deny the existence of a problem in the partnership, or an attempt to deflect attention away from it. When a relationship problem is acknowledged, relatively few people are likely to consult a couple counsellor or therapist about it, although the trend is rising (Simons, 1999). Once a marriage breaks down, lawyers, mediators, counsellors, health professionals, social workers and other professionals working in what has been described as the 'family justice system' (Murch and Hooper, 1992) are likely to be invited into the closed world of the family as the couple go public about their private sorrows. In the context of divorce, indirect communications to social workers are most likely to be couched in the language of child welfare, for clients quickly learn that this is the language that is most likely to engage their attention. But it is important to note that, for example, many contact and residence disputes are centrally related to the adult partners' unresolved feelings about their marriage or partnership having come to an end. In working with families during the process of separation and divorce, the subtext of many communications about the practical difficulties of accommodating to a changed situation will be feelings of anger, guilt and distress about the couple going their separate ways. Ignoring this dimension may limit the effectiveness of what can be done by social workers in their primary concern for children.

But there are many pressures acting to deflect practitioners from engaging with the couple, not least those emanating from the couple themselves when the partners are reluctant to acknowledge their feelings of loss as well as of anger and injustice. In a study of clients attending social services departments in the 1970s it was apparent how many of the practical difficulties they faced had their roots in relationship problems, but how seldom they were thought about in those terms by those who were on hand to help (Mattinson and Sinclair, 1979). Three features characterised the ways couples in that study concealed their need of each other: ambivalent behaviour, an obsession with blame and an intolerance of third parties. When one partner was feeling at their most vulnerable they were most likely to tell their spouse to go away; when efforts were made to spend more time together they often took the form of complaints about absences, and in talking to third parties about these matters attempts were made by each partner to forge an alliance with the third against the other. These three features of behaviour are often displayed by couples at stressful times during their divorce.

In responding to them, social workers will not be immune to the distress of their clients, although the wish to be so may result in a collusion to avoid what underlies the problems presented by them, the courts and others as the manifest site of concern. Yet to be able to help with the emotional distress of families, practitioners need to be open to the distress of what their clients are going through and to use their own feelings and experiences to make sense of what is happening during the transition of divorce. Anxiety is infectious, and the behaviour of practitioners with clients and colleagues will to some degree reflect the anxieties and feelings of the families they are there to help (Clulow, 2000; Woodhouse and Pengelly, 1991). The challenge for practice is to create the conditions in which this anxiety can be known for what it is, thought about and de-toxified.

In this chapter we shall consider the nature of anxiety affecting adults going through separation and divorce, and some implications of this for professional practice. We shall be drawing on attachment and object relations theories to provide a conceptual basis for this task and using illustrative vignettes already in the public domain from work undertaken by us at the Tavistock Marital Studies Institute. We hope that, despite the context of our work being different from that of other practitioners, the ideas will have a utility that is not limited to any one discipline.

Separation anxiety and the experience of change

At the heart of the divorce process is the experience of change. Change involves a mixture of loss and gain. The balance between the two will depend on many factors, and notably on whether a partner has instigated or been a reluctant party to the decision to end a marriage. Loss relates not simply to the legal contract of marriage, or to an understanding of the informal commitment entered into, but to the many and various connections that bind couples together in partnership. Separation disrupts the ordinary rituals of living together, and the sense of a common history and continuing conversation that is rooted in it. It disrupts sexual activity and a boundary of privacy surrounding the couple. As knowledge of the breakdown becomes public it affects the alliances within families, most notably between children and their parents but extending also to other kith and kin. One household becomes two, with the financial and logistical problems this generates for its members as they manage a new balance between being together and being apart. Networks of friends are restructured, and changes may be required at work. New, and sometimes unwelcome, networks are created as couples are drawn into the machinery of divorce and exposed to the public gaze. The habits of a lifetime are disrupted, a framework for living dismantled and there is the loss of love. These multiple changes, clustering around the central transition of divorce, will impact on a person's sense of identity, sometimes for good and sometimes for ill. The experience will have different meanings for the partners and those that surround them, especially in relation to the person initiating the break and the one who is left behind.

The picture is complicated by the reality that most marriages end, at least in emotional terms, well before a physical separation takes place. It is not uncommon for one partner to register that all is not well in the marriage and to attempt to engage the other about this. If the attempt is successful, the marriage can develop. If not, the emotional and practical investment in the partnership may gradually be withdrawn until the 'bank' becomes empty. A cycle of detachment and denial may result in the breakdown of communication until one partner, perhaps years into the process, takes advantage of an opportunity to leave. When both partners have accepted the problem between them and their inability to change it, separation may simply constitute the next step in what both regard as an inevitable outcome of what has happened between them (although the circumstances of the actual break are still likely to carry an emotional charge, especially when a third party is involved). When one partner has chosen to deny the problem, the separation may come as a shocking and wholly unexpected event, and there may be a flurry of activity to try and reverse or control the actions of the one who has left. Separation then triggers high levels of anxiety.

Bowlby's theory of attachment (Bowlby, 1969, 1973, 1980) identifies separation anxiety as one driver of attachment behaviour. He asserted that such anxiety is generated by the fear of separation and/or the experience of loss. Anxiety is a natural and inevitable response to the unaccountable and unwanted absence of an attachment figure. That figure may be an external person or an internal object. If things go well developmentally, the growing child learns that his or her attachment figures are available and responsive when needed. With time, these figures become internalised so that the child does not need the actual presence of the attachment figure to manage every potentially threatening situation or uncomfortable experience. But, equally, when that person is needed, there is confidence in seeking out the help of an actual other to cope with increased threats to physical safety and emotional security.

While he was principally concerned with the relationship between children and their primary caregivers, Bowlby believed that separation anxiety and the need for attachment continued to motivate behaviour across the life-span, and in contexts other than that of the child–parent relationship. He also believed that the responses of young children to being separated from their attachment figures had their adult counterparts.

Early responses of children to the experience of separation were marked by intensive activity to try and restore the relationship with the attachment figure. Searching and protest were specifically directed towards finding, and recruiting others to find, that which had been lost. If these efforts proved unsuccessful, the child would lapse into despair and a detachment from others. These responses are evident in the grief reactions of bereaved adults who may also turn away from the knowledge of absence if the reality is too much to bear (Parkes, 1986). Denial, protest and depression are predictable and normal responses to bereavement. It is not hard to discover similar responses during separation and divorce. Sometimes they occur in extreme form.

Denial

> A woman had been separated from her husband for 18 months. He had left her for another woman and subsequently petitioned for divorce. His wife spent much of the period after he left visiting doctors, psychiatrists and social workers to ask what could be done to treat what she considered to be the consequences of his mental ill-health. The divorce petition was read by her as yet further confirmation that he was not well. She said his behaviour towards her had changed following an accident at sea when he had suffered from concussion. She believed he could not be held responsible for his subsequent action of leaving her for another woman, and wanted to know what might be done to cure this sickness and restore to her the man she once used to know. She became angry when told there might be nothing to be done other than for her to try and come to terms with the end of her marriage. She would then tend to move on to consult another specialist whom she hoped would be more helpful.

It is not hard to see in this vignette how for this woman the story of mental illness had the purpose of denying the reality that she had been abandoned. It constituted a kind of life-belt to which she clung in order to avoid facing the reality that her marriage was on the rocks. She was searching for a man who used to be, and angry with anyone who came between her and the hope of recovering him.

Disbelief works like an emotional anaesthetic. In the short term it can protect against being overwhelmed by the magnitude of something traumatic that has happened. Over time it can turn into a pathological form of denial that works against recognising reality and adapting to change.

Protest

It is not uncommon for those who have been left to expend psychological effort not only on blocking out the reality of change, but also on trying to recover the person who has been lost. Searching and protest can be understood as behaviour directed towards this end:

> A man turned up at a counselling agency demanding an emergency appointment. He angrily and energetically explained that his wife had left him the previous day, leaving a note that did not disclose her where-

abouts. He was engaging the services of a private detective to track her down, and he wanted to know if the counsellor would see them to 'talk some sense into her' when he'd found where she was. He also said he was consulting a solicitor later that day and might file for divorce as a way of shocking her into a realisation of what she had done.

As with denial, searching and protest can be self-defeating, especially in the context of divorce. Stalking, harassment and legal action may be motivated by the wish to compel, if not coerce, a partner into believing there is no option other than returning to the marriage. One of the sad facts about divorce is how easily anxiety about loss can be transformed into feelings of anger, and how long it can take for anger to abate, how destructive it can be (not least when it perpetuates negative patterns of relating through endless court skirmishes) and how pyrrhic the victories won in the service of self-justification.

But anger does have its positive side. It can help people to give up the hopeless quest of putting the clock back, and provide a break-through when ambivalent feelings are serving to perpetuate a frozen situation in the marriage. One husband, faced with the offer of joint meetings to work at the implications of his wife's wish for him to leave the matrimonial home, was clear he could not bear to be in the same room as her. 'If I am to leave, I must hate her in order to go', he said (Clulow, Dearnley and Balfour, 1986). As it turned out, they eventually decided to stay together. The emotional separateness that can follow the expression of anger may some-times make an actual separation unnecessary. It may also galvanise partners into reappraising how important they are to each other.

Depression

When the loss is real and irreversible, depression and despair may be an indication that work is going on to relinquish the past in order to allow something else to take its place. Feelings of sadness may replace those of anger and apprehension, and pave the way to reintegrating the self and recovering new life and meanings. However, depression may also indicate the turning of anger in upon the self, or a chronic retreat from allowing anyone or anything to make a difference:

A woman who had been left by her violent husband was reluctant to allow the social worker into her home. When, at last, she consented, she was flat and uncommunicative in her manner, only stirring to life in pointing out the damage to sink and furniture inflicted some months previously by her husband before he had left for another woman. It was as if the evidence of damage needed to be preserved, and she sat in silent attendance on the debris of an earlier time.

In these circumstances the road to recovery is impeded by an inability to let go of the other and recover a sense of self.

Responses to current experiences of loss will be patterned by previous attachment experiences. During the course of growing up people develop their own particular strategies for protecting themselves against the fear of loss in the hazardous business of making and sustaining relationships with others. For those who feel secure in their attachments there is a confidence that others will be available and responsive when needed, and an ability to be available and responsive to others when they make an approach. This reciprocity is the hallmark of secure attachment in adult partnerships (Crowell and Treboux, 2001; Fisher and Crandell, 2001). For those whose childhood experience has been of consistently unresponsive parents, an insecurely patterned strategy directed towards maintaining contact while keeping an emotional distance and playing down the import of attachment may characterise their response to the threat or experience of loss. At its extreme come Bowlby's compulsively self-reliant, care-giving or detached responses to anxiety, strategies that aim to avoid the vulnerability associated with depending upon others. For those whose childhood experience has included inconsistently responsive parents, an insecurely patterned strategy of bidding for or coercing others into providing care, and accepting it ambivalently or aggressively, may be the prominent feature of their attachment orientation. This strategy approximates Bowlby's anxiously attached, clinging response of children to the prospect of separation, a response that can unwittingly provoke the very rejection that is consciously avoided.

Responses to loss usually have temporal continuity. There is a predictable sequence to the process of mourning, and the process itself is influenced by how previous experiences of separation and loss have been integrated within a person's psychological make-up. However, patterned ways of managing loss may break down if the nature of the event unlocks anxiety associated with earlier histories of loss or abuse which have remained unresolved and excluded from consciousness. Then, a person may be overwhelmed by the experience in a way that neither s/he nor others would have predicted.

Persecutory anxiety, depressive anxiety and the management of change

As we have indicated, divorce involves not only the loss of a partner and all that goes with it, but also a loss of self. It is not only that people have to reconstruct their view of their circumstances, they also have to reconstruct their view of themselves. With the loss of one's 'other half' – be that a 'better' or 'worse' half – comes the loss of that part of one's own identity that finds expression through the person one has chosen to become intimately associated with. With his or her departure goes part of the self. The loss of self in the other can trigger intense persecutory anxiety. Persecutory anxiety is associated with a state of mind that Klein described as the 'paranoid-schizoid' position (Klein, 1946). In this state of mind individuals unconsciously deal with threats to the self by splitting off and projecting into others all that is felt to be bad, shameful or blameworthy in order to try and preserve a core of the self as good and deserving of better. Negative qualities are attributed to former partners and all who might associate with them. Allegations are made and reinforced in ways that amplify complaints and provide a positive feedback loop in the social system of the couple, further alienating them from each other and themselves in a rage that feels good – in the same way that it feels good to identify an enemy and go to war. By these means some sense of solidity and solidarity is achieved. But there is a price to be paid.

The paranoid anxiety of externalising all that is experienced as hostile and destructive is one means of protecting against the fear of personal disintegration, although not one suited to adapting to change in the long term. When the actions of others who had once been soul-mates are experienced, as one man put it, 'a declaration of war', the world divides into enemies and allies. The capacity to be concerned about others is limited by the energy expended in sustaining the self. This narcissistic preoccupation, perhaps necessary in the short term, embraces most warmly involvements and activities that absolve the self and vilify others.

It is not hard to see how well-matched psychological processes driven by persecutory anxiety are to inquisitorial and adversarial systems. Fault-based divorce is a more intelligible concept than 'irretrievable breakdown', and meets the needs of people who feel persecuted, besieged and deeply wronged. Litigation is a means of constructing for and conveying to the individuals concerned, and those around them, a story about how they come to be where they are. The purpose of the story is to retain some semblance of identity and integrity by prosecuting blameworthiness in others and seeking vindication for the self. Report recommendations and court decisions can be received as a form of public absolution and acquittal or, conversely, as a conviction and life sentence. In the nightmare world of monsters and villains to which divorcing parents may sometimes temporarily regress, the concepts of 'fault' and 'matrimonial offence' are eminently more comprehensible than some of the assumptions underpinning the unimplemented Part 2 of the 1996 Family Law Act. As one man in our research sample put it: 'I think adultery is a crime. Full stop. It's a terrible crime'.

Countering defensive systems, whether at private or public level, can be very difficult. Practitioners working in the family justice system are particularly exposed to invitations to join the 'greek chorus' of divorce, muttering favourably or unfavourably about the different players. They will be under pressure to declare for one party and against the other, and are likely to have difficulty holding the middle ground. When they seek to bring embattled protagonists together they may underestimate just how alarming can be the prospect of being in the same room with someone who has mentally been transformed into the embodiment of evil. Attempts to engage the rational parts of those in conflict through mediation and other non-adversarial processes may contain such feelings in a constructive way. But they may also operate as a defence for practitioners against the pain of those they see. When the family justice system denies the messy aspects of divorce by trying to sanitise procedures there is a risk of hindering people rather than helping them to move on (Sclater, 1999).

Persecutory anxiety is linked with psychological processes that split off aspects of the self, locating them 'out there' rather than 'in here'. It is essentially linked with a failure in the capacity to distinguish others from self. In contrast, depressive anxiety is associated with feelings about the loss of an actual other person, rather than an aspect of the self located in that person. In what Klein (1946) described as the 'depressive position', there is a recognition of the other as a separate person with legitimate agency to behave as s/he might wish. Feelings of sadness, guilt and concern characterise this state of mind, and there is awareness of the part the self has played in bringing about an unhappy situation. Reparation replaces retribution. The world becomes a less threatening place; the self a wiser, and perhaps sadder, being, at least in the short term.

Some implications for professional practice

Some years ago the Tavistock Marital Studies Institute researched the work of a specialist team of family court welfare officers (Clulow and Vincent, 1987). The aim of the project was to explore the feasibility of welfare officers mediating between parents over contact and residence disputes while preparing court-ordered reports concerning the welfare of their children. The research involved us in working with a core sample of 30 families who were the subject of welfare enquiries. By definition, they were a particularly contentious section of the divorcing population. Three-quarters of the petitioners had used the behaviour clause of the 1969 Act to establish 'irretrievable breakdown', the same proportion had involved one partner taking the decision to divorce unilaterally, and there was ambivalence about the marriage ending in 25 of the 30 cases. All these factors have been associated with high levels of conflict and poor adaptive responses in relation to divorce. A recent study similarly indicates how distressed a group are the parents and children who become clients of family court welfare services, and indicates the significance of the reporting process for alleviating or aggravating their beleaguered state (Buchanan *et al.*, 2001).

Despite the role tensions of combining reporting, mediating and therapeutic functions (and it can be argued that the conflict between private ordering and public adjudication is not one for welfare officers to attempt to manage), agreement was recorded in over half of the core sample of cases at the end of the enquiry period, and in over two-thirds of these the parties were judged by the welfare officers to have moved closer to a joint position during the enquiry period. These figures probably overstate the role played by practitioners in achieving this outcome (the prospect of a court order deterred some couples from pursuing their dispute, some agreements were arrived at to deflect unwelcome attention and some were paper agreements that masked unchanged positions).

Our classifications of divorces into three groups allowed us to make some assessment of which couples were most amenable to change. The *nominal* group of divorces consisted of parents who remained ambivalently attached to each other, unable to acknowledge their relationship as durable or to implement a decision to part. Not knowing their own mind they pressed others to take responsibility for decisions, and elicited a therapeutic response from welfare officers that could neither be sustained nor was appropriate to their role. They could absorb a lot of the welfare officer's time to no good effect, resisting referral to agencies that might help reconcile them and any moves that would finalise the divorce.

At the other end of the spectrum were *long-lease* divorces, where the prognosis was equally poor. These parents remained distantly but chronically attached, as if they could never quite disengage from a sense of belonging together. A lengthy history of divorce-associated litigation, highly discrepant accounts of events, a determination and ability to 'play the system', plus a preference for bypassing direct communication, made them unlikely candidates for out-of-court assisted settlements.

The key indicator of a favourable prospect for achieving agreement was a degree of accessibility in the ways parents approached each other. This was most often found in our *shot-gun* category of divorces (in which one party clearly wanted out and the other felt they had had no opportunity to establish what they wanted), and was partly determined by the situation existing between the parties at the time and partly a product of the opportunities afforded them by their welfare officers. Accessibility implied a capacity, however limited, to hear what others were saying and to take it into account, to press for claims in an assertive but not self-defeating way, and to show a certain amount of flexibility towards the claims of others when circumstances warranted it. Parents were most likely to be accessible when they were far enough removed from the trauma of separation not to feel their lives were in pieces, but not so far removed that patterns of conflict had become entrenched and embittered.

Most of the parents we saw in the study were intensely preoccupied with their own psychological survival. Their emotional and social viability had been seriously disturbed. The roles of parent and spouse had acted for them, as with most people, as life-support systems. The couples were facing an existential crisis. Perhaps unsurprisingly, the fight for survival was carried out in relation to partners and children. Shock, fear, outrage and intransigence were their understandable reactions to the threat and realisation of being dispossessed. 'The argument simply wasn't rational', one mother observed with hindsight, 'I felt I would lose my rights. I think my husband felt the same way'.

This had a clear impact on the welfare officers who needed to survive the verbal abuse and emotional battering that were frequently part of the work. In surviving the impact it was essential for the team to feel supported and together as a group in relation to their role and tasks. Co-working was sometimes helpful as a way of feeling less fragmented by family dynamics. Having a partner to confer with – and occasionally to fight with – helped preserve some balance between partisan interests. Agreements were more likely to be achieved when we worked in pairs than when we worked on our own. Supervision was also a vital support in managing the boundaries of the task in a world where boundaries were collapsing and being redrawn in sometimes astonishingly rapid succession.

Part of the stress of the work was related to how family experiences resonated with the emotional life of the practitioner. This is particularly true in relation to the highly emotive issues of family dissolution and child welfare, both of which are likely to activate transference and counter-transference responses in the client–practitioner relationship. Such resonance also provided an opportunity for creative work.

Transference is used here to describe the unconscious process of attributing to a current relationship properties that derive from a person's representation of past (usually family) relationships. Boundaries distinguishing the past from the present, and internal phantasy from external reality, are collapsed or breached in the process. Counter-transference refers here to 'out of the ordinary' feeling and thinking states clients induce in their professional helpers. Provided that helpers know about their professional boundaries and role – something that cannot be taken for granted and which has led to the publication of a practice guide for those working in the family justice system – they are in a position to register when boundaries are being broken as a result of unconscious pressures exerted by clients. Members of divorcing families are capable of 'getting under the skin' of those to whom they turn for help, which is a colloquial way of expressing the idea that people can disown feelings and states of mind they cannot bear to know about, projecting them into others in whom they might be recognised and related to from a safe distance.

Wallerstein (1990) charts different ways in which the experience of divorce can unconsciously engage practitioners. There is the practitioner's responses to marital breakdown, inviting identifications and counter-identifications in response to the betrayal of trust, sexual jealousy, fear of loneliness and the many other emotions that surround divorce. This may be at the near conscious level of evoking disapproval and censure, or at a deeply unconscious level of evoking anxiety states and the fear of annihilation that speaks to, but is not consciously linked with, the client's experience. It is not uncommon for practitioners to find themselves drawn into the persecutor or persecuted role in relation to those they see, as the nature of a client's anxiety is unconsciously communicated through enactments of one kind or another. Diminished parenting can also engage the practitioner in different ways, inviting anguish, rage, impotence, judgemental responses and fantasies of rescuing the 'victim' child. Alternatively, the desire to be noncondemnatory and even-handed may result in a cool remoteness where feelings of anger or alarm may be more appropriate. There are also gender factors that may reverberate in the transference, conflating this man with all men, or that woman with the 'other woman', and so infusing the professional relationship with hostile, vengeful or erotic overtones.

A study undertaken at the Tavistock Marital Studies Institute sought to identify the emotional challenges encountered by workers offering brief interventions to couples and individuals going through the divorce process. This study distilled three counter-transferential roles that workers were unconsciously invited to take up by divorcing spouses who were in the grip of persecutory anxiety: *the judge, the magician* and *the servant*.

The wish for a 'judge' captures a recurring expectation placed on practitioners to save an impossible situation from proceeding on its seemingly never-ending course by deciding in favour of one party at the expense of the other. Cases in which this expectation was present were nearly always referred from other professionals – court welfare officers, social workers, solicitors – who had reached an impasse in their attempts to help arrive at a settlement. These cases might be in the middle of protracted and unresolved court hearings, allegations of abuse were likely to be rife and, as likely as not, a multiplicity of other agencies would be involved. Yet the expectation was that the practitioner would be able to resolve a matter that had defeated all other approaches. In particular, there was an expectation that decisive action would be taken that would remove the offending party from the picture. Faced with these impossible expectations the task of the practitioner was to help the couple, and sometimes the referrer, to face the disappointment that such a power in the land did not exist.

Interventions where practitioners were asked to be a 'magician' similarly involved a process of relinquishing an omnipotent fantasy that there was a magic wand that could 'disappear' the problem. Partners with this fantasy frequently referred themselves and came alone to the session. They were often at an early stage of the divorce process and would frequently express their dilemma in the form of a question such as 'what do I tell the children?' Behind this question lay an anxiety about openly facing conflict with a partner, and about bearing the guilt of inflicting the consequences of a separation on their children. The result was an unconscious hope that the consultant had a magic formula that would allow the divorce to proceed without turmoil and pain.

While the wish for a judge or magician involved expectations of an omnipotent kind, there were other experiences that left practitioners feeling helpless and ineffective. Rather than being elevated to a position of specialist with potentially enormous powers and abilities, the prescribed role for the practitioner was one of 'servant'. Here, the power appeared to reside with the client. Appointments would be cancelled without warning. Frequent, lengthy and demanding telephone calls would convey an expectation that the practitioner should be at the client's beck and call, or that s/he should accept being treated in a rather demeaning way as a 'go-between' or 'letter-drop' facility, conveying messages between warring parties. What needed working with in these situations was the fear of becoming out of control and subject to the power of others, something that the practitioner might experience as a result of strategies that, on the surface, portrayed the client as being powerful and seemingly in control.

In the following example it will be clear that while the focus of the work is determined by the prospect of separation, it addresses matters that extend beyond the transitions of separation and divorce and link with emotional communications that the practitioner picked up in the counter-transference. This, we believe, is often the case, and argues against regarding work in the divorce arena as in any sense encapsulated from the rest of life. Family transitions of any kind can generate symptoms that have dynamic roots that can be remarkably unchanging over time. We have selected an illustration coming from the 'magician' group of cases because the therapeutic possibilities are often greater for these than for the two other categories:

A woman referred herself for an interview about what she described as her 'dead' marriage. She was hesitant about seeking advice, and described walking up and down her local High Street wondering whether to make an appointment with a solicitor's practice or with a counselling organisation.

She said that she and her husband had not been close for years. She had tried to talk about the distance in their relationship early on in the marriage but had given up in the face of his withdrawal. She described her disappointment with herself for having put up with a dead marriage for so long. She told herself she had done so for her teenage daughter, who had a close, affectionate and protective relationship with her father that was reciprocated. The main reason she gave herself for not leaving her husband was the emotional distress it would cause both him and her daughter.

She described her daughter as a very bright girl who was doing well at school and who had many friends. This picture contrasted strongly with the one the practitioner formed of the mother from her flat and anxious manner. Yet she had a mental picture of how life might be if she left her husband, and said she could imagine the cosy and bright flat she might create for herself if she were on her own. In this new setting she had thought about how she could juggle her commitments as a parent and also develop her career. But as she talked about the optimistic pictures of her life after marriage she checked herself, insisting she could not go ahead for the damage it would do to her daughter and husband.

The practitioner was puzzled by her struggle, and asked her to say something about her background. She described the large family she had grown up in where she had been a late developer and opportunities had been limited. She sketched in a background of under-achievement, and of being trapped in circumstances from which she wished to escape but could never quite get free. It was striking that she equated 'getting free' in her current situation as being something that could only be achieved at her daughter's expense. There was a sense in which she wanted her daughter to achieve all that she felt she had been unable to achieve for herself, but that she might also envy her for having opportunities that she had missed out on.

Reflecting on the links between her childhood experiences and her current problems in the marriage, the practitioner thought that, stuck as she was and tempted to make do with second best, she harboured a fantasy of a different life away from her parental family and separate from her husband. This plan could never be translated into reality because of a fear that it would wreak havoc and be very destructive. He thought that he was expected to take responsibility for overcoming the impasse she found herself in by providing a magical solution that would bring about a pain-free happy ending.

He responded by commenting upon what he understood her dilemma to be. First, she needed something to be different, but was anxious about separating because of the feelings of guilt that were associated with acting on her own initiative. He said that she hoped he might help her get round this problem by providing a 'magical' solution that would cause no-one distress. Second, he put forward the idea that by avoiding taking responsibility for herself she preserved her daughter's view that her parents, and especially her father, needed looking after and could not take responsibility for their own lives and difficulties. He suggested that she might be relieved if both her parents took responsibility for their problems and left her to get on with her life.

The mother felt particularly helped by this idea, and could identify with it both as a parent and also from her experience of growing up in a family where she felt unduly responsible for others. The single session ended with her saying that she would try to persuade her husband to come with her for a joint discussion of their problems.

Such cases were not of the entrenched variety, often presented themselves early on in the separation process and typically would define the problem as not knowing what to tell the children. Anxiety was more depressive than persecutory, and therefore there was more space to think about the problem and its various ramifications. Nevertheless, the consultant was facing pressure to act in omnipotent, magical ways, and there was a hope that personal responsibility might be handed over to external expertise. As is so often the case, the work needed to focus on the implications of there being no magical pain-free option, and on galvanising a sense of personal responsibility for understanding and managing the stress of effecting change.

We want to conclude by drawing attention to seven broad questions that practitioners working with divorcing couples might want to keep in mind. These constitute potentially useful arenas in which the experience of separation and divorce might be processed in constructive and creative ways. They delineate important aspects of the emotional work required when marriage and partnerships end.

What meanings do separation and divorce carry for those involved?

The significance of any change depends not just upon its nature and extent but also upon what it represents for the adults and children concerned. What has been invested in the relationship? How exclusively has it been relied upon and for what kinds of things? How much of a gap will be left? For couples parting early on in their relationship there may be losses about giving up a fantasy of what might have been rather than the experience of what actually was. For older couples, a lifetime of shared history may seem to be at stake, questioning assumptions that had hitherto been taken for granted.

Why is this change taking place now?

The understood causes and circumstances in which a marriage breaks are likely to be very important, both in relation to the reactions it provokes and the process of adjustment that the changes require. Divorce, unlike most deaths, follows the exercise of choice. Feelings of rejection, betrayal and injustice are likely to be intense for one or both partners. Who is thought to be to blame for what has happened? Was it thought to be avoidable? How does one live with the feelings of physical, sexual and emotional exclusion that follow from one's spouse becoming involved with someone else? These questions are relevant to children as well as the grown-ups, and involve emotional work as well as cognitive recognition.

How much forewarning has there been?

The more predictable change is, the more manageable it is likely to be. We have referred to how devastating sudden and unexpected departures from the matrimonial home can be for those who are left behind. Yet we have also observed that when partners cannot bear to know that the marriage is in trouble it may be impossible for them to pick up the signals that herald change. These observations can be applied to the legal and para-legal processes that are set in train following an application for divorce. The more informed people are about what happens if they initiate divorce proceedings, where they can go for different kinds of help and what they can expect to receive in terms of response, the less stressful the experience is likely to be. This is mainly because information is power. Change is best accomplished when people feel empowered in relation to it.

What about the balance of power?

When relationships break down the imbalance of power between partners can sometimes be starkly revealed. The manipulation of assets, physical violence and emotional coercion may be brought to bear by one partner against the other. Many women are fearful of leaving violent marriages because of the repercussions they expect to follow, and threatening attitudes may lead either partner to settle for an arrangement that falls short of what they might be entitled to, or what is in their own and their childrens' best interests. Mediators are trained specifically to be alert to such imbalances when facilitating the private resolution of disagreements over post-separation arrangements. Social workers need to have this dynamic in mind, and to remember that they, too, have power, and need to exercise care in how it is used.

How will family and friends respond?

The support of family, friends and colleagues has a major impact on the management of change. These people provide a thread of continuity with ordinary life. They can provide encouragement, support, counsel and the vitally needed thinking space in which events can be talked about, replayed and reworked. When divorce involves moving away from familiar people and surroundings an important supply of 'social oxygen' is cut off. Even when no physical moving away is involved, people who are divorcing, and those around them, may enter a conspiracy of silence and avoidance because they do not know whether and how to talk about what is going on. Sometimes family members and friends feel so strongly about what has happened that they may contribute to the polarisation of the parties and become part of the problem.

What professional help is at hand?

Closely related to the social and emotional support of family and friends comes the practical support available to parents and children once a marriage comes to an end. Financial worries can be all-consuming, and information about benefits and entitlements is much needed at this time. So, too, is information about services that can help families manage the transition they are going through. The attitudes of teachers towards children going through family upheaval, and of schools towards them and their parents, can act as helpful and unhelpful influences. Practitioners need to be aware of the part they play, unwittingly or not, in fashioning the experience of divorce. The ways in which divorce is – and is not – ritualised by society, the processes that people go through, their access to rites that help them refashion meaning from experience, will all be relevant to how able they are to integrate their past with their future.

How has change been managed previously?

Highly relevant to the management of loss in the present is how people have experienced and managed loss previously in their lives. Current events provide a hook on which past traumas can be hung, with all the confusions and emotional charge that attend fusing the past with the present. A man in our study of divorce-court welfare enquiries vigorously pursued an application for his children to live with him, irrespective of practical and other difficulties that made the proposition unrealistic. When confronted with the impracticality of his proposals he brushed objections aside, saying he had lost contact with a child from a previous marriage and was not going to let that happen to him again.

Linking past experience with current meanings attributed to separation and divorce brings us full circle. The central task for those undergoing divorce is to come to terms with the emotional, social, existential and practical upheavals that accompany marriage breakdown in order to accomplish the shift in identity and organisation of relationships that the change requires. One route to arriving at new meanings and purposes is through the telling and retelling of experience. For practitioners, as well as their clients, this involves knowing about and making sense of their emotional responses to experience as well as the events in which they are involved. Through this process, sense can be made of what has gone before and secure foundations laid for what is to follow. As the stories told and retold gain in coherence and consistency, the past is integrated into the present rather than banished from it or allowed to take it over.

In our study of welfare enquiries the core sample of 30 families were followed up around one year after completion of their report. We were surprised by how many parents had kept the reports and referred to them. These reports had attempted to represent, with greater and lesser degrees of success, the stories of all the parties to the dispute. The welfare officer's story was superimposed upon those of the other players in a way, it was hoped, that would allow for the maximum of consensus between private ordering and child welfare considerations to emerge. Having a story to tell and arriving at a point of view were important for family members and practitioners alike in surviving a fragmented world.

Fact or fiction, everyone needs a story to stand by. The best stories are those that serve people well in their present circumstances, and which are open to review and updating. The challenge for parents, children and all who come into contact with them during the refashioning experience of separation and divorce is to construct and reconstruct stories that have integrity and work well for the tellers and those around them.

References

Bowlby, J. (1969) *Attachment and Loss: Attachment* (Vol. 1). London: Hogarth Press.
Bowlby, J. (1973) *Attachment and Loss: Separation* (Vol. 2). London: Hogarth Press.
Bowlby, J. (1980) *Attachment and Loss: Loss, Sadness and Depression* (Vol. 3). London: Hogarth Press.
Buchanan, A., Hunt, J., Bretherton, H. and Bream, V. (2001) *Families in Conflict: Perspectives of Children and Parents on the Family Court Welfare Service*. Oxford: Polity Press.

Clulow, C. (2000) 'Supporting Marriage in the Theatre of Divorce', in M. Thorpe and E. Clarke (eds), *No Fault or Flaw. The Future of the Family Law Act 1996*. Bristol: Family Law.

Clulow, C., Dearnley, B. and Balfour, F. (1986) 'Shared Phantasy and Therapeutic Structure in a Brief Marital Psychotherapy', *British Journal of Psychotherapy*, vol. 3(2), 124–32.

Clulow, C. and Vincent, C. (1987) *In the Child's Best Interests? Divorce Court Welfare and the Search for a Settlement*. London: Tavistock/Sweet & Maxwell.

Crowell, J. and Treboux, D. (2001) 'Attachment Security in Adult Partnerships', in C. Clulow (ed.), *Adult Attachment and Couple Psychotherapy. The 'Secure Base' in Practice and Research*. London: Brunner-Routledge.

Fisher, J. and Crandell, L. (2001) 'Patterns of Relating in the Couple', in C. Clulow (ed.), *Adult Attachment and Couple Psychotherapy. The 'Secure Base' in Practice and Research*. London: Brunner-Routledge.

FPSC (2000) *Family Change: Guide to the Issues* (Family Briefing Paper no. 12). London: Family Policy Studies Centre.

Klein, M. (1946) 'Notes on some Schizoid Mechanisms', in M. Klein (ed.), *The Writings of Melanie Klein* (Vol. 3). London: Hogarth Press.

Mattinson, J. and Sinclair, I. (1979) *Mate and Stalemate. Working with Marital Problems in a Social Services Department*. Oxford: Blackwell.

Murch, M. and Hooper, D. (1992) *The Family Justice System*. Bristol: Family Law.

Parkes, C. M. (1986) *Bereavement. Studies of Grief in Adult Life* (2nd edn). Harmondsworth: Penguin.

Sclater, S. D. (1999) *Divorce: A Psychosocial Study*. Aldershot: Ashgate.

Simons, J. (1999) 'How Useful is Relationship Therapy?', in J. Simons (ed.), *High Divorce Rates: The State of the Evidence on Reasons and Remedies* (Vol. 2). London: Lord Chancellor's Department.

Vincent, C. (1995) 'Consulting to Divorcing Couples', *Family Law*, vol. 25 (December), pp. 678–81.

Wallerstein, J. S. (1990) 'Transference and Counte transference in Clinical Intervention with Divorcing Families', *American Journal of Orthopsychiatry*, vol. 60 (3), pp. 337–45.

Walsh, E. (ed.) (1998) *Working in the Family Justice System*. Bristol: Jordan.

Woodhouse, D. and Pengelly, P. (1991) *Anxiety and the Dynamics of Collaboration*. Aberdeen: Aberdeen University Press.

7

Working with Family Change: Repartnering and Stepfamily Life

Jane Batchelor

Professionals working with families at any stage of their life-cycle are likely to find that an understanding of stepfamily issues helps them in their practice. The feelings aroused and the tensions and strains experienced in stepfamilies are not confined to those raising children, as many adults who have experienced parents repartnering in later life will know. There are important issues to be addressed in relation to stepfamilies of all ages and at different points in their life-cycle; for example, stepfamily obligations in caring for elderly relatives in the extended kinship networks (Bornat *et al.*, 1999). However, an understanding of such issues is of particular value to all of us working with children and families in the field of social care since we are bound sometimes to work with stepfamily members. Even if the crux of a problem or difficulty is not centred on a stepfamily issue, an understanding of the particular stresses and strengths of stepfamilies will positively inform our practice.

Definitions

A stepfamily is created whenever a parent takes a new partner through cohabitation or marriage. Defined in this way it encompasses the households of both parents, their new partners, the children (dependent and independent) and the extended families of all the adults in these two households. For the purposes of this practice guide to working with families, this broad definition will be used but the focus will be upon those stepfamily households with dependent children.

Today most stepfamilies in Britain are created following divorce, separation or elective single parenthood, rather than death. Numbers are hard to come by, partly because different definitions have been used. For example, the Office for National Statistics (ONS) defines a stepfamily as a married or cohabiting couple with dependent children living in their family, at least one of whom is not the biological child of both the man and the woman. Such a definition excludes same-sex couples with children and older couples whose children have reached adulthood.

This definition also carries an implicit assumption that a stepfamily is only created when a child's resident parent repartners. Many children who live in lone-parent households may acquire a stepparent when their non-resident parent repartners, though present methods of counting stepfamilies would not necessarily record such households as stepfamilies. Yet it is known that non-resident parents and their partners experience many of the stresses that full-time stepfamily households do (Batchelor *et al.*, 1994). To exclude or ignore these part-time stepfamily households when looking to improve professional practice with children or to develop family policies is a serious omission.

How many stepfamilies are there?

Using the ONS definition (which excludes part-time stepfamily households and same-sex couples) in the mid-1990s it was estimated there were over half a million stepfamilies in Great Britain; that is, 1 in 14 of all families with dependent children (Haskey, 1996). They contain about a million dependent stepchildren plus over 300 000 children of the new couples (Parentline Plus, 2000). It has been estimated that, in addition, about a million children in Great Britain are members of part-time stepfamily households, visiting a parent (probably their father) and stepparent at weekends or holidays (Schlosser and De'Ath 1994). Thus about 2.5 million of the 12 million dependent children in the UK today – that is, about 1 in 5 of all children – are involved in stepfamily life in some way. The rise in divorce rates over the past 30 years, combined with high remarriage or repartnering rates, has resulted in an increase in the number of stepfamilies in Britain (although numbers created following the death of a parent have declined dramatically over the past century). More than half of divorced parents will go on to acquire a new partner and so form a stepfamily. It has been predicted that by 2010, divorce or separation followed by settling down with a new partner will be the norm (Parentline Plus, 2000).

Stepfamilies are different from nuclear families by virtue of their history and their structure. The ways in which they differ have implications for all our work with children and families, from assessment of needs and strengths to planning and implementation of interventions and evaluation of outcomes. Yet there is mounting evidence that, despite the stresses that stepfamily members may experience by virtue of their unique and often complex structure, they can be happy and sustaining settings for children and for adults (Gorell Barnes *et al.*, 1998). When a parent repartners, children become part of an extended kin network. They have opportunities to experience different models of family life and to build close and mutually satisfying relationships with adults other than their birth parents and with children other than full siblings, some of whom may become significant figures in their lives. However, as professionals we need to be sensitive to stepfamily issues if we are to help such families overcome or weather the stresses and maximise their potential as nurturing environments.

Policy issues: rendered invisible or labelled a failure?

In many child and family policy discussions in Britain, stepfamilies have been and continue to be invisible. The fact that most stepfamilies are created following the breakdown of a relationship rather than death may in part account for society's ambivalent views. Whilst a parent is rarely held responsible for the death of a partner (and repartnering by a widow or widower is usually viewed benignly), a level of culpability is often attributed to a lone parent, whatever the circumstances.

The position of stepparents in England and Wales has been partially addressed in recent legislation. Permanency of parenthood is enshrined in the 1989 Children Act, built on the principle that parents are responsible for their dependent birth children unless that tie is severed through adoption. The potential for stepparents to be granted Parental Responsibility through the making of a Residence Order under the 1989 Children Act goes some way towards enabling stepparents to establish legal status in relation to their stepchildren without recourse to adoption, should they so wish. As predicted, (Masson, 1992), the number of adoptions by stepparents has declined over the past 10 years. Yet they continue to account for about a half of adoption orders made in England and Wales (Utting, 1994); in 1996–97, of the 5,000 adoption orders granted, 2,700 were to stepparents (DoH, 1999).

Adoption has received much political attention recently, but chiefly in relation to meeting the needs of looked-after children. It remains to be seen whether current proposals under the Adoption and Children Bill will result in an increase in the numbers of stepparents acquiring Parental Responsibility (and a parallel decrease in numbers that adopt their stepchildren). This may depend on the motivation of stepparent adopters, about which little is known. For some, it may be an attempt to erase their stepfamily status and leave the past behind, establishing themselves as a 'normal' family. If this is the case, then acquiring parental responsibility is unlikely to offer what the adults may be looking for, yet may be in the best interest of the child since legal ties with the non-resident birth parent are not severed. For others it may be a means of securing the stepparent-stepchild relationship in case of early death of the resident birth parent, or of ensuring a stepchild has the same status in the family as a new half sibling when the parent and stepparent have their first joint child.

When stepfamilies are not being rendered invisible by policy-makers and practitioners, they often fall prey to the myths attached to stepparents. Most of us are familiar from childhood with stories of 'wicked stepmothers'. If we add to these myths the media coverage given to stepfamilies, usually relating to the behaviour of 'abusive stepfathers' and the consequences for 'neglected stepchildren', we should not be surprised that, in the face of such labels, many stepfamilies choose to 'pass' as a nuclear family. The unflattering terms commonly used to describe stepfamilies, such as 'blended', 'second' and 'reconstituted' are hardly likely to encourage stepparents and stepchildren to identify themselves as such. These terms also perpetuate a deficit-comparison model (Ganong and Coleman 1994) whereby assumptions are made that a stepfamily should be measured against a nuclear or first family and, on this basis, is necessarily found wanting.

Thus it is that stepfamilies are either pathologised or ignored. Berger (1998) suggests the paucity of stepfamily studies prior to the 1980s may be due to 'a societal tendency to ignore their unique issues' (p. 4), perhaps compounded by the challenges presented in researching such complex family situations. The new framework for the assessment of children in need and their families (DoH, 2000) makes some references to stepfamilies but the implications of stepfamily status for assessment are only briefly referred to, despite the acknowledgement in accompanying literature that parenting in a stepfamily '... is common and applies to up to a third of all families' (Jones, 2001, p. 266).

From the foregoing discussion it is clear that that there are significant numbers of stepfamilies in the population, that they differ from nuclear families yet these differences may not immediately be visible. Stepfamily members (especially the adults) may have no wish to challenge this invisibility. As most stepfamilies are born of loss – a death, divorce or separation – the new couple may have a personal agenda to leave painful pasts behind and make a fresh start within this "new" family. If problems are later experienced there is a risk that the professionals consulted will, because of a lack of awareness of stepfamily issues, fall into the trap of making assumptions that they are the same as a nuclear family and inadvertently exacerbate problems.

What do we know about stepfamilies?

Some preliminary thoughts on stepfamily research

Until the 1980s research addressing stepfamilies was extremely thin on the ground. In Britain, Margaret Robinson's paper published in 1980 was one of the earliest in this country to draw attention to stepfamily issues and their implications for practice, based on the author's extensive clinical experience. This was followed by the groundbreaking study of stepfamilies by Burgoyne and Clark (1984) who conducted in-depth interviews with 40 stepfamily couples, looking at the ways in which they made sense of their experiences. At about the same time, there was published a study of stepchildren based on secondary analysis of data from the National Child Development Study. Since then there has been an exponential increase in studies, both here and in the USA, ranging from single-case analyses based on clinical practice through to large-scale epidemiological research.

Whilst studies from other parts of the world (particularly North America) have much that may be helpful in understanding stepfamilies in Britain today (for example Ganong and Coleman, 1994; Visher and Visher, 1996; Berger, 1998), we always need to be mindful of differences in the economic, social, cultural and political contexts of the UK and the USA. In addition, there are various methodological limitations to the research that has been undertaken in both countries, making comparison of study outcomes difficult and requiring that some caution be applied in interpreting findings.

A basic problem is the lack of consistency in what is defined as a stepfamily. There are also many variables that may influence outcomes for children in stepfamilies. The quality of the birth parents' relationship before separation or bereavement, the age of children at parental separation and at the point of repartnering, the gender of the child *vis-à-vis* that of the stepparent, length of single parenthood, and prior parenting experiences of stepparents are all important. However such variables are rarely controlled for; this can be a particular problem when undertaking secondary analysis of existing data-sets.

There has also been an early reliance in the research on clinical samples. This in part accounts for the perpetuation of the deficit-comparison model used for so long when examining outcomes for children in stepfamilies. Whilst clinical studies are valuable, outcomes for such families may not be applicable to the full population of stepfamilies and it is hardly surprising if their findings are at odds with those of researchers using, say, subsets drawn from large-scale longitudinal studies.

Child abuse in stepfamilies has been a longstanding concern for practitioners. At first glance there appears to be some research evidence that children with stepparents are at increased risk of abuse compared to those living with birth parents. However, without denying that abuse may occur in stepfamilies, caution must be applied in interpreting the findings since methodological problems are rife in this work (Brodie and Berridge, 1996). There is a lack of consistency in definitions of abuse used in research, which is compounded by similar problems regarding definitions of a stepfamily, as noted earlier. If abuse is attributed to a stepparent, was he or she a longstanding member of the child's household or one of several transient adults in that child's life? Men who have problems in forming close attachments and who have a history of violent relationships may have a series of relationships with vulnerable women, some (or many) of whom may be single parents. These men may come into contact with and abuse a series of children, any or all of whom may be classed as their stepchildren, regardless of whether they have taken on what may be understood to be a parenting role.

Similarly, paedophiles may seek out and build relationships with single parents as a means of having ready access to children; their sexual abuse may figure in research as 'abuse by a stepparent'.

There is also the issue of increased visibility of stepfamilies who, by virtue of their 'deviant' structure may be more likely to come to the attention of public service workers, making any abuse in such families more likely to be detected. It may also be that children sometimes feel more able to disclose abuse by a stepparent than abuse by a parent, so increasing rates of detection in such families. All these factors may skew rates of reported abuse in stepfamilies and point to the need for more sophisticated research in this area.

Finally, as researchers we are not immune to bringing our own beliefs to bear on our work and, as already noted, as a society we have ambivalent views about stepfamilies who have either been pathologised or ignored. It has been suggested by one family researcher (Amato, 1994) that the differing beliefs researchers hold about stepfamilies account for some of the contrary findings regarding outcomes for stepchildren, since their interpretation of data will be shaped by those beliefs.

With these methodological problems in mind, we should not be surprised that different studies sometimes point to different outcomes. However, many of the problems inherent in the early stepfamily research have been addressed as the quality of the work has improved in recent years. Studies have explored more theoretical questions in relation to stepfamilies (Collins, 1995; Ribbens *et al.*, 1996), as well as the meaning of stepfamily status across different cultural communities and ethnic groups (Hylton, 1995). Large-scale epidemiological research has also been undertaken (for example Dunn *et al.*, 1998), reducing the reliance on clinical samples. Gender and power issues in stepfamilies are now being attended to (Crosbie-Burnett and Giles-Sims, 1991), including the position of gay stepfamilies (Berger, 1998). Finally, the voices of children who have grown up in stepfamilies are beginning to be heard (Gorell Barnes *et al.*, 1998; Dunn and Deaker-Deckard, 2001).

Ways that stepfamilies differ from nuclear families

There is now a substantial body of knowledge about the ways in which stepfamilies differ from nuclear families, but many practitioners are ill-informed about these differences. Visher and Visher (1996) who have long been working with and studying stepfamilies in North America recently conducted a survey of nearly 300 remarried couples about their experiences of therapy. They found that lack of familiarity with the issues and dynamics of stepfamily life was a major limiting factor of the counselling process. Visher and Visher go on to provide a succinct description of seven key differences in stepfamily structure. These are detailed below with some discussion of tasks that stepfamilies face as a result of these differences, supplemented by research findings relating to achieving these tasks and the role that practitioners might play in helping both the adults and the children.

Loss and change

As noted earlier, the formation of a stepfamily today is usually preceded by breakdown of at least one couple relationship. Thus, when we consider stepfamily issues, we need to do this in the context of what we now understand about the consequences of parental separation for children and for adults. There is a growing body of research looking at the implications of family change for children (Richards, 1991; Amato and Keith, 1993), and Cockett and Tripp (1994) concluded from their pilot study of the impact of family breakdown on children that '... although most children do not exhibit acute difficulties beyond the initial stage of family breakdown a significant minority of children encounter long-term problems' (p. 59). Loss of contact with one parent deals a profound blow to children's self-esteem, rendering them at risk of such problems as a decline in their school performance or difficulties in peer relationships. This may then be compounded by the impact of poverty as post-separation households adjust to a diminished income.

More recently, Rodgers and Pryor (1998) reviewed 200 research studies on divorce and separation and reported on the outcomes for children, comparing those in 'intact' families with lone-parent families and stepfamilies. Like Cockett and Tripp they concluded long-term adverse outcomes usually only apply to a minority of children whose parents are going through the process of separation. Most will experience unhappiness and low self-esteem, but in time they will develop normally. However, there is a greater probability of poor outcomes for children from separated families. Adverse outcomes such as behavioural problems, poor school performance, leaving home when young and becoming sexually active at an early age are roughly twice as prevalent amongst children of separated parents compared with children of 'intact' families.

Health and social care practitioners have an important role to play in helping those going through the process of separation to minimise the negative consequences for the children. For example, Rodgers and Pryor (1998) found that clear, open and regular communication between both parents and the children about what is going on helps them understand they have not been abandoned. At the time of separation many parents will need help and encouragement to achieve this. Quality contact with the non-resident parent (so long as there are no issues of child protection) is also known to improve outcomes for children after divorce but again parents may need support to establish this.

When a parent repartners, children may face further changes (which may be experienced as a loss) in levels of contact with non-resident parents, sometimes combined with move of house or school. There may be loss of the familiar; mealtimes may be organised differently to fit with the new family routines, a child may have to share a bedroom with a stepsibling for the first time or lose their status as eldest child, or only girl. The legacy of these losses is reactivated at times of transition in any part of the stepfamily. The birth of half-siblings or a change of residence or contact for children can stir up the feelings present at the time the stepfamily was first created. Events that superficially appear more 'distant' can still reactivate these feelings; for example, the death of a non-resident parent's own parent.

The impact of loss on stepfamily members has been well-documented (Robinson and Smith 1993, chapter 3). Helping adults and children express their sadness and working towards ensuring that some continuity is maintained for children (for example, by enabling them to keep links with old school friends or maintain a routine of visits to a grandparent), can ease the experience whilst new routines are established. Gorell Barnes *et al.* (1998) studied the long-term impact of stepfamily life, using life-story interviews with adults who had entered a stepfamily in their childhood. They found that one of the important factors that helped stepchildren was the way change was handled by parents.

Stepparents can be influential adults in children's lives; for example, they may facilitate or hinder children's contact with their non-resident parent. The research (Rodgers and Pryor, 1998) indicates that quality contact with the non-resident parent improves outcomes for children but resident parents and stepparents may be unaware of this. They may obstruct such contact in the mistaken belief that this will be to their and the child's benefit. In such circumstances practitioners can usefully share the research evidence regarding post-divorce parenting and successful stepfamily functioning with the adults concerned. Rodgers and Pryor (1998) also ascertained that family conflict before, during and after separation contributes to children's behavioural problems, so work with stepfamilies to enable them to develop skills in conflict resolution will again benefit the children. Finally, multiple changes in family structure were found to be especially detrimental to children. Supporting stepfamilies at the point of formation may be particularly beneficial, giving them the best chance of achieving long-term stability.

Different life-cycle positions

Adults and children in a stepfamily come together at different points in their various individual and family life-cycles. For example, a father of adolescents may partner with a young woman looking forward to having children of her own. Two years later she may be facing sleepless nights with a crying baby at the same time as her stepchildren require emotional and practical support from their father as they face the demands of final school examinations or the frustrations of limited youth employment opportunities.

Stepfamilies are often helped by having the complexity of these competing life-cycle stages acknowledged. The differences in life-cycle position mean that meeting everyone's needs all of the time is nigh on impossible, but with flexibility, tolerance and support much can be achieved. For example, health visitors can play a crucial role when a child is born to the new couple by helping them anticipate the strains this may put on an already complex set of relationships.

Expectations of family life

When two adults enter their first couple relationship, each will bring expectations of family life from their family of origin. They will gradually develop shared values and behaviours; these will then be absorbed by their children. If one of the adults then enters a new couple relationship they will take those values and behaviours with them, as will their children. The new stepfamily members then find themselves having to negotiate agreed ways of going about family life. Support to couples when forming a stepfamily might focus on developing skills for negotiation; for example, between parents to facilitate ongoing contact with the children, or between parent and stepparent to establish common family rules over such issues as discipline. Establishing some agreement about behaviour and values takes time but the process can be aided if the adults openly share their expectations of one another and of the children.

Differing expectations often relate to food and mealtimes; for example, one parent may allow children to help themselves to biscuits from the tin and eat in front of the television whilst the other might expect children to ask for snacks and eat all meals at a dining table. The couple might need help to negotiate a joint rule; for example, free access to the biscuit tin but no eating in front of the television. In addition the new stepfamily can start to build up its own traditions, such as a weekend fry-up breakfast together or all having fish and chips on a Friday night.

Issues of discipline often arise because of differing expectations of the adults, combined with a testing out by the children. In the early days of stepfamily life it helps if the parent takes the lead in disciplining their own children, having negotiated with their partner that each will support the other in this until such time as the stepparent has a sufficiently strong relationship with their stepchildren to take on this role as well. The adults will undoubtedly have different ideas about family life but it helps if they can present a united front to the children whilst working out their differences in private.

The parent–child relationship predates the new couple relationship

The parent and children share a history of which the stepparent has not (usually) been a part. As a result the parent may struggle to be loyal to their children whilst also meeting their new partner's wishes. For example, children may want to reminisce about past shared events of which the stepparent was not a part; the parent may want to protect the stepparent from feeling excluded from this yet not want to stop their children remembering the past.

The new couple relationship can easily be overlooked in the hurly-burly of stepfamily life with children. Couples need to ensure they devote some time and energy to this relationship. However, this should not preclude the birth parent continuing to have time with their children on their own; this is of particular importance if they were previously in a single-parent household and the children are accustomed to high levels of parent–child time. In addition, the stepparent will require opportunities to build relationships with the stepchildren, although taking it at the children's pace. To achieve this, a non-resident parent having his children to stay for weekends might take them to the park himself on a Saturday morning, spend the rest of the day at home with them and their stepmother, but on the Sunday ensure she has an opportunity to be involved in an activity with them, such as playing a board game, whilst their father prepares a meal.

It should not be assumed that stepparents can or should take on parental roles or have parental feelings towards their stepchildren, especially in the early stages of stepfamily life. There is no reason why stepparents and stepchildren *should* love one another; this is a powerful myth, especially for stepmothers. In time, stepparents may build warm and mutually satisfying relationships with their stepchildren. However, for some, managing a way to get along together without too much antagonism may be the best that can be achieved.

A birth parent exists (in life or in memory) outside the household

Children are tangible evidence that the parent had a prior relationship, and whether the other parent is living or dead, they exert an influence over the stepfamily household. Children retain loyalty to both parents, so enabling them actively to remember their non-resident parent is important. It is the adults who usually struggle with this, sometimes expecting children to forget the past and 'choose' their new stepparent as a replacement for the absent parent, so facing their child with an intense conflict of loyalty. The best outcomes for children are achieved when they can maintain relationships with both parents. The stepparent may then become, in time, a significant but additional person in the children's lives.

Building a 'parent coalition' (Visher and Visher, 1996, p. 25) between the two birth parents can be of benefit to everyone, but is not always achievable. Failing this, finding a way to reduce acrimonious exchanges and avoid putting children in the position of 'go-between' is important. It can help if parents focus on just that – parenting – whilst accepting that they cannot control what happens in the other parent's household. It is well-documented in the research that a home environment that is low in criticism and high in warmth is important for all children (DoH, 1995); this applies to children in stepfamilies as well as nuclear families or single-parent households. All children find overt criticism of one parent by the other distressing and this can be particularly so for a child whose parents are separated.

Children are part of two households

When parents separate, children's future development is generally enhanced if they maintain contact with their non-resident parent (so long as it is safe to do so). Many children in stepfamilies live with one parent whilst visiting the other; they may have a stepparent in each of these households and possibly step or half-siblings too. Children can learn from the experience of being part of two households (for example, of different lifestyles and values) but also experience great stress if they hear the adults in one household running down the other.

The moving of children between households (or exchange of letters and telephone calls) can be difficult for the adults to accept but is of great importance to children. However, the children also need help with these transitions, for example by not being quizzed by one parent about the other after a visit or telephone call. For visiting children, having even a small space that is their own – such as a cupboard or drawer – where they can leave personal belongings between visits can enhance their sense of belonging.

Stepparents and stepchildren are not legally related

Legislation has taken time to catch up with changes in family life. The permanency of parenthood under the 1989 Children Act ensures adults maintain responsibility for their children, at least in the eyes of the law. As noted earlier, it is possible for stepparents to obtain Parental Responsibility under the Act, yet many choose adoption as a route to securing their relationship. This may have major drawbacks for many children since it severs their relationship with one set of birth relatives.

For many stepfamilies the adults and children have to find a way of living their lives in a society that gives them little support in their new roles. Yet stepparents and stepchildren may, over time, develop positive relationships. Despite the ambiguity of their role in the eyes of the law, a stepparent maintaining that relationship should the stepfamily subsequently break down can be important for the children concerned.

In view of the complexity of structure and the many tasks that have to be negotiated, it is clear that in many ways stepfamilies have the odds stacked against them when it comes to achieving a nurturing environment for adults and children alike. There are three additional key areas which can create stress for stepfamilies, in addition to structural differences, that we need to remember in our work.

Gender and stepfamily life

Firstly, we need to be mindful of gender issues in stepfamilies. As Burgoyne and Clark (1984) noted, studying stepfamilies inevitably requires us to reflect upon the nature of family life in general. Gender is central to all our lives, regardless of family form or structure. However, in stepfamilies the common gendering of parenting roles in families is constantly thrown into question, not least because a stepchild will have an extra male or female parenting figure (and possibly both) in their lives.

The problems that adults in stepfamilies with dependent children raise often relate to two areas: tensions in the stepparent–stepchild relationship, and difficulties with stepchildren's behaviour (Batchelor *et al.*, 1994). Both of these areas of concern have specific gender dimensions to them. At one extreme some stepparents report feeling shut out by the birth parent from involvement in the lives of their stepchildren. This may be stepfathers who want to take a greater role in the raising of their stepchildren, for example by disciplining them, but find the children's mother blocks them from doing so. They would like to have greater involvement but experience being excluded; this is sometimes accompanied with reports of feeling they always come second to the stepchildren in the eyes of their partner. At the other extreme, stepparents may report feeling overloaded in their new role, with expectations upon them that they will take on full parenting responsibility with little support. This can be a particular issue for stepmothers (Smith, 1990), most of whom are in part-time stepfamily households since it is not the norm for children's main residence after divorce to be with their father.

Consider a scenario in which Matt and Ellen have divorced and their son Andrew remains with his mother. Ellen then repartners with Steve. If Matt pays child support, takes Andrew to football once a week and attends school open evenings, what role is there for Steve? Similar issues arise for women in stepfamilies. The expectation that women should 'mother' children in their care is powerful. If Matt remarries, what are the expectations on his new wife Lisa when Andrew visits? Should she cook nutritious meals and ensure he gets to bed at a reasonable time? If these responsibilities rest with Matt when his son visits, where does this leave Lisa? She may feel overloaded (if it is all left to her) yet excluded if she has no part in caring for Andrew. The four parents and stepparents (and Andrew himself) may all have different expectations of one another, shaped to a large degree by gender.

The expectations of the adults regarding the roles each will play in their stepfamily will be a combination of internalised societal expectations and the individual beliefs brought from their own families of origin and subsequent family life (for example, time in a single-parent household). Many may be inappropriate in the context of a stepfamily which, by virtue of the structural differences discussed earlier, has the potential for adults to be competing for the same role, to the detriment of the children involved. For successful step-family functioning, the adults (assisted by those working with them) need to move beyond highly prescribed, gendered parenting roles to creating newly negotiated relationships with children (Gorell Barnes *et al.*, 1998).

Material disadvantage

Secondly, not only do stepfamilies *differ* from nuclear families in the ways already identified, but recent research by Ferri and Smith (1998) has also identified the ways in which resident stepfamily households with dependent children are *disadvantaged* in comparison to 'first' families. They conclude that the former are very similar to nuclear families but they experience greater economic disadvantage. Thus it is particularly hard for them to meet the material needs of their dependent children. In addition stepfamilies often have to manage very complex financial arrangements, with child support money sometimes both going into and being paid out by the one household. Ermisch and Francesconi (1996) stress that we should view the increased incidence of separation in second relationships against this back-drop.

Stepfamilies are not all the same

Thirdly, along with remembering that stepfamilies are different from nuclear families, we should avoid assuming all stepfamilies are the same as one another. For example, there are important differences between those step-families created following a separation and those following the death of a partner. One member of the new couple may have extensive experience of heading a lone-parent household, whilst the other may have no parenting experience at all. These differences may be further compounded by issues related to culture, class, ethnicity and religion.

Theoretical frameworks and practice tools for working with stepfamilies

Having reflected upon the ways that stepfamilies differ from nuclear families and upon some of the implications of these differences, we can turn to look at the theoretical frameworks and practice tools that might be of use to practitioners. When we work with stepfamilies, it is not necessary for us to abandon what we already know. In view of the fact that a stepfamily is created when parts of other families are brought together, it is not surprising that attachment theory, systems theory and an understanding of the development of family rules and of life-cycles are of immense value when working with stepfamily members. These are all addressed elsewhere in this volume, so what follows is a brief outline of each with reflections upon their use in work with stepfamilies.

Attachment theory is of particular help in informing us of the nature, for example, of attachments children may have with birth parents and other caregivers. Our understanding of stepfamilies differences can then alert us to the variables we should take into account when using this theory; for example, a child's age at separation from a parent and at the introduction of a stepparent will be highly significant. Using a systemic approach in step-family work helps us make sense of some of the complexities in such families and avoid simplistic linear thinking when looking to help resolve difficulties. Firstly, who is the family? Where does it begin and end? What is realistic to expect in terms of a boundary between the two households of separated parents? As Robinson and Smith (1993) state:

> Most stepfamilies, by definition, are part of a network of households which are more or less linked, and the boundaries between them often become contentious, particularly in the early stages. (p. 215)

An understanding of the importance of family rules, how family members evolve shared patterns of behaviour and build up shared understandings can help us to make sense of what happens in stepfamilies. In addition a life-cycle perspective on stepfamilies is essential in understanding some of the stresses such families experience. Transition points in the life-cycle, particularly when members join or leave, are hard for all families. At such times, old ways of coping may no longer be appropriate yet we all tend to revert to tried and tested ways when faced with problems or difficulties. For example, physical disciplining of an unruly child is unlikely to work once they reach adolescence. Parents need to develop new strategies as their children mature and move to the next stage in their individual life-cycle. For stepfamilies the issues are compounded as they may simultaneously be dealing with several different family life-cycle transition points at one time. The child of the new couple may be starting school as the adult stepchildren leave home; a remarried father may reach retirement at the time his second wife starts her career; an older woman may feel under pressure to have a child with her second partner when she is just enjoying the end of childcare responsibilities now her children are grown.

Using a life-cycle perspective may not change any family's life course; nor can it halt the transitions they have to face. However, it can help stepfamilies understand the stages they are moving through. Robinson and Smith (1993) detail seven such stages, from 'new beginnings' through to acceptance by the whole family that the stepfamily is 'good enough'. Understanding this process may also enable them to be more realistic about the time it may take to reach this final stage (Papernow, 1993) and to anticipate the changes they will face, so feeling more in control of their lives. It can reduce their sense of isolation and of failure if they know they are not alone in experiencing such difficulties and that the problems are not of their making but arise as a consequence of their family structure.

Practice tools for work with stepfamilies

All the skills that are used in our everyday work with families and children, whatever our professional setting, are applicable to stepfamilies. We do need to ensure that we take account of the differences between stepfamilies and nuclear families, as discussed earlier. However, there is one tool that can be considered essential to effective stepfamily work and that is the construction of a family tree or genogram.

Genograms

A genogram is a pictorial representation of a family. When completed it helps convey a full picture of the family structure; for a stepfamily it will immediately make apparent the complexity of structure and so go some way to helping family members make sense of the stresses they face at times. No genogram is complete unless in contains at least three generations; grandparents are significant figures in all families and this is no less so in stepfamilies. It should include those family members who have died, including still births and miscarriages as well as absent members (such as those who have lost contact or emigrated).

The process of constructing a genogram can in itself be very powerful for the family members involved. For this reason it should be done with forethought and care, and the worker needs to be sensitive to the issues it might raise. For example, it is important to start a stepfamily genogram by drawing the present couple plus the children in their household. They can then be enclosed in a circle before other stepfamily members are added. Birth children living elsewhere (including those with whom there is no contact) would usually be added next, although the worker should take their lead from the family members present. Some families may chose to include very close friends who are thought of as 'family' or even put in the pets. Others may not want to recognise the existence of certain relatives; sensitive exploration of who is included and who is left off can be valuable for the worker in making sense of difficulties a particular family is facing.

Normalise and inform

Drawing on these practice skills, what form should our work with stepfamilies take? Clearly this will largely depend upon our professional background and the nature of our contact with families. Youth workers, teachers, health visitors, social workers, nursery nurses and GPs, to name a few, all come into contact with children and their families as part of their daily work. Some will have opportunities to use their knowledge of stepfamily issues in a broadly educational way to help stepfamilies (and other professionals who work with them), so reducing the stigma and isolation that stepfamily members can experience. The value of such work is well-established and is in part what prompted the formation of the stepfamily associations in America (founded by Visher and Visher) and more recently in England (now incorporated in Parentline Plus) and in Scotland. Parenting helplines are available as are publications in print and on line for adults and children in stepfamilies as well as for the professionals (see Useful Contacts at the end of this chapter). There is also scope for parenting programmes (some of which address post-divorce parenting) to provide input on parenting in a stepfamily (see Kahn, 1995). In addition, all professionals can challenge the myths that surround stepfamilies, such as 'instant love' for stepchildren, and can avoid colluding with the notion that stepfamilies are the same as nuclear families whilst not pathologising them as deviant or deficient – just different.

Use a knowledge of family systems

More generally, an understanding of family systems can help us keep the full stepfamily network in mind when changes occur or interventions are planned. For example, antenatal classes might, as a matter of course, specifically look at the impact of the impending birth on step and half-siblings and the contrasting experiences of the couple if it is a first child for one and not for the other. School staff providing support to a child displaying behaviour problems might sensitively explore the home circumstances and take account of stepfamily differences when advising parents and staff on ways to handle the situation.

Other professionals will be working with families already identified as at risk of problems. In such cases they might again bring their stepfamily knowledge to bear but can use it more directly to inform the type of intervention or support they provide themselves or seek from others. For example, we need to be prepared to work with unresolved issues from the separation, divorce or death that preceded the creation of a stepfamily. On occasions it may be appropriate to undertake some work with the separated birth parents. This requires sensitive negotiation with the new couple, reassuring them that bringing the ex-partners together is to focus solely on current parenting and not on their previous couple relationship.

Children in need in stepfamilies

From the preceding discussion it is clear that we all need to be sensitive to stepfamilies in our day-to-day work, but this does not mean that stepfamilies cannot be mutually satisfying and nurturing environments for adults and children. However, there will be occasions when we are working with stepfamilies for whom there are concerns about whether a child is 'in need' in terms of the 1989 Children Act, although not necessarily simply by virtue of their stepfamily status. We might then be looking to provide additional family support to ensure that a child's development is not hindered or impaired.

It is inevitable that some stepfamilies, by virtue of their history, will have experienced discontinuity of care arrangements for children. As a result, stepfamilies may figure largely in the work of health and social care professionals. There is some evidence that children from stepfamilies are over-represented amongst those looked after by local authorities (Schlosser and De'Ath, 1994). We might then draw on materials specifically developed for work with stepfamilies, such as that by Loughran and Riches (1996) on working in partnership with children looked after and their parents and stepparents. We also need to be aware of particular risk factors that might exist for children in stepfamilies in terms of need for protection from abuse (Brodie and Berridge, 1996), whether that be abusive incidents or an increased risk of experiencing low warmth and high criticism.

Using the Framework for Assessment with stepfamilies

Whether we are working with a child in need or a child in need of protection, the Department of Health's (2000) *Framework for the Assessment of Children in Need and their Families* will be an important tool. This framework and accompanying materials (see for example Horwath, 2001) have been compiled for use with all families, whatever their structure. A full description and analysis of the *Framework* can be found elsewhere in this book. What follows here are some reflections upon the framework from the perspective of use with stepfamilies.

We are all aware that assessment should be an ongoing process, not a one-off event. Ongoing assessment is particularly important when families are going through changes in their structure. We may start work with a child and parents at a point when they are together in a nuclear family but later there may be a period of lone parenthood followed by creation of a stepfamily household when one of the parents repartners. For this reason we need to maintain our awareness of stepfamily issues in all family situations as they may be of relevance at any time.

At various points in the framework and associated publications, the term parent is broadened out to include care-givers. There are some specific references to stepparents within the framework, for example step-relations are included as one of 'a wide range of adults ... [who] may have a significant role in caring for a child' (DoH, 2000, p. 22). However, beyond occasional references to care-givers and significant adults, stepparents (whether resident or non-resident) are rarely referred to in the framework. It is for the worker to remember the significance of step relationships when assessing children in need and their families. Consideration will be given here (in reverse order) to the three domains of the assessment framework – child's developmental needs, parenting capacity, family and environmental factors – and the way that an understanding of stepfamily issues can inform such assessment work.

Family and environmental factors

Family history and functioning are key when assessing a child's needs within a stepfamily. As practitioners we need to be aware of the transitions that precede the creation of every stepfamily and the impact these may have on adults and children. Constructing a genogram is often the best way to build an understanding of these experiences. In addition, the wider family's view of the new partnership will be key to understanding whether they are able to offer support to the stepfamily. Factors such as housing and income should be addressed. When a parent repartners, housing may prove too small as bedrooms must be shared with stepsiblings. Finances are often complex, with incoming and outgoing child support payments.

Parenting capacity

Many questions need to be addressed when assessing parenting capacity in a stepfamily. Firstly, who is – or could reasonably be expected to be – acting in a parenting capacity in relation to this child? It is important not to assume that a non-resident parent no longer parents; nor that a stepparent should take on that role, particularly in the early stages of stepfamily life.

Assumptions should not be made in relation to any of the six dimensions of parenting capacity suggested in the framework. For example, basic care in a stepfamily household may more appropriately be provided by a resident father than a new stepmother. The level of emotional warmth a stepparent can provide will depend on such factors as length of time in their stepparenting role and previous parenting experiences, as well as the age and gender of the child and stepparent. A stepparent may, in time, build a good relationship with their stepchild. This can then provide the foundation from which they provide guidance to the child, but this takes time. A new stepparent is likely to be greeted with 'Who are you to tell me what to do?' if they attempt to set boundaries for their stepchild too soon.

Children's development

Stepparents may impact on all seven dimensions of children's developmental needs that are addressed in the assessment framework. However, three of these dimensions – emotional and behavioural development, identity, family and social relationships – are of particular importance when assessing the developmental needs of a child in a stepfamily.

A child in a stepfamily is likely to have experienced some disruption of attachments, but may also have the opportunity to form important new attachments with significant adults in the stepfamily. It should be remembered that delays in emotional and behavioural development may be partly due to family conflict that preceded the stepfamily formation. As quality contact with the non-resident parent can improve outcomes for children (Rodgers and Pryor, 1998), assessment of the development of children of separated parents should include an evaluation of this contact. Rodgers and Pryor (1998) also found that multiple changes in family structure were especially detrimental for children so the impact of such changes in terms of children's developmental needs should be attended to.

In conclusion, if we do nothing else in our work with stepfamilies we should ensure we remain mindful of the differences identified by Visher and Visher (1996) and that we reflect on their implications when working with parents and children. Key factors in stepfamily living include allowing time for new relationships to grow and the stepfamily's identity to develop, sharing expectations of each other in the newly created household and the stepparent aiming to be an additional adult rather than a replacement parent in their stepchild's life (Robinson and Smith, 1993). Remembering that stepfamilies are not the same as nuclear families is a vital first step towards ensuring that our practice is effective and that stepfamilies have the best chance to succeed in the demanding task of raising children.

Useful contacts

Parentline Plus (incorporating the National Stepfamily Association), 520 Highgate Studios, 53–79 Highgate Road, London NW5 1TL. Parentline Helpline (confidential 24 hour freephone number) 0808 800 2222; Textphone 0800 783 6783
Head office telephone number 020 7284 5500
Website: www.parentlineplus.org.uk

Stepfamily Scotland 5 Coates Place, Edinburgh EH3 7AA
Helpline: 0131 225 5800
Head office: 0131 225 8005
Website: www.stepfamilyscotland.org.uk

References

Amato, P. R. and Keith, B. (1993) 'Parental Divorce and the Wellbeing of Children: A Meta-Analysis', *Psychological Bulletin*, vol. 110, pp. 26–46.
Amato, P. R. (1994) 'The Implications of Research Findings on Children in

Stepfamilies', in A. Booth and J. Dunn (eds), *Stepfamilies: Who Benefits? Who Does Not?* Hillsdale, New Jersey: Lawrence Erlbaum Associates.

Batchelor, J., Dimmock, D. and Smith, D. (1994) *Understanding Stepfamilies: What Can be Learned from Callers to the STEPFAMILY Telephone Counselling Service.* London: STEPFAMILY Publications.

Berger, R. (1998) *Stepfamilies: A Multi-Dimensional Perspective.* New York and London: The Haworth Press.

Bornat, J., Dimmock, B., Jones, D. and Peace, S. (1999) 'Stepfamilies and Older People: Evaluating the Implications of Family Change for an Ageing Population', *Ageing and Society*, vol. 19(2), pp. 239–61.

Brodie, I. and Berridge, D. (1996) *Fact File 4: Child Abuse and Stepfamilies.* London: STEPFAMILY Publications.

Burgoyne, J. and Clark, D. (1984) *Making a Go of It: A Study of Stepfamilies in Sheffield.* London: Routledge and Kegan Paul.

Carter, E. and McGoldrick, M. (eds) (1989) *The Changing Family Life Cycle: A Framework for Family Therapy*, 2nd edn. Boston: Allyn and Bacon.

Cockett, M. and Tripp, J. (1994) *The Exeter Family Study: Family Breakdown and Its Impact on Children.* Exeter: University of Exeter Press.

Collins, S. (1995) 'Ideological Assumptions in the Lives of Stepchildren', in J. Brannen and M. O'Brien (eds), *Childhood and Parenthood*. London: University of East London/Institute of Education, pp. 79–92.

Crosbie-Burnett, M. and Giles-Sims, J. (1991) 'Marital Power in Stepfather Families: A Test of Normative Resource Theory', *Journal of Family Psychology*, vol. 4(4) pp. 484–96.

Department of Health (DoH) (1995) *Child Protection: Messages from Research.* London: The Stationery Office.

— (1999) *Adoption Now: Messages from Research.* London: The Stationery Office.

— (2000) *Framework for the Assessment of Children in Need and Their Families.* London: The Stationery Office.

Dowling, E. and Gorell Barnes, G. (2000) *Working With Children and Parents Through Separation and Divorce.* Basingstoke: Macmillan–Palgrave.

Dunn, J., Deater-Deckard, K., Pickering, K., O'Connor, T. G. and Golding, J. (1998) 'Children's adjustment and pro-social behaviour in step-, single-parent, and non-stepfamily settings: findings from a community study'. *Journal of Child Psychology and Psychiatry*, vol. 39(8) pp. 1083–95.

Dunn, J. and Deater-Deckard, K. (2001) *Children's Views of Their Changing Families.* York: York Publishing Services.

Ermisch, J. F. and Francesconi, M. (1996) *The Increasing Complexity of Family Relationships: Lifetime Experiences of Single Motherhood and Stepfamilies in Great Britain.* ESRC Research Centre on Micro-social Change Working Paper, University of Essex

Ferri, E. and Smith, K. (1998) *Step-parenting in the 1990s.* London: Family Policy Studies Centre.

Ganong, L. H. and Coleman, M. (1994) *Remarried Family Relationships.* Thousand Oaks, Ca: Sage.

Gorell Barnes, G., Thompson, P., Daniel, G. and Burchardt, N. (1998) *Growing Up in Stepfamilies.* Oxford: Clarendon Press.

Haskey, J. (1996) 'The Proportion of Married Couples Who Divorce: Past Patterns and Present Prospects', *Population Trends*, vol. 83, pp. 28–36

Horwath, J., (ed.) (2000) *The Child's World: Assessing Children in Need – The Reader.* London: NSPCC.

Hylton, C. (1995) *Coping with Change: Family Transitions in Multi-Cultural Communities.* London: National Stepfamily Association.

Jones, D. P. H. (2001) 'The Assessment of Parental Capacity', in J. Horwath (ed.) *The Child's World: Assessing Children in Need.* London: Jessica Kingsley Publications, pp. 255–72.

Khan, T. (1995) *Learning to Step Together: Building and Strengthening Stepfamilies.* London: National Stepfamily Association.

Loughran, G. and Riches, P. (1996) *Working in Partnership with Stepfamilies.* London: STEPFAMILY Publications.

Masson, J. (1992) 'Stepping into the Nineties: a summary of the legal implications of the Children Act 1989 for stepfamilies', in B. Dimmock (ed.) *A Step in Both Directions; The Impact of the Children Act 1989 on Stepfamilies.* London: National Stepfamily Association.

Papernow, P. (1993) *Becoming a Stepfamily: Patterns of Development in Remarried Families.* San Francisco: Jossey-Bass.

Parentline Plus (2000) *Stepfamily Facts and Figures*, April 2000. London: Parentline Plus.

Ribbens, J., Edwards, R. and Gillies, V. (1996) 'Parenting and step-parenting after divorce/separation: issues and negotiations', *Changing Britain*, issue 5, pp. 4–6, Swindon: ESRC.

Richards, M. P. M. (1991) 'The effects of parental divorce on children', *Archives of Diseases in Childhood*, vol. 66, pp. 915–6.

Robinson, M. and Smith, D. (1993) *Step by step: focus on stepfamilies.* London: Harvester Wheatsheaf/The National Stepfamily Association.

Robinson, M. (1980) 'Stepfamilies: a reconstituted family system', *Journal of Family Therapy*, vol. 2(1) pp. 45–69.

— (1991) *Family Transformation Through Divorce and Remarriage: A Systemic Approach.* London: Routledge.

Rodgers, B. and Pryor, J. (1998) *Divorce and separation: the outcomes for children.* York: Joseph Rowntree Foundation.

Schlosser, A. and De'Ath, E. (1994) *Fact File 2: Keeping In Touch – Looked After Children and Their Stepfamilies.* London: STEPFAMILY Publications.

Smith, D. (1990) *Stepmothering.* Hemel Hempstead: Harvester Wheatsheaf.

Utting, D. (1994) *Stepfamilies and Adoption.* London: STEPFAMILY Publications.

Visher, E. B. and Visher, J. S. (1996) *Therapy With Stepfamilies.* New York: Brunner/Mazel.

8

Working with Families where there are Child Protection Concerns

Stephanie Petrie

Introduction

Childcare policies since the late 1990s have been directed towards mitigating the consequences of poverty, particularly child poverty, and childcare professionals are expected to participate in the 'major strategies to tackle the root causes of poverty and social exclusion, (DoH, DfEE, HO, 2000: 1 par. 1.1). Professionals working with children and their families where there are child protection concerns are required to assess a child's needs from a holistic perspective, and consider the impact of poverty, recast as social exclusion, as a factor undermining parenting capacity (*ibid.*, 2000). Current child protection policy and practice has been heavily influenced by research studies showing the correlation between poverty and concern about child maltreatment as significant numbers of poor families were found to have been involved in formal child protection investigations leading to no futher action (DoH, 1995). The message to childcare professionals was that the 'child rescue' approach, which dominated child protection activity in the 1980s and early 1990s, left many vulnerable children and their families without any services at all. This approach, it was suggested, focused on investigating the family care of children, considered 'at risk' to determine if the legal test of 'significant harm' (Part IV Children Act 1989 s.31(2)) had been met, to the exclusion of any other needs the child or family might have (DoH, 1995). Current government guidance to childcare professionals in all sectors (DoH, DfEE, HO, 2000) draws attention to the two key legal duties of *safeguarding* and *promoting* the welfare of children contained in Part III of the Children Act 1989, and stresses they are not separate activities but '... two sides of the same coin' (*op. cit.*, 2000, p. 5)'. The concept of 'child protection' is meant to cover a wide spectrum of circumstances from those situational episodes due to the pressures of socio-economic factors to the more pathological.

This change of emphasis in child protection policies and practice recommended by government is taking place in a system of welfare that has also changed considerably in the last decade, away from Welfare State provision to a 'mixed economy' of welfare. The role of the State as the main provider of welfare services has diminished and the role of independent sector agencies as service providers has increased (Petrie and Wilson, 1999) although the role of the State as regulator and commissioner (purchaser) of services has been strengthened. The National Health Service and Community Care Act 1990, in relation to services for adults, placed requirements on local authorities to purchase a percentage of services from the independent sector. They were also required to separate the management of their own provision from the management of assessing individuals and commissioning appropriate services. Although the same budgetary and structural requirements were not imposed on local authorities by the Children Act 1989 a duty was placed on them to enable the provision of services by others (Children Act 1989 s.17(5) (a). Since both Acts were designed to be 'consistent and complementary' (Stace and Tunstill, 1990, p. 1), children's services, influenced by the imposed structures and policies for adult services, have also become 'marketized' during the last decade (Petrie and Wilson, 1999). During the same period comprehensive research and practice developments have strengthened the knowledge base of those working with families where there are child protection concerns, and current approaches to child abuse, based on eco-systemic theory, has much to offer as a common model of practice (DoH, 2000). Understanding child abuse in this way is 'currently the most comprehensive model we have for understanding child abuse, providing a systemic framework in which to conduct both research and child protection practice (Sidebotham, 2001, p. 97)' and is reflected in the *Framework for the Assessment of Children in Need and their Families* (DoH, DfEE, HO, 2000).

However, if vulnerable children are to be protected there are critical factors in the current context that need to be addressed. The impact of the 'mixed economy' of welfare could mean that the substantial research and practice knowledge about child abuse located primarily within local authorities (Corby, 2000) will not be sufficiently accessible to agencies now likely to be first-line service providers. The range, number and size of service providing agencies in the 'mixed economy' means that the ability of agencies to work together is even more critical than when local authorities were the primary providers of family support services. Furthermore, as many child abuse inquiries have shown, organisational and management effectiveness is an essential foundation for best practice, and inadequacies in these areas have been significant factors in many failures to protect children (DoH, 1991). These issues are emerging in the latest inquiry into the death of the eight-year-old child Victoria Climbié where the bureaucratic complexity and demands of the 'mixed economy' appears to have contributed to the breakdown of child protection services (*Guardian*, 18 October 2001). Finally increasingly prescriptive government policy and practice guidance, whilst providing a unifying framework for all agencies and professionals involved, may deflect attention away from the uniqueness of individual children and their families. Ultimately it is professional judgment, drawing on best practice founded on research evidence, that must be relied upon to determine the level of protection an individual child requires. This may be within their family, with appropriate interventions to support their safety and optimal development, or in respite or short-term or permanent substitute care.

However, it is important to begin with what is known about protective and effective work with children and their families before considering the implications of current policy. Whatever the policy context, research knowledge or practice developments, working with families where there are child protection issues demands highly competent practitioners. Practitioners have to manage a complex environment, keep themselves informed of legislative, policy and practice changes whilst establishing and maintaining helping relationships with individual children and adults. This chapter is concerned with examining 'best practice' for professionals working with families where there are child protection concerns in the current context. The legal and policy framework will be outlined before three important aspects of working with vulnerable children – child development, attachment relationships and communication approaches – are examined. Ways of working with family adults 'in partnership' will also be reviewed followed by an anonymised case study showing how inter-agency work, beginning with services provided under s.17 of the Children Act 1989 in the context of the 'mixed economy' of welfare can effectively protect children. Implications of the policy context for practice will precede a summary of the chapter and final comments.

The legal and policy framework

Changing attitudes, laws and practices towards children have been frequently explored (Frost and Stein, 1989; Corby, 2000). In the four decades since Kempe and his associates in the USA recast nineteenth century child cruelty concepts into twentieth century child abuse, there has been a huge increase in research studies and debates about definitions, types, causes and effects of child abuse particularly in complex affluent societies (Sidebotham, 2001). During the same period knowledge and understanding of the lives and experiences of maltreated children has increased, often though their own narratives as adult survivors of child abuse (Gordon, 1989). As a result the law reflects a greater awareness and willingness to recognise that children are not merely possessions of parents but autonomous human beings, whatever their age. For example the requirement of the court to establish the 'ascertainable wishes and feelings of the child concerned (considered in the light of his [*sic*] age and understanding' before making or discharging any order (Children Act 1989 Part I Section 1(3)(a)). The UK and European legal framework, including the Children Act 1989 (with the central definition of 'child in need' as a passport to services), the UN Convention on the Rights of the Child 1989 (ratified by the UK in 1991) and the Human Rights Act 1998 share key principles. These can be summarised as recognising that children are citizens with independent rights, that the best place for them to grow up is within their birth family, and the duty of the state is to support families in rearing their children. Statutory intervention in family life to protect children is a measure of last, not first resort. The guidance documents *Working Together to Safeguard and Promote the Welfare of Children* (DoH, HO, DfEE, 1999) and the *Framework for the Assessment of Children in Need and their Families* (DoH, DfEE, HO, 2000) were drafted to reflect these principles and are promoted by government as best practice.

Recent policies, such as *Modernising Health and Social Services* (DoH, 1998a) and *Quality Protects* (DoH, 1998b), including funding programmes such as Sure Start (established to increase family support programmes for vulnerable young children and their carers), have driven the 'refocusing' initiative placed on local authorities by government. The aim is to direct more resources towards supporting 'children in need' and their families in the community and away from resource-heavy procedural and legal interventions that offered little to children and did not ameliorate the adverse impact of poverty on families. However, these programmes are not universal, aimed at all children, but are distributed according to eligibility criteria and targets, albeit criteria not restricted to children for whom there are protection concerns but including all 'children in need'. Nevertheless, many of these services are those that childcare professionals will make available to families where there are child protection concerns in order to reduce situational stress that may undermine parenting capacity. Guidance recognises that family support services are important resources yet raises concerns that accessibility has been primarily through formal child protection systems. Responding to child protection concerns initially from the perspective of 'children in need', it is advised, will be more beneficial to children.

It is anticipated that although specific policy remains in place for child protection investigations and the processes to be followed if significant harm is suspected (DoH, HO, DfEE, 1999), children in families where there are protection concerns will be offered services outside formal child protection procedures.

[W]orking with local communities and agencies, taking a broader-based approach to helping vulnerable children and their families will lead to:

- A slight increase in childcare referrals.
- The majority of referrals more appropriately dealt with under s.17 [Children Act 1989].

- Proportionately fewer child protection s.47 enquiries [Children Act 1989].
- Fewer children's names being placed on the child protection register.
- A decrease in the numbers of children being 'looked after' [s. 20, s.31 Children Act 1989].
- A decrease in the numbers of children accommodated [s. 20 Children Act 1989]on an unplanned basis.
- A reduction in the anxiety levels of all staff in child and family work.

(DoH, DfEE, HO, 2000, p. 3)

It is likely, therefore, that children in need of protection and their families may receive services from a number of different agencies and workers, and be subject to specialist interventions, before, during or after completion of the new core assessment recommended in policy (*ibid.*, 2000, fig. 5: 35). Since assessment is promoted as an ongoing process to guide plans and interventions, rather than an end in itself, child protection concerns may emerge or diminish at any point in work with families. Whatever the circumstances or agencies involved, the focus of any intervention must be on the child and their well-being can be identified and monitored if attention is paid to their development, attachment relationships and their own wishes and feelings.

The child

There are several levels of information about children that reveal the nature of the protection concerns, and the foremost among these is child development information. Child development information is crucial and routine monitoring and collation of such information is essential. Health professionals are important partners in this process – whatever the level of protection concerns. However, all childcare professionals must have a good understanding of child development that is not culturally specific or ill-attuned to the differential development of children with special needs or specific health issues.

Developmental milestones are generalised guidelines influenced by dominant social and cultural values, not absolute standards, and measures commonly used reflect child behaviour typically found in complex, affluent societies. Department of Health guidance (2000) highlights the importance of child development information and includes the comprehensive checklists developed by Mary Sheridan (*ibid.*, p. 23). However, these helpful tools have some limitations. For example one measure of the social behaviour and play of a two-year-old is 'Follows mother round house and copies domestic activities in simultaneous play (*ibid.*, p. 26)' which is gender-specific and could lead to inappropriate conclusions if, for instance, the family structure is not normative. That is if the family is not composed of a mother who is the primary care-giver and a father who earns the family income. Similarly a child of two and a half years who doesn't 'Eat skillfully with spoon and may use fork (*ibid.*, p. 27)' may not be suffering developmental delay but be part of a family that uses different eating tools, such as chopsticks or bread, with different customs relating to meal etiquette. However, recognising the limitations of these tools does not mean assuming any difference observed in a child is solely due to culture. During the latest child abuse death inquiry it was revealed that the withdrawn and passive demeanour of Victoria Climbié, unusual in a child of that age, was interpreted by professionals as showing the 'normal' respectful behaviour of West African children towards adults:

> [T]he social worker admitted that her handling of Victoria's case was adversely affected by misguided assumptions about the African girl's ethnic background. She had interpreted the girl's timidity around her great-aunt, Marie Therese Kouao and her other killer, Carl Manning, as a cultural show of respect rather than fear. (*Guardian*, 20 December 2001)

Such assumptions are themselves discriminatory and there is a danger that the individual experiences of children will not be identified if stereotypes are assumed.

Rates of developmental achievements vary from child to child, especially children who have physical and/or learning impairments. Such children may achieve all the major developmental milestones but more slowly, or may never achieve some aspects of development but will achieve beyond the 'norm' in other respects. It is more useful to conceptualise a child's acceptable rate of development as 'optimal' rather than 'normal'. That is, h/er rate of development equals h/er individual potential for development. Or rather, since childrearing and childhood are rarely without some deficits, the rate of development is 'good enough' (Adcock and White, 1985). It is clear that developmental achievements once acquired are not lost unless the child is experiencing some difficulty. Of course this does not always mean a child has suffered 'significant harm' but will always indicate some issue needing attention, such as ill-health, reaction to the birth of a sibling or parental separation for example. A child's developmental history will indicate the nature of harm they may be experiencing, however, only if the information gathered is consistent and comparable since developmental patterns only emerge over months not days. Comparison is undermined, for example, if different scales are used to weigh children, especially very young children, or if they are sometimes weighed clothed and sometimes unclothed. The accuracy of scales varies enormously and the weight young children gain or lose is often very small so patterns can either be overlooked or falsely observed. However, comparable and consistent information over time can show whether or not development continues to be optimal, whether there has been a sudden adverse change in development or whether the pattern is indicative of factors that are chronic and long-term. Children continue to develop throughout their childhood, and child development information remains an indicator of their well-being. If a child moves from family to

substitute respite care or vice versa, or is allocated daycare, their development must be monitored carefully before, during and afterwards. Any
changes in developmental patterns, whether adverse or positive, will reveal
the times and circumstances where they did not flourish and circumstances
that support their well-being. The *Framework for Assessment* (DoH, DfEE,
HO, 2000) recommends that all assessments and interventions should be
rooted in child development. Awareness of a child's development in any
programme of work also ensures s/he is not seen solely in deficit terms and
provides evidence that care is good enough. If a child's development is
optimal within their family, however deficient circumstances appear, family
care is likely to be the best option for them. The Looked After Children
ongoing developmental records (LAC) are also recommended as useful
tools for reviewing a child's well-being (*ibid.*, 2000) for children in the
community as well as 'looked-after' children, although there are indications
that the check-list approach has not been conducive to good practice and
may be revised (DoH, 2002).

Attachment theory is also important (Fahlberg, 1991). Attachment
theory seeks to explain the nature and development of parent/child relationships and the impact on a child's development if this relationship is
removed at an early age or is inadequate according to a range of classifications. Attachment patterns are well-researched in a range of cultures and
countries and, apart from minor differences in rates of attachment classifications, all types are evident (Howe, 1995). Attachment assessments in this
country have been used primarily as a description or explanation of observable parent/child relationships as part of evidence gathered about parenting
capacity (Adcock and White, 1985). Use of this theory to inform specific
interventions is a comparatively new development and is being used increasingly in work with parents to strengthen their understanding of and respon-
siveness to their children (Howe, Brandon, Hinings and Scofield 1999).

Little known in the UK but influential in other parts of Europe and the
USA is the work of Dr Emmi Pikler, Director of the Loczy Institute in
Hungary from 1948 until her death in 1984. Dr Pikler pioneered ways of
group care for infants that promoted attachment between infant and carer
and many of her methods have been used in the USA, enhanced by Dr
Pikler's friend and colleague Magda Gerber, in daycare settings and also
parent/infant classes (Gerber, 1997; David and Appell, 2001). These ways
of caring for infants and young children could also be used in UK to assist
parents unable to understand or respond to their child adequately by offering a practical approach to infant care that promotes attachment. The
methods are also applicable to group care for infants offered by child
minders, daycare establishments and creche facilities, now a major service in
many child protection plans for pre-school children (Statham, Dillon and
Moss, 2001). Respite childcare for parents means a change in routine for
young children and often lack of continuity as they move between different
caring regimes (Novak, Owen, Petrie and Sennett, 1997). These services are
sometimes at the expense of the child who becomes more difficult to care

for at home because of these changes. The well-researched approach to group care for infants and toddlers developed by Dr Pikler and others in Hungary and Magda Gerber in the USA offers the possibility of an approach to respite childcare that benefits not only the family adults but the child too.

Children are autonomous human beings and have rights to give and receive information and participate in decision-making in ways suitable to their age and understanding. John Fitzgerald, former Chief Executive of the Bridge Child Care Development Service, points out that professionals rarely seem to listen to children, or if they listen may not believe what they say:

> When their words are heard the results can be dramatic ... The youngest children of Fred and Rosemary West were removed because of allegations of sexual abuse. They eventually started to tell their new carers they had another sister, Heather, who was 'under the patio'. This statement could not have been more bizarre. However, gradually the carers, social workers and police started listening carefully to the children ... and the full story of the horrific events in the West household were discovered. The failure to comprehend what some abused children are saying is often because of our inability to imagine the grotesque world in which some children live. (NSPCC, 2001, p. 93)

The *Framework for Assessment* (DoH, DfEE, HO, 2000) identifies five dimensions of direct work with children – seeing, observing, engaging, talking and sharing activities – through which workers can acquire knowledge and understanding of the child. No specific approach has been identified or recommended and it would seem all of the above steps could be taken without children feeling involved or empowered. Non-directive play therapy, drawing on the work of Axline (1947), would appear to offer a great deal to children, including children with communication impairments and those whose first language is not English. Non-directive play therapy offers a way in which professionals can develop a listening ear by communicating with a child through their own language of play. It is non-intrusive and child-centred and does not undermine the parent/child relationship. Even if the child does not engage with the process the consequences are not harmful to her/him, indeed the theory underpinning this approach is to give the child, however young, maximum control over the process (Wilson, Kendrick and Ryan 1992; Ryan and Wilson, 1996). Without understanding of the child's perspective any plans will be inadequate and non-directive play therapy is a highly protective service as it attunes the professional network to the child's world.

Parents and adult family carers

Adult family members and their relationships with professionals are significant elements of any child protection work. In the same way that a child's perspective must be understood, so must the situation of parents. Guidance to childcare professionals (DoH/SSI, 1995) states that professionals should work *in partnership* with parents and other significant family adults. Although the concept of 'partnership' is mentioned frequently in guidance it is not referred to in statute nor defined (Petrie and Corby, 2001). The nature and level of partnership practice depends on the ability of agencies involved to agree an operational definition. When agencies fail to agree the consequences fall most heavily on those with least power – children – as evidenced in the Cleveland debacle (Campbell, 1988). Guidance identifies four approaches to partnership: providing information, involvement, participation and partnership. Full partnership is seen to involve openness, mutual trust, joint decision-making and a willingness to listen to families and capitalise on their strengths. Guidance points out, however, that partnership is not an end in itself and the objective is the protection and welfare of the child. Child development information is a good starting point for work in partnership with family adults. Even if the significance of their child's developmental history is not understood by the family adults they are nearly always aware of how their child behaves and so can began to focus on specific aspects of their child's needs in practical and understandable ways. The paper tools used for recording aspects of a child's developmental pattern and history need, therefore, to be understandable to all adults and older children involved in programmes of work whatever their cognitive capacity. Guidance publications for many years have included examples of useful paper tools that convey written information visually as well as textually, and can easily be used in a participatory manner if adapted to individual circumstances (DHSS, 1985; DoH, 2000). Gathering, collating and sharing information with families permits recording of different perspectives and helps separate perceived fact from attributable opinion. In this way the uniqueness of each situation can be recognised whilst drawing on the core knowledge of child protection practice.

Involving family adults (and older children) in decision-making as far as is possible is recommended by guidance. One way of doing this is through Family Group Conferences (FGC). FGCs were developed in New Zealand with Maori communities and are recommended by guidance in certain circumstances (DoH, HO, DfEE, 1999). However, their use at present is limited in the UK due, it is argued, to the reluctance of social workers to engage in the process (Marsh and Crow, 1998). However, involving families in decision-making in this way has a number of advantages. It can be safer for all concerned if difficult issues are considered in a group setting, since all family members are then privy to the same information. Any individual accustomed to dominating others by misinformation or physical behaviour, whether family member or professional, becomes less powerful in a group setting if the chair of the meeting can ensure equity of participation for all. Failing to confront frightening adults with child abuse concerns has been a feature in many child death inquiries (DoH, 1991). Involving such individuals can be easier in a group setting where time, venue, participants and content are pre-planned. Family involvement can also reveal protective factors and family strengths that can be built upon. Chairing and coordinating FGCs demands a high level of interpersonal skills and a high degree of ownership and active participation from agencies involved. Detailed discussion as to how partnership with parents can be approached has been discussed elsewhere (Petrie and Corby, 2001), but two points are important when working with family adults.

First professionals need to be able to ask difficult questions. Some adults and families are frightening to workers and as a result issues of concern may be minimised or avoided. Research examining male violence within families, for example, has shown how damaging this is to children, and yet their mothers, also assaulted and abused, are often held solely responsible for controlling the behaviour of violent men and protecting their children from them (Farmer and Bushel, 1999). Studies have consistently revealed that about half of the men who abuse their partners also abuse their children (Campbell, 1995). Workers and agencies, with due regard for personal safety and the impact on vulnerable family members, must involve those adults whose violent behaviour raises child protection concerns. This issue was raised as early as 1987 during the inquiry into the death of the child Tyra Henry (DoH, 1991):

> It may sound absurd now to talk about involving Andrew Neil in plan-
> ning for Tyra's wellbeing. The true starting point was not that he was a
> violent young man who had if possible to be kept away from Tyra. It was
> that he was Tyra Henry's father … It would have fulfilled a necessary
> function, which common fairness requires. That the father of a child
> should be told why he cannot play any part in her upbringing. It should
> have performed the task, which instead was invidiously left to Claudette
> and Beatrice Henry [Tyra's mother and grandmother] of warning
> Andrew Neil off. (*Ibid.*, p. 82 par. 4.4).

Second, the inter-agency context is critical. Unless all involved are aware of the protection agenda, plans will fail. This requires transparent and accountable inter-agency plans that involve family members. Furniss (1991), in his clinical work with children and families in the aftermath of the discovery of child sexual abuse, identifies the ability of agencies to work together effectively as a major factor in successful therapy:

> [I]f therapeutic intervention is to have any success there needs to be
> agreement at the beginning of the intervention between legal and thera-
> peutic agencies on the overall approach. The aims and means and degree
> of involvement of each professional sub-group need to be clearly defined.
> (*Ibid.*, p. 64)

If the family adults and professionals are not sharing the same agenda, however unwilling the family adults may be, most work will be fruitless.

Working within formalised child protection systems, it has been argued, can bring benefits because of the level of information-sharing with families that legal intervention requires, and the sometimes necessary coercive power of the State needed to ensure compliance (Dale, Davies, Morrison and Waters, 1986; Furniss, 1991). However, these elements of openness and honesty about child protection issues and possible consequences must be evident in all child protection work even when taking place on a voluntary basis.

The horrific lives and deaths of children killed by their parents (NSPCC, 2001) reveals one end, the most severe, of the child abuse spectrum:

> Sukina, aged five, died on 6 December 1988 following a sustained and ferocious attack upon her by her father... She was beaten first with a ruler, then with a short length of rigid plastic tubing and finally with a length of kettle flex which had the kettle attachment at one end, but not the three pin plug. We do not know how long the attack lasted, but at least fifty blows were rained upon her, interspersed with repeated demands that she spelled her name. Sukina, at one stage, when she was too weak to stand, tried to crawl out of the room to the stairs, asking her father to stop hitting her. Sukina's mother tried to intervene and was herself assaulted, causing injuries to her face, which required a hospital examination. The attack on Sukina however continued until she was barely conscious, at which point she was taken by her parents, to the bathroom and placed in a bath of warm water in an attempt to revive her... As she slipped into unconsciousness, Sukina told her father she was sorry. Although an ambulance was called, Sukina was already dead on arrival at hospital. (The Bridge Child Care Consultancy, 1991, p. 7)

The above description of Sukina's death is taken from an evaluation of the circumstances, commissioned by the Department of Health, and the relevant local and health authorities. The report highlights the challenge for professionals:

> [Professionals have to] differentiate between those parents who, because of pressures of life, from time to time hit out at their children and those where the abuse is of a sadistic and continuous nature ... At the time these two kinds of families may not appear very differently in the way they act and behave. (*Ibid.*, p. 2)

At the other end of the child abuse spectrum from child death are situational abuses of which many parents are capable but usually sidestep because needed relief or help is there before self-control is lost. Identifying the degree of protection a child requires depends on an accurate understanding of the child's world. Child abuse inquiries of the last two decades reveal the dangers for children when professionals lose sight of them whilst endeavouring to make a positive relationship with their parents or care-givers (DoH, 1991). The absence of the child's perspective has also been shown to occur when crucial information about their circumstances does not pass from one agency to another.

Similar themes concerning 'best practice', in any work with families where there are child protection concerns, are evident in practice research and literature and have been referred to earlier. These approaches can be used when working with families within formal child protection procedures or with families where agreements for work are within the framework of services to 'children in need'. The following case study demonstrates some of the elements of effective work in the current context. Comprehensive assessments and direct work with children drawing on non-directive play therapy approaches were central to the services offered. Openness and clarity about the protection concerns with the family adults was possible because the agencies involved, independent and statutory sector, had agreed an operational definition of 'partnership' and their agency roles and responsibilities and these were clear to those working within and using the services.

Case study

The agency

The agency was a joint voluntary/statutory sector family centre with an open-access/service-user involvement philosophy. The team included qualified social workers with specialist training in aspects of child protection, a manager seconded from the local authority, and other workers with varied childcare training, experience and practical skills. In-service training was ongoing and responded to staff needs. A range of services was provided from cleaning, 'baby-sitting' and school holiday activities for children to specific assessments or interventions, often in relation to ongoing legal proceedings commissioned by the local social services department. Individualised programmes with families began with a four-week assessment process. All children were allocated their own worker for regular 'special time', drawing on non-directive play-therapy techniques. Ongoing work usually included family therapy using the systemic (Milan) model (Bentovim, 2002) and this approach also informed the regular review meetings. Family members, adults and children, attended initial and review meetings and all recording was shared with family members. Records clearly distinguished between factual information that could be amended by family members and the opinions and judgments of the workers involved. In the latter case family members, if they wished, could record their disagreement and with the support of advocates make formal challenge through available channels. The meaningful participation of adults and children was supported by pre-meeting preparation and advocacy. All agencies involved, including education and health authorities supported and participated in this approach.

The family

Pat Brown and Keith Brown parented six children, three by earlier relationships of Mrs Brown and three children of the marriage. The children ranged in age from 12 years to six months, and included two boys and four girls. The elder boy, not the child of Mr Brown, had been assessed as having a mild learning disability as had his mother when a child. The family was well-known to social services and other agencies because of long-standing concerns about the level of care and supervision of the children. The family lived in economic hardship and home conditions were poor. Mrs and Mr Brown attended the family centre on a voluntary basis for intensive assistance in order to improve their parenting skills. The service was requested and paid for by social services with the agreement of Mrs and Mr Brown.

Assessment

Practical services, such as debts counselling, requested by parents were provided during the initial assessment. The information gathered about the children and family covered the elements discussed above in addition to information gathered from the parents about their history and circumstances. It quickly became apparent that, for the elder children in particular, a range of developmental concerns, a worrying pattern of minor injuries and bruises and recorded remarks of theirs to various professionals were indicative of significant harm. Furthermore the children's play indicated they were apprehensive about some adults and situations in their lives. Mrs Brown's own family story revealed long-standing and serious child abuse, particularly sexual abuse, through several generations. Mr. Brown's family history was more difficult to determine.

Intervention

Within a short time it was recommended that social services consider protective action. Mr and Mrs Brown were compliant with the suggestion the children be 'accommodated' (Part III s.20 Children Act 1989) with supervised contact, followed by a further period of assessment centred on issues of significant harm. Neither Mr nor Mrs Brown disputed the information about their children and said they too had wondered if the children were being abused but they didn't know by whom. The children were accommodated and kept together as a sibling group with frequent and purposeful contact with Mr and Mrs Brown. Once the children felt safe they revealed a catalogue of harms they, and other children outside their immediate family, had experienced, including physical and sexual abuse by a number of male family members. Within a short time an interim care order was granted followed by a full order with plans to seek carers for the sibling group as a whole. During the next year Mr Brown and his brother-in-law were prosecuted for sexual and physical abuse of a number of children within and outside their own families and received substantial prison sentences.

Reflection

The messages given by children, through their developmental history, behaviour, pattern of injuries and what they had said to a range of professionals, had gone unrecognised for many years. Mr and Mrs Brown lived in economic hardship and they were offered supportive services on the assumption their parenting capacity would increase and their children benefit as a result. Mr Brown was rarely seen by any service provider and was not involved in any previous work. Mrs Brown's vulnerabilities and powerlessness was apparent to all and her need for nurturing dominated professional attention. As a result the children suffered avoidable significant harm. It was only when each child's developmental and chronological history was pieced together and opportunities given to them to share their wishes and feelings in a safe environment that the extent of their abuse became known. All the children received modest sums from the Criminal Injuries Compensation Fund but will have to deal with the consequences of their childhood experiences throughout their lives.

Implications of policy – the 'mixed economy' of welfare

Professionals have to identify those situations/adults that cannot meet a child's needs, and those where appropriate intervention will ensure a child's experiences are 'good enough'. Identifying 'appropriate intervention' is critical and depends on comprehensive, dynamic, multifaceted and inter-agency assessments that link a family's needs to the full range of social work/social care interventions:

> An important underlying principle of the approach to assessment in the Guidance, therefore, is that it is based on a [*sic*] inter-agency model in which it is not just social services departments which are the assessors and providers of services. (DoH, DfEE, HO, 2000, p. 14)

Child protection interventions are therefore likely to include services provided by independent sector agencies. These agencies now provide a range of family support services including children's daycare, family centres, child protection assessments, specialist therapeutic/protective programmes, and respite or short-term substitute care. Daycare for young children is now purchased by the state almost solely as part of child protection programmes, and daycare providers are, in the main, small neighbourhood agencies or women working in their own home (Statham *et al.*, 2001). The 'mixed economy' of welfare in relation to services for children and their families where there are child protection concerns has many implications for inter-agency work.

Childcare professionals in all sectors must be aware of the indicators pointing to child harm and be able to work with families and other agencies on this issue. For small agencies and single providers, for whom remuneration is often very low and cover for staff training unavailable (Statham *et al.*, 2001), acquiring and keeping up-to-date in child protection knowledge may prove difficult. Similarly, the level of administration and networking associated with child protection programmes may be beyond the capacity of some of the smaller service providers. The failure of agencies to share information and work together in a way that afforded vulnerable children protection from avoidable harm caused by family carers has been a feature identified in many child abuse inquiries (DoH, 1991). Sadly, the level of inter-agency cooperation necessary for protecting children often takes place only after a child has died rather than during work with the family:

> It would seem that only when a child dies is time set aside for the task of piecing the story together. If records are not read and information is not extracted or shared with other agencies, then the professionals involved are creating a dangerous context within which decisions are made. In effect, professional judgment is reduced to guesswork. (NSPCC, 2001, p. 92)

Those who know children best are those who spend most time with them and, apart from their families, this means the service providers not the service commissioners. In this context child protection concerns cannot be the sole responsibility of social services departments. As Tilman Furniss (1991) points out, there are implications for the range of professionals working with children, such as teachers and youth workers, hitherto accustomed to only a marginal role in child protection work. This issue has been powerfully addressed in the NSPCC Report *Out of Sight* (2001):

> Ultimately, the protection of vulnerable children must become the concern of us all and the focus should be on all children who are significantly harmed, not only on extreme cases. Services need to be put in place which families in distress feel comfortable to seek out before they reach the point where they harm their children. (p. 15)

Families where there are child protection concerns may not always come to the attention of social services by reason of a child protection investigation under s.47 of the Children Act 1989, but may receive services under s.17. Local authorities frequently commission family support services from independent sector providers with major implications for their responsibilities in work to protect children. Without attention to staff skills and training across all sectors and intra and inter-agency operational functioning, 'best practice' will be difficult to achieve.

Implications for practice

It has been recognised that protecting children ultimately depends on professional judgement:

> [D]espite increasing sophistication in the design and evaluation of risk assessment tools, the variables for assessing children, in the context of their families, are so complex that professional judgment underpinned by theory and research still remains the cornerstone of good practice. (DoH, 2000, p. 12)

The balance between protection and prevention, family support and child rescue, highlighted time after time in the child abuse inquiries of the 1980s (DoH, 1991) is difficult to achieve. However, current knowledge of the aetiology of child abuse is now substantive and suggests the most severely abused children suffer abuse across more than one dimension. Specific indicators that signal when a child's welfare is seriously compromised by the actions or lack of care they suffer within their families are well-known (Corby 2000).

Notwithstanding the barriers facing inter-agency child protection work arising from differing agency cultures, knowledge bases, resources and responsibilities, current approaches to child protection based on an eco-systemic understanding, have much to offer as a common model of practice. The model identifies harm to children occurring in the context of their environment with multiple determinants at individual, family, community and societal level. Understanding child abuse in this way suggests causality is a dynamic process rather than a static and predictable occurrence. An ecological approach enables protective factors to be identified too. The importance of 'buffers', that is family or community resources that support parenting and ensures a child's well-being, cannot be underestimated. Working with families where there are child protection concerns must involve breadth of understanding in relation to all aspects of the child's and the family's life, including socio-economic factors, and depth in relation to the core body of knowledge on the aetiology of child abuse.

However, there may be dangers in linking a comparatively unusual phenomenon, child maltreatment, with a common one, child poverty. The scale of child poverty has increased enormously in three decades (Jones and Novak, 1999; Burden, Cooper and Petrie, 2000). By 1996 over 4.3million children, a third of the total child population, were living in households with below half average income compared with just 10 per cent in 1968 (Gregg, Harkness and Makin, 1999). Professional attention may become focused on an aspect of child harm, child poverty, which they can only ameliorate on an individual level but which requires political will and public support to eliminate. To imply poverty can be eradicated through professional activity defines poverty as an individual not a structural issue. Conversely, significant harm to children, if understood ecologically, requires an individualised response to each child and family. Recognising the impact of socio-economic pressures on parenting capacity must not be at the expense of abandoning practice knowledge gained, through the tragic lives and deaths of numbers of children, during the last three decades. This requires childcare professionals in all sectors to understand the spectrum of parenting problems from those resulting from unusual pressures and stresses to those that are cruel and abusive.

Summary

Recent government policy has been influenced by research suggesting child protection processes developed through the 1980s and 1990s were unhelpful for many children. Large numbers of parents and their children were subjected to highly intrusive child protection investigations that resulted in no further action and no services. In response to this and in recognition of the large numbers of children living in poverty, with adverse consequences for their health and welfare, the current policy framework and government guidance place child protection concerns within a more holistic framework. It is expected that the *Assessment Framework for Children in Need and their Families* (*op. cit.*, 2000), drawing on an ecological explanation of child abuse, will be the baseline from which interventions and services, appropriately protective, can follow. It is anticipated that more families where there are child protection concerns will be dealt with through s.17 of the Children Act 1989, and fewer s.47 investigations will result. Many families where there are child protection concerns will not enter the formalised child protection system. Some, albeit a small minority, will be causing serious child harm that is unrecognised. However, the elements of effective work with families where there are child protection concerns have been emerging through practice research and professional debate during the last three decades and remain relevant. First, this requires childcare professionals to focus on the child, through direct communication and comprehensive, ongoing, development and attachment observations. Second, the quality of the work with parents is also important, especially how to work openly and honestly in situations where adults may be threatening and aggressive. Last, although especially critical in the current context of the fragmentation of the welfare state, is the quality of inter-agency communication and joint work. This has implications for the skills, training and management of childcare professionals in all sectors, not only local authority social workers.

Final comments

The current situation may bring benefits for children and families where there are child protection concerns since there is more substantial research available to professionals about all aspects of child maltreatment than ever before. However, whilst it was true that many children were subjected to protective investigations but received no services, it is also true that there have been some children, as with the Brown children above, who received services but no protection. Whatever the service provided and whichever agencies provide them, all children deserve the same attention to their well-being. This is clearly in line with our duties under the Human Rights Act 1998 which requires all 'public authorities' to act in accordance with fundamental human rights principles (NSPCC, 2001). There is substantial knowledge available about the aetiology of child abuse and the ecological approach offers a model that has utility for all childcare professionals in all sectors. A common knowledge base and effective inter-agency work is an essential prerequisite of an effective child protection system and it is essential this knowledge base is not lost in a laudable desire to respond to the savage impact of poverty on children in the UK.

References

Adcock, M. and White, R. (1985) *Good-Enough Parenting*. London: British association for Adoption and Fostering.
Axline, V. (1947) *Play Therapy*. New York: Ballantine Books.
Bentovim, A. (2002) 'Work with Abusing Families', in K. Wilson and A. James (eds), *The Child Protection Handbook*, 2nd edn. London: Balliere Tindall, pp. 456–80.
Burden, T., Cooper, C. and Petrie, S. (2000) *'Modernising' Social Policy: Unravelling New Labour's Welfare Reforms*. Aldershot: Ashgate.
Campbell, B. (1988) *Unofficial Secrets. Child Sexual Abuse: The Cleveland Case*. London: Virago.
Campbell, J. C. (1995) *Assessing Dangerousness. Violence by Sexual offenders, Batterers and Child Abusers*. Thousand Oaks: Sage.
Children Act 1989. London: HMSO.
Corby, B. (2000) *Child Abuse. Towards a Knowledge Base*, 2nd edn. Buckingham: Open University Press.
David, M. and Appell, G. (2001) *Loczy. An Unusual Approach to Mothering*. Budapest: Pikler-Loczy Institute for Young Children.
Department of Health (DoH) (1991) *Child Abuse. A Study of Inquiry Reports 1980–1989*. London: HMSO.
— (1995) *Child Protection. Messages from Research*. London: HMSO.
— (1998a) *Modernising Health and Social Services: Promoting Independence, Improving Protection, Raising Standards*. London: The Stationery Office.
— (1998b) *Quality Protects Circular: Transforming Children's Services*, Local Authority Circular LAC (98) 26. London: Department of Health.
— (2000) *Assessing Children in Need and their Families: Practice Guidance*. London: The Stationery Office.
— (2001) *Studies informing the Framework for the Assessment of Children in Need and their Families*. London: The Stationery Office.
— (2002) *Integrated Children's System*. Briefing paper no. 3, http://www.doh.gov.uk/qualityprotect/work–pro/framebrief3.doc

Department of Health, Department for Education and Employment, Home Office (2000) *Framework for the Assessment of Children in Need and their Families*. London: The Stationery Office.

Department of Health, Home Office, Department for Education and Employment (1999) *Working Together to Safeguard and Promote the Health of Children*. London: The Stationery Office.

Department of Health/SSI (1995) *The Challenge of Partnership in Child Protection: Practice Guide*. London: HMSO.

Department of Health and Social Security (1985) *Social Work Decisions in Child Care. Recent Research Findings and their Implications*. London: HMSO.

Fahlberg, V. (1991) *A Child's Journey through Placement, UK edition*. London: BAAF.

Frost, N. and Stein, M. (1989) *The Politics of Child Welfare: Inequality, Power and Change?* New York: Harvester Wheatsheaf.

Farmer, E. and Boushel, M. (1999) 'Child Protection Policy and Practice: Women in the Front Line', in S. Watson and L. Doyal (eds), *Engendering Social Policy*. Buckingham: Open University Press.

Furniss, T. (1991) *The Multi-Professional Handbook of Child Sexual Abuse. Integrated Management, Therapy and Legal Intervention*. London: Routledge.

Gerber, M. (ed.) (1997) *The RIE Manual: For Parents and Professionals*. Los Angeles: Resources for Infant Educarers.

Gregg, P., Harkness, S. and Makin, S. (1999) *Child Development and Family Income*. York: JRF/YPS.

Gordon, L. (1989) *Heroes of their Own Lives: The Politics and History of Family Violence, Boston 1880–1960*. London: Virago.

Guardian 'Overstretched Child Care Service "Unravelled"', 18 October 2001. http://society.guardian.co.uk/climbie/story/0,10939,576651,00.html accessed March 2002.

Guardian '"Political Correctness" Puts Children at Risk', 20 December 2001. http://society.guardian.co.uk/climbie/story/0,10939,623077,00.html accessed May 2002.

Howe, D., Brandon, M., Hinings, D. and Schofield, G. (1999) *Attachment Theory, Child Maltreatment and Family Support* Houndmills, Basingstoke: Macmillan–Palgrave.

Howe, D. (1995) *Attachment Theory for Social Work Practice*. Basingstoke: Macmillan–Palgrave.

Jones, C. and Novak, T. (1999) *Poverty, Welfare and the Disciplinary State*. London: Routledge.

Kellmer-Pringle, M. (1986) *The Needs of Children: A Personal Perspective*. London: Hutchinson.

Marsh, P. and Crow, G. (1998) *Family Group Conferences in Child Welfare*. Oxford: Blackwell.

Novak, T., Owen, S., Petrie, S. and Sennett, H. (1997) *Children's Day Care and Welfare Markets*. Hull: University of Lincolnshire and Humberside.

NSPCC (2001) *Out of Sight. NSPCC Report on Child Deaths from Abuse 1973–2000*, 2nd edn. London: NSPCC.

Petrie, S. and Corby, B. (2001) 'Partnership with Parents', in K.Wilson and A. James (eds), *The Child Protection Handbook*. London: Harcourt.

Petrie, S. and Wilson, K. (1999) 'Towards the Disintegration of Child Welfare Services', *Journal of Social Policy and Administration*, vol. 33(2), June, pp. 181–97.

Ryan, V. and Wilson, K. (1996) *Case Studies in Non-directive Play Therapy*. London: Jessica Kingsley.

Sidebotham, P. (2001) 'An Ecological Approach to Child Abuse: A Creative Use of Scientific Models in Research and Practice', *Child Abuse Review*, vol. 10, pp. 97–112.

Stace, S. and Tunstill, J. (1990) *On Different Tracks. Inconsistencies between the Children Act and the Community Care Act.* London: Voluntary Organisations Personal Social Services Group.

Statham, J., Dillon, J. and Moss, P. (2001) *Placed and Paid For. Supporting Families through Sponsored Day Care.* London: The Stationery Office

Staffordshire County Council (1991) *The Pindown Experience and the Protection of Children: The Report of the Staffordshire Child Care Inquiry 1990.*

The Bridge Child Care Consultancy Service (1991) *Sukina: An Evaluation Report of the Circumstances Leading to her Death.* London: The Bridge Child Care Consultancy.

Wilson, K., Kendrick, P. and Ryan, V. (1992) *Play Therapy. A Non-Directive approach for Children and Adolescents.* London: Balliere Tindall.

9

Working with Families where there is Domestic Violence

Margaret Bell

Practitioners from all the helping professions – housing, refuges, education, health, social services, court welfare, police, criminal justice – come into contact with families who have experienced domestic violence. However, because of the secrecy and fear that silences families who are experiencing violent behaviour at home its existence often goes unrecognised. There are many reasons for this. Accounts by professionals (Bell, 1996) and by women themselves suggest that mothers do not disclose it because they fear retribution. Many are afraid of being judged incompetent as parents and of having their children removed if they approach statutory agencies. It is probable that women from Asian communities in the United Kingdom experience even greater family and social pressures to maintain silence, pressures exacerbated by problems of language or ignorance of available services, and by racism (Adams, 1998). Male partners avoid discussion or minimise violent events – often by blaming alcohol (Ptacek, 1988), while children use a range of strategies to avoid discussing it (Mullender, 1996). Research also provides evidence of a reluctance on the part of professionals to see domestic violence. In perusing social work files, Milner (1996) found that social workers failed to record the existence of violence or to mention it in meetings, often referring to it in gender-neutral terms, where it was reframed as marital conflict or fighting. In Bell's (1996) study, social services staff report that the process of identification by the range of professionals involved was *'almost incidental – very sort of pot luck'*. Professionals only became aware of the violence sometime after the child presented with symptoms of distress, the child or the family member trusted the professional enough to tell, or another professional involved passed on the information.

Statutory agencies have been slow to respond to issues of domestic violence, and the way in which services have been traditionally organised has militated further against statutory agencies taking on responsibility for policy and practice development. In the 1970s and 1980s, refuges, informed by feminist perspectives based on self-help and self-determination, predominantly met the needs of women, providing immediate support and safety. The needs of children, especially when defined in child protection terms, were met by social services, whereas responsibility for working with men was seen to lie outside the voluntary and social services sector and was generally located within the criminal justice system. Stanley (1997) argues that this culture of separateness both reflects and pervades attitudes to and service provision for violent families. making progress towards more appropriate and responsive inter-agency services slow and difficult.

The size of the problem

Largely due to feminist voices, the 1980s witnessed growing public awareness of the violence women suffered in their own homes. A policy statement by the Home Office (Circular 60/1990) directed police to treat assaults in the home as criminal acts, and Domestic Violence Units were set up. A more proactive response emerged, including the beginnings of work with violent men in the probation service. Developments in 1992 were seminal. The British Crime Survey, 1992, revealed a minimum of half a million domestic violence incidents a year, of which 87 per cent are assaults on women. Subsequent research confirms the relatively high rate of incidence of violence against women although, as suggested above, prevalence rates are almost certainly much higher than reported incidents – especially in Asian communities. The best available data to date from the new British Crime Survey (Mirlees-Black, 1999) covered men and women aged 16 to 59 and found that, over their lifetime, 22.7 per cent of women and 14.9 per cent of men reported being a victim of domestic assault. Women were more severely affected than men, were twice as likely to have been injured and to have suffered multiple assaults. Physical violence is the most frequently reported and it is now recognised that violence takes many forms, including rape, mental cruelty and, in some cases, homicide. Criminal statistics for England and Wales (1997) showed that 47 per cent of female homicide victims were killed by their partners compared to 8 per cent of men. The most robust risk factor is that of previous assault. Other risk factors include poverty and social exclusion, that women who are separating from their partners are at much higher risk and the risk is increased by marital dependence (where women are unemployed) and lack of economic resources (Walby and Myhill, 2000). Women in Asian communities who may, in addition, be socially isolated and not speak English, are at increased risk; from a woman in Adam's study (1998):

> Since I could not speak English I could not talk to anyone ... I didn't know of any help available ... I was imprisoned in my own home.

Research has also provided evidence of the close relationship between domestic violence and child abuse – whether physical, sexual or emotional. Cleaver and Freeman (1995) found that between a fifth and two-thirds of children with social services involvement were also living in situations of domestic violence. More recent research suggests higher rates. McGee (2000) estimated that children were present during the violence in 85 per cent of the 41 families she surveyed. The complexity of the links between domestic violence and child abuse is also now better understood. Edeslon (1999) found that children were vulnerable to being abused themselves in incidents, and Farmer and Pollock (1998) have drawn attention to the prevalence of domestic violence in cases of child sexual abuse. Cleaver *et al.* (1999) highlight the coexistence in violent families of mental illness and problems of substance abuse. Additionally, there is now increasing awareness of violence against men, against elderly people – both at home and in residential care (Harbison, 2000) – amongst people in gay and lesbian relationships and between siblings. The focus of this chapter, however, is on men's violence against women with children at home.

The effects of domestic violence on women and children

The effects of domestic violence on women and children are serious. For many women the violence often begins when they are pregnant (Mezey and Bewley, 1997) and increases when the children are small (Abraham's, 1994). Youth is an added factor – as women become older the risk decreases. The effects on the physical and mental health of women are multiple and lasting. As well as physical harm, many women experience loss of self esteem leading to isolation and depression (Mcgibbon, Cooper and Kelly, 1989). This, then, has adverse effects on their capacity to parent, including emotional unavailability, resulting in insecure attachments which then produce difficult behaviours. In the words of a mother interviewed in a NCH survey (Abrahams,1994):

> You put a protective barrier around yourself that stops you from completely crumbling – there was no room for that extra cuddle. (p. 46)

The multiple ways in which children suffer emotionally, behaviourally and physically in both the short and long term has been the subject of much research. Developmental delays may result from unmet needs and lack of concentration in school. Ezell (2000) categorises externalising problems such as aggressive and delinquent behaviour, and internalising problems such as withdrawal and anxiety. McGee (2000) reports general and specific fears, including for mothers' safety and draws attention to the feelings of powerlessness invoked by repeatedly leaving home. There is evidence that children who witness sexual assaults develop post-traumatic stress disorder

(Sylvern, Karyl and Landis, 1995). Peled (1997) suggests that there are particular issues for children's relationship with their fathers because of the confusing feelings they have towards them. Less is known about the influence of age and race, much of the research being on younger children. Gender can be an influencing factor – there is some evidence that boys are more vulnerable than girls – and some children are more resilient than others. One protective factor may be the quality of attachment between the non-abusing parent and the child, another the existence of secondary attachment figures in the child's network (Bell, 2002). The need to recognise the interconnections between physical, sexual and emotional abuse in the context of domestic violence and that children in such situations are experiencing significant harm (Brandon, 1996) is now more widely understood.

The policy framework

The extent and nature of the problems caused by domestic violence, the various ways in which it can present itself and the cost and issues raised now have a high media profile. While some policies continue to limit women's ability to create safety for themselves – such as the Child Support Act and recent revisions of definitions and rights in relation to homelessness (Mullender, 1996) – the Family Law Act 1996 has introduced the new concept of 'associated persons' and provides for two main orders: *occupation orders* regulating the occupation of the family home, and *non-molestation orders*, providing protection from violence. However, recent changes to the Legal Aid system now make these costly. Part 1V also amends the Children Act 1989, so that an order can be made to exclude a suspected abuser from the house. The Housing Act 1996 (sec. 18.9) is relevant in entitling people who are homeless and in priority to temporary accommodation, although they need to secure it beforehand. Recent government guidance, the *Framework for Assessment* (DoH, 2000), has heightened the profile of domestic violence in assessments of children in need by including questions about domestic violence, although there is little in it about working with men. And *Working Together* (DoH, 2000) now requires agencies to produce clear guidance on domestic violence interventions which, as Humphreys *et al.* (2001) point out, presents opportunities to Area Child Protection Committees to include domestic violence within the framework of inter-agency child protection procedures.

Inter-agency work

The need for the range of agencies involved to work together has been a key focus in developing services for work with violent families. Many areas now have coordinating domestic violence fora, or inter-agency groups, which have representatives from the range of statutory and voluntary services and sometimes service users. Refuges and other women's support services are often linked to these. Their aims include increasing agencies' awareness of each others' roles, promoting their cooperation in developing services, raising public awareness, providing information and examining causes of domestic violence. Leeds has one of the best known inter-agency fora, being rooted in an active women's movement, and initiating a range of innovative projects such as a schools project and the commissioned survey mentioned above (Bell, 1996). However, in researching multi-agency work, Hague *et al.* (1996) found that while some sites are the focus of ongoing attempts to create change, elsewhere it is a struggle with much depending on where women live.

Humphreys *et al.*'s (2001) more recent survey of statutory and voluntary provision for families where there is domestic violence tells the same story, finding that less than half (45 per cent) of the responding departments had policies in place. Local and regional variability is influenced by existing relationship between agencies, the strength of women's community groups, the nature of the community and the degree of activity of police, probation and other agencies in the inter-agency work. Most importantly, resources essential for effective inter-agency working are not always forthcoming and need to be properly established.

Social work policy and practice

Turning to social work services, Mullender (1996) suggests that social service departments are not in the forefront of progress and she paints a picture of inconsistency and widespread bad practice. She suggests social workers do not see domestic violence as relevant to their work, and lack skills and confidence in helping women and confronting men. Following on their more recent survey, Humphreys and Mullender (forthcoming) also identify structural and organisational barriers, such as the separation of services for children from services for adults and the incident-focused nature of child protection, which have prevented the development of more sensitive and effective intervention in the statutory sector.

A psychodynamic understanding of the difficulties for practitioners is an equally important part of this complex picture, adding to the frame an exploration of the inter and intrapersonal factors which influence professional responses. Bell (2000) points out that families in which there is violence arouse feelings of anxiety and helplessness in those who are there to help them which are deskilling and disempowering. Additionally, there is danger. Practitioners expose themselves to physical violence, intimidation and harassment, sometimes of a sexual nature, and may not in these cash-strapped days have the support from their agencies such as mobile phones or co-workers to make their work safe. Agencies rarely offer the quality of supervision necessary for such responses to be constructively contained and managed. Also confusing is the policy and legal framework within which social workers operate. The Children Act 1989 requires families to be kept together, yet makes no suggestions as to how the relative rights of men, women and children should be weighted – or by whom. Society also imposes conflicting paradigms – supporting family rights to privacy on the one hand, and the need to protect vulnerable people on the other. Finally, there is uncertainty about what interventions are helpful and, related to this, what theoretical framework is most apposite. In particular, uncertainty surrounds whether or not couple or family work should be undertaken. On the one hand working with couples where there is violence may be both unsafe and perceived as blurring issues of criminal responsibility. On the other, since over half the women who seek refuge do continue their relationship (Frude, 1993), there is a strong argument for working with the couple to effect change.

Increasingly – and, in part, due to the now wider definition accorded to children in need – a broader range of practice interventions with families where there is domestic violence are now considered necessary. A number of developments have enabled social workers to shift from their 'either remove the child or help the mother escape' syndrome to more thoughtful and flexible approaches. One of these is the recognition that working only with mothers is oppressive and ultimately unproductive. It risks reinforcing women's sense of helplessness and low self-esteem rather than tackling it; it objectifies men by assuming they are incapable of change and unworthy of help; and it fails to address the needs of children. Another is that the range of interventions for men – especially when placed alongside work with women and children – are becoming more available.

Most importantly, the policy context within which work with violent families is located is gradually becoming more robust. Returning to Humphreys *et al.*'s survey (2001) of policy documents, while, as reported above, less than half of the social service departments surveyed had policies and guidelines in place, they identified as the best those which adopted strategies for addressing issues of safety and confidentiality, clarifying referral systems, providing information to the public and providing practice guidelines for front-line workers. The ways in which providing practice guidelines improves social work practice in situations of domestic violence is well-demonstrated by Hester and Pearson's (1998) awareness raising work with an NSPCC team. Where the workers asked the mothers they were working with directly about domestic violence, evidence of its existence rose by 33 per cent. This allowed cases to be looked at in a wider context, leading to more holistic and sophisticated practice responses such as an increase in work with both child and mother and promoting inter-agency links.

The next section will discuss and illustrate ways of working with families where there is domestic violence. As the interventions presented derive so clearly from the theoretical framework upon which they are based, I will first briefly describe the three main approaches and illustrate their connection with particular interventions.

Theoretical frameworks and associated interventions

The feminist approach

This approach to understanding and explaining domestic violence is that men's violence against women is the product of a patriarchal culture which condones men's domination of women. Within this framework, family conflicts should be addressed from a perspective which focuses on structural factors and requires social and institutional change in all the individuals and organisations involved. Individual work with women is seen as being unhelpful in that it may reinforce women's blame and guilt for behaviour which is not their responsibility. Individual work with men is regarded as risky and as potentially offering them the opportunity to excuse and 'explain' rather than confront their violence. Family and couple work is seen as problematic in viewing causality as a circular process within which violence is regarded as a symptom and not the cause of family problems. And working with the couple is inappropriate because it ignores and feeds into unresolved power issues and because the focus on the family can exclude an understanding of wider social forces.

The feminist approach highlights the need to prioritise the physical safety of women and children and to align family support provision alongside interventions which effectively challenge men's paternalistic attitudes to women. Focused group work with women, with children and with men in conjunction with a range of community and educational initiatives are seen, generally, as being the most effective interventions. So:

- At the primary level of prevention, a good example is the educational work developed in primary schools by the Leeds inter-agency forum to teach children that violence is never a solution and there are other ways of expressing anger.
- At the secondary level, the Killingbeck police project illustrates how neighbourhood support systems can be activated to enhance women's safety. This project aimed to reduce repeat victimisation by encouraging victimised women to report all incidents while at the same time adopting a proactive approach to the offending man. Improvements were found in that police responses became more consistent, the number of women seeking police support increased, chronic offenders were identified and closer inter-agency partnerships were established (Hanmer and Griffiths, 2000).
- At the tertiary level, the Domestic Violence Intervention project in London provides an example of how group work with violent men can be combined with crisis-oriented support services and group work with women. Men are accepted onto the programme of structured group sessions with mixed gender facilitators either on a court-mandated or a

voluntary basis. The groups work on helping men to understand why they use abusive behaviour and how they can change. They are encouraged to take responsibility for and change attitudes to their violence and, where relevant, alcohol abuse. For women one-to-one safety assessment sessions are run alongside a group. At the same time, advocacy work is undertaken with agencies such as housing, police and lawyers. Burton *et al.*'s (1998) evaluation provided some evidence of success where men had completed the 32-week programme. However, there was a high attrition rate (two-thirds dropped out), and changes in behaviour were heavily dependent on motivation to change. They concluded that the proactive support offered to the women was also crucial to success.

The systemic approach

Systems theory provides a perspective on the family as a system rather than a set of individuals, and suggests people's behaviour is best understood in the context in which it occurs and within the belief systems of the family over time, including families of origin and former partnerships. All family members' behaviour is seen as a reaction to the behaviour of others which becomes self-regulatory. Thus people in close emotional proximity set up stable patterns of interaction which are interconnected, made up from a series of sequences and produce a family pattern. This in turn assumes that there are no victims or villains as both partners complement one another's behaviour.

A systems approach to understanding relationships takes into account that couples often remain together in spite of the violence, and that, rather than being the cause of the couple's difficulties, the violence is part of a wider problem in relationships. From this perspective, interventions should be focused on family roles and communication patterns, generally within a family or couple-work intervention. Change, therefore, requires that both partners are involved in relation to the abuse of women by men. This would imply that the woman, while not responsible for the mans behaviour, has to learn to identify the signs and different ways of responding as well as modifying her own behaviour, while the man has to accept full responsibility for his abusive behaviour and make concerted efforts to change. The content of couple work should be:

- to enable the victim to release her anger and tell her story, and for the perpetrator to listen;
- to increase positive and solicitous behaviour;
- to develop problem-solving skills; and
- to provide opportunities for conflict resolution on specific areas, such as childcare.

As well as looking at ways of improving communication, couple therapy also offers opportunities to work with both partners on issues related to their past, such as attachment disorders. The following case example illustrates how working with the couple together can be helpful:

> Mr and Mrs Clark, a married couple in their early 30s, have been together since aged 18 and have a close relationship. They have two children, a boy aged 7 (Gary jnr) and a girl aged 8 (Flo). Mr Clark (Gary snr) is employed as a foreman and works long hours. He was sexually abused as a child. His mother provides some support to the family. Mrs Clark has, for some years, misused alcohol and has received treatment from a substance-misuse clinic. Her family are estranged by her drinking habits. Gary jnr has behavioural problems, including fire-setting and anger outbursts.
>
> A pattern exists whereby Mr Clark gets home from work late and tired, Gary jnr has been difficult and Mrs Clark has been drinking. Arguments escalate and Mr Clark hits Mrs Clark. Police have been involved. On more than one occasion Mrs Clark has taken out an injunction, but subsequently invited her husband back into the home.
>
> Identified problems: father's violence towards mother; mother's long-standing alcohol abuse; Gary jnr's behavioural problems. The family have been receiving help from the community mental health team for sometime. Mrs Clark is in treatment for her alcohol misuse and she and Gary jnr did attend a parenting class for help with her childcare skills and his emotional difficulties. Mr Clark was not involved.
>
> Recently a new referral was made by the school to the substance-misuse team and taken on by the social worker. Taking into account the couples history, the established patterns of behaviour and their wish to stay together, the social worker agreed to work with the couple, together. The goals negotiated were to work on:
>
> - helping them to look at the ways in which the children were being hurt and the possible child development and child protection consequences;
> - learning new parenting skills, in particular the need to supervise Gary jnr more closely and to provide him with stimulation and praise;
> - basic ways of changing their pattern of interaction as a couple. Mr Clark to stop complaining about his wife's drinking and to end his violence. Mrs Clark to find ways of drink reduction and to stop raising the history of abuse. Both to chart situations seen to lead to violence and try other ways of dealing with the situations – for example, to try time-out when Gary's behaviour was a trigger.

The social worker meets the family weekly to discuss progress in the above areas and plan for the next week's work. Both parents are beginning to see a connection between their behaviour and Gary's. Mr Clark spends more time with Gary when at home, and tries to get home early two nights a week to help at bedtime. Mrs Clark is drinking less and has more energy when with the children. Violent episodes still take place, but less frequently. Mr Clark is beginning to see when his violence will erupt and sometimes goes to his mother's house to cool off. Separate sessions are to be offered to him to look at his own early sexual abuse and related attachment issues. There are child protection concerns and these are being carefully charted by the social worker in conjunction with the school and the clinic treating Mrs Clark for her alcohol misuse.

After years of evaluative research with abusing men, Edelson and Tolman (1992), suggest that cautious and responsible use of couple work has its place – especially after group work with both partners has successfully been completed. Sinclair (1985) adds that the degree of intimidation and fear must be significantly reduced so as not to interfere with open discussion of marital issues, that the couple's goals are mutually agreed and the work is entered into freely by both partners. In recognition that there are some situations where couple work would not be appropriate, domestic violence cases are often screened out of wider conflict resolution work, such as by Relate.

Individual pathology

Traditional explanations of family violence have focused on personal characteristics that can cause violent behaviour. These include psychobiological (Lorenz, 1966) and social learning (Bandura, 1973) explanations which emphasise the role of internal conflicts such as suppressed anger and learned responses in aggression.

An example of an intervention that attempts to change aggressive behaviour by challenging beliefs that condone violence is the Duluth programme. Here a power and control wheel is used to focus discussion in a men's group on the tactics they use to control relationships (Robertson, 1999). What the men found helpful were discussions on denial, discussion to identify triggers to violence and learning to take 'time out' (Dobash *et al.* 1996).

Evaluations of effectiveness of such interventions are complex because they need to address both the safety of women and children and the degree to which they achieve change in the behaviour of men. What studies there are of success are mixed, and there are significant problems with evaluation – not least being women's lack of confidence in reporting truthfully. Edelson (1996) found evidence of some success in that 53–85 per cent of the men in the programmes reviewed stopped physical battering over an 18-month period. However, drop-out rates in all of the programmes researched are substantial, with less than a third completing (Burton *et al.*, 1998).

Alternative explanations for violent behaviour draw on early childhood experiences which are traumatic, conflictual or unresolved. Attachment theory has been widely used to link aggression with childhood experiences, and Malan (1979), for example, has drawn connections between aggression and early maternal deprivation. Evidence suggests that poor attachment experiences predispose to adult mental health problems, including loss of control and low self-esteem. Socialisation processes impact further, so men are more likely to see violence as an acceptable means to gain control whereas women internalise their anger because they are conditioned to believe they are to blame.

Interventions based on psychological explanations include those that take as their focus the need to work on attachment issues. Such work would encompass individual work with men or women on their early attachment experiences, couple work, such as that being undertaken with Mr and Mrs Clark, and conjoint work with mothers and children together as a way of enabling mothers to become more attuned to children's needs, especially by play and observation. Individual work with children, for example on their sometimes deeply ambivalent feelings toward their fathers (see Saunders, 1995), is another intervention indicated by this approach.

The next section expands upon the above by providing more detail about interventions which are largely based upon systems and attachment approaches to working with children and families who have experienced domestic violence. The framework outlined for assessing the needs of women and children follows the structure outlined in the *New Framework for Assessment* by focusing on need, parenting capacity and environmental factors. The content of individual and group work is then discussed.

Assessment and associated interventions

Work with women

Disclosure

- **Screening**. Given the research reported above – that the most robust risk factor for domestic violence is that of previous assault, and that women are more likely to self-report at point of separation – the need for all professionals to sensitively enquire into and document incidents of domestic violence is obvious. Many women will not be able to trust and the question will need to be repeated, always when the woman is alone. For black women race may be a key factor in disclosure. Some of the women interviewed in Adam's (1998) study described forceful family pressures not to disclose, and women were inhibited by the fact that the community leaders were male. Agencies should have guidance about what confidentiality can be guaranteed and what not.
- **Monitoring**. All social work records, referral and assessment forms should include a specific category on domestic violence. Of course, the existence of screening and monitoring procedures does not ensure that they will be complied with. Some workers fear that asking questions that appear routine will alienate families, others feel uncomfortable asking them, and yet others that, in a hierarchy of traumatic life events more general questions are preferred (Kelly, 2001). Training is essential to ensure specificity.

Safety

Women's safety is paramount, and it is important to work closely with other primary healthcare settings, including mental health and antenatal services. Advice and information about temporary accommodation, housing and support services should be offered, including telephone contacts, help with alarms, mobile phones and legal advice. Advocacy may be necessary where women are exhausted and disempowered. Outreach services for women not wanting to leave their partners and for women from ethnic minority groups should be available. Aftercare for women who have been rehoused and need help with resettlement and support, including counselling, should also be offered.

Assessment

Assessments should be of:

- risk of further violence,
- risk to physical and mental health
- need for a range of service provision, and
- capacity and motivation to affect or engage in a process of change.

Assessments of risk would take into account:

- knowledge of the degree, type and circumstances of the violence being perpetrated, and of the perpetrator;
- knowledge of local resources for women experiencing domestic violence;
- information about current housing and finance; and
- judgments as to the woman's capacity to defend herself, including to mobilise supportive formal and informal networks (where they exist).

Assessments of need are likely to be of:

- short-term need, such as for legal advice, money and safety, including refuge;
- longer-term need, such as for a range of family support services and therapeutic help.

Assessments of capacity for and motivation to engage in a change process will be on different levels, as follows:

- *Individual* – careful assessments should be made of both partners' physical and mental health, family background and history and of what is currently experienced as stressful. Young children may, for example, be experienced as impossible or as providing comfort. The Family Scales in the Framework for Assessment could be of use here – especially daily hassles and adult well-being.

- *Relationships* – the quality, nature and duration of (1) the couple relationship, its strengths and weaknesses, including the place and function violence has within it, (2) the mother/child relationship, in particular the quality of attachment and parenting capacity, and (3) the father/child relationship, as above.
- *Environment* – assessment of environmental strengths and weaknesses would include the quality of extended family and community support, the nature of services available in the locality, as well as the contribution of financial, housing and employment factors which may add to or diminish stress.

Interventions

The nature of the interventions offered will depend upon the assessment of what the woman wants to do, what is likely to decrease risk and what is available. As suggested above, these may include or begin with enabling resettlement to take place, encouraging legal and police help or enlisting support from the wider family network or community. Running alongside and, in the longer term, family support and therapeutic help – individual or group – should be offered in the following areas:

- Work on self-esteem. Whether the work is short or long-term, there is a particular need to address women's sense that they are to blame. Many have been sensitised to feel they have provoked the violent behaviour (Jukes, 1999) and feel helpless and out of control. Women who have suffered depression can benefit from following the stages outlined below:
  (1) The first stage is the self within the conflictful relationship, characterised by role expectation and depletion.
  (2) The second requires 'seeing the abyss' – a turning point where a decision is made to no longer be powerless.
  (3) Following this is learning about self in relation to the world – 'who am I?', providing a chance to remodel behaviours, to take legal action and to exercise choice.
  (4) This leads to the fourth stage of self-awareness, and realisation that change requires action.
  (5) Finally, seeing where things have gone wrong and moving to change, for example by taking up education, changing attitudes and feeling powerful.

- Work on parenting skills
  (1) Ability to parent. The need to avoid reinforcing the view that children come first and mothers second must be balanced with increasing women's confidence in their parenting abilities. Domestic violence affects women's experience of motherhood, having profound effects on their feelings and behaviour towards their chil-

dren, including inconsistent responses. Kelly (2001) describes how the community mental health team workers she interviewed reported that supporting the mother to establish herself as the authority in the family, setting boundaries and containing the child's feelings was at the foundation of their approach. A key factor was establishing good communication between mother and child, so that offering information about the effects on children is important, combined with providing practical help with parenting tasks, such as by Home Start volunteers.

(2) Understanding of children's needs. Again, a balance must be held between enabling women to understand children's needs and avoiding them feeling solely responsible. Stressing the joint responsibility of parents to their children is important as is using the discourse of children in need, rather than of children in need of protection in order not to increase anxiety. Hague *et al.* (1996) give an example of successful work with a woman in a refuge:

> *The refuge worked with other agencies with an 'off the wall' family: the mother was abused as a child – sexually, physically – and had seven children. The whole family were known to have been victims of abuse. In-depth work resulted in mother eventually living in the community with her children. It involved learning to be an adult and a mother learning to protect her children and living as a single parent. With care the family have moved forward.* (1996, p. 27)

Other aspects of working with women on their children's needs include enabling them to become aware that they may be using their children as protectors, allies or confidantes, and that their negative feelings toward their child could be because they perceive similarities between that child and the abusing parent.

- Work on changing behaviours. Women need to be helped to make effective choices, including ending relationships safely, renegotiating them and changing their own behaviours. Individual, couple or group work can be used. Groups run for women who have experienced domestic violence can be supportive in reducing isolation, in sharing information about available resources and in prompting proactive responses and advocacy. Kelly and Humphreys (2000) found that, in an Islington initiative, support groups were the most effective element in combating the shame, self-blame and the destruction of self-belief which inhibited their attempts to end the violence. The Domestic Violence Intervention project in London (described above) provides details of how one-to-one safety assessment sessions for women are run alongside a group which uses techniques such as a graph to enable women to chart and track a man's behaviour over time to see patterns of abuse, as well as self-esteem work and exploring ways domestic violence affects children.

Work with children

While work with mothers and children together can promote the children's interests, it is important to remember that children's interests are not the same as their mother's. Work with children can involve, separately and together, individual work, group work and work with both abusing and non-abusing parents.

Disclosure

As with adults, many children go to great lengths to hide the existence of violence because they fear the consequences of telling. They may also have learnt that adults do not want to hear. Research (McGee, 2000) and practice (Sylvern, Karyl and Landis, 1995) with children strongly suggests that – as with child sexual abuse – children need to be helped to disclose and respond over time by employing sensitive questioning or through play techniques. This may take a long time and constant reassurance that what they say will be believed. Where the violence runs alongside physical or sexual abuse, the child may only feel safe enough to tell if the abuser has left the home (Forman, 1995).

Assessment and safety

In any event, the need to thoroughly assess the child's immediate safety needs by enquiring into detail about the incidents, whether weapons or drug use is involved and what the child tries to do by way of personal defence, is paramount. Sec. 47 enquiries under the Children Act 1989, resulting in statutory intervention may be necessary. Taking age into account, a personal safety plan should then be developed ensuring, among other things, that children know how to contact emergency and other services. This should be accompanied by an assessment of significant harm, including considering the known emotional effects as well as listening carefully to how the child has experienced the violence. There is a need to look also at protective factors. Resilience is known to affect how children deal with trauma (Gilligan, 2001), so it is not just the severity and form of the violence that has to be considered in relation to emotional abuse. Gilligan helpfully draws attention to the important role of school and teachers in promoting self-esteem through social activities and personal support.

While there may not be pressing issues of physical safety, all agencies where children present with physical, emotional, educational or behavioural problems should take the possibility of domestic violence into account in their assessment.

Interventions

While children will react differently and their needs vary, it is likely that all children will benefit from some support and validation of their experiences, including that they are not responsible for the violence. Some, depending upon the assessment of need, will require longer term therapeutic help. Some interventions are:

- Individual work that is age appropriate. The range of therapeutic approaches can include talking, such as telling and retelling the story, and play therapy. In non-directive play therapy the approach might be to enable the child to reflect upon and explore their feelings, or to discuss feelings of guilt and responsibility. The therapist provides a safe place, positive attention and containment for the child's often angry feelings.
- Exploring children's personal constructs can aid in helping children to resist taking on inappropriate family roles, such as assuming a parental role towards a sibling. Cognitive-behavioural approaches have also been found helpful in dealing with children's self-perceptions. Grych (2000) discusses the impact of living with violence on working models and the need, therefore, to work on understanding relationships. In contributing to understanding the difference between anger which is OK, and violence which is not, re-education might include teaching different models of how to manage anger and conflict. Such work should not be done in isolation, so it is important to feed back to the parent what is being done.
- Group work is of value, providing the opportunity to share experience in a safe place. This can help to reduce feelings of stigma and isolation. The younger the child the more activity-based the group should be, focusing on recovering from the impact. Two programmes in Canada provide models of group-work interventions, both requiring an intake assessment interview and that mothers also join a treatment programme. The Ontario model, for children aged 8–13, focused on enabling children to understand their feelings, deal with anger, develop self-esteem and explore safety skills; and one part of the Domestic Abuse Programme (DAP) in Minneapolis employed groups with children working on 'breaking the secret', defining violence and assigning responsibility. In evaluating the DAP, Peled and Edelson (1992) reinforced the need to also work with mothers in finding that, while the objectives outlined above were largely met, an unintended outcome was that mothers became frustrated because the children did not tell them what was going on in the group. In the UK, such groups as have got off the ground have taken place mainly in refuges, or in voluntary agencies such as Family Service Units.

Work with men

Only in the last decade, and with the shiftings in attitude described above, has the need to work with men become accepted in the UK. Most work with men has been under compulsory schemes, generally run by Probation. Otherwise, and increasingly, work is being undertaken largely by voluntary organisations, sometimes with statutory funding or in conjunction with domestic violence fora. This development is important because many men do not appear before the courts, and few are placed on probation. The big issue is, are men motivated to change? Even where attendance on a programme is part of a court order, Wallace (2001) found that assessments of suitability often did not include judgments about men's motivation, and only a tiny number of perpetrators came forward for help in any event. One-to-one work assessing men's motivations and suitability for group work is therefore an important preliminary to any intervention, and may suggest group work to be inappropriate. A history of mental ill-health or substance abuse may preclude or suggest delay to a treatment programme, while strong denial or a history of abuse may indicate the need for individual sessions (as with Mr Clark, above).

The literature suggests that the most effective interventions share similar characteristics, such as that men accept that their behaviour is abusive and take responsibility for it and are prepared to track violent incidents and the associated emotions and events. Dobash *et al.* (1996) provide a framework delineating the process of change in working with men achieved through talking, learning, listening and thinking, and dependent on the following:

- men need to see change as possible and desirable;
- men need to have reasons to change (which may include awareness of the costs and benefits, as well as other means of promoting their low self-esteem);
- men change from object to subject (they develop an awareness of their own behaviour and choices);
- men move from external to internal constraints;
- men shift their language and thinking to expand their emotional and cognitive landscape;
- men identify specific elements of change in both behaviour and attitudes.

Scourfield (1995), found that most work with violent men is carried out in groups. There are over 30 projects in the UK of mainly group work and some offering individual and couple therapy. Most group work is focused, using profeminist cognitive behavioural approaches, and may include groups with an educational element such as the DVI described above. Group workers maintain that groups are more effective in addressing feelings and defences and in helping men to develop alternative strategies for dealing with their violence. Individual and couple work may be more useful for working on personal or relationship difficulties. Developing self-esteem and a sense of agency in other areas of their lives, such as employment or through education, may help to reduce the need to feel powerful by resorting to violence in relationships. Work on communication skills was found by Moran and Wilson (1999) to be particularly useful in enabling men to develop understanding of the need to communicate with their partner, rather than simply their ability to communicate. Where they recognised the need to communicate – and then did so – their behaviour and attitudes began to change. Teaching anger management is another method used to enable men to think differently about dealing with situations that make them angry so that they can control their impulsive aggression, while at the same time suggesting new ways of communicating feelings and reducing stress. However, critics suggest that anger is not a necessary component of violence and that the issue of power and control is not addressed by this approach.

The need to evaluate one-to-one work taking place between practitioners and offenders is pressing. As stated at the beginning of this chapter, many social workers working in situations of family support and child protection, as well as the range of workers in health, education and criminal justice, will be working with families where there is domestic violence. They may well not have the confidence to engage with a violent man, and suggestions have been made as to how such engagement could be encouraged by training and sustained by good supervision and agency support. As Heard has suggested in Chapter 4, agencies need to mirror the support to and nurturing of their staff. One-to-one work is necessary for assessment purposes and as a necessary prelude to group-work. However, since the numbers referred to group work programmes represent a tiny proportion of male perpetrators, there is an urgent need for practitioners to develop skills and confidence in engaging and working with violent men. The aims could be to help men to identify cues for violence, to acknowledge the effects on women and children, to rebuild relationships where violence has taken place, or to let go of relationships where the partner wishes it to end. Whatever the intervention it should not be based on an objective of keeping partners together, and contact should be maintained with the woman throughout.

Conclusion

This chapter has reviewed the research on domestic violence, its impact on women and children and explored initiatives in place to enable families and communities to prevent violence from happening in the first place, as well as to mitigate some of its most damaging effects. It has suggested areas that it would be helpful for practitioners to focus on in making their assessments so that the interventions can focus on need as well as risk, taking into account individual motivations and capacity to change as well as the broader structural issues at play. The theoretical framework found most apposite for enabling practitioners to work with individuals, families and communities in the ways described is a systemic one. More than any other area of social work practice, what seems essential to help these families is for every locality to provide a range of services within all statutory sectors, to fund provision in the voluntary sector and to ensure that professionals working at primary and secondary levels within their community develop preventative services for families experiencing domestic violence. The case for focused as well as general provision is also clear, as is the need to provide a range of individual, couple and group-work services for the men, women and children involved.

References

Abrahams, C. (1994) *The Hidden Victims – Children and Domestic violence*. London: NCH Action for Children.
Adams, E. (1998) *Asian Survivors of Domestic Violence*. Social Work Monographs, Norwich: University of East Anglia.
Bandura, A. (1973) *Aggression: a social learning analysis*. Englewood Cliffs, N.J.: Prentice-Hall.
Bell, M. (1999) *Child Protection: Families and the Conference Process*, Andover: Ashgate.
— (2000) 'Social Work Responses to Domestic Violence within the Context of Child Protection', in U. McCluskey and C.-A. Hooper, *Psychodynamic Perspectives on Abuse: The Cost of Fear*. London: Jessica Kingsley.
— (1996) *A Survey of the Needs of and Service Provision for Children and Young People in Leeds who have Witnessed/Experienced Domestic Violence*. York: University of York.
— (2002) 'Promoting Children's Rights through the Use of Relationship', *Child and Family Social Work*, vol. 7(1), pp. 1–11.
Burton, S., Regan, L. and Kelly, L. (1998) *Supporting Women and Challenging Men: Lessons from the Domestic Violence Intervention Project*. Bristol: Policy Press.
Brandon, M. and Lewis, A. (1996) 'Significant Harm and Children's Experiences of Domestic Violence', *Child and Family Social Work*, vol. 1(1), pp. 33–42.
Change Project, The (1996)
Cleaver, H. and Freeman, P. (1995) *Parental Perspectives in Cases of Suspected Child Abuse: Studies in Child Protection*. London: HMSO.
Cleaver, H., Unell, I. and Aldgate, J. (1999) *Children's Needs – Parenting Capacity: The Impact of Parental Mental Illness, Problem Alcohol and Drug Use and Domestic Violence on Children's Development*. London: HMSO.
Department of Health (DoH) (2000) *Working Together to Safeguard and Promote the Welfare of Children*.
— (2000) *The New Framework for the Assessment of Children in Need and their Families*, London: HMSO.
Dobash, R., Dobash, R. E., Cavanagh, K. and Lewis, R. (1996) *Research Evaluation of programmes for violent men*. Edinburgh: HMSO.
Edelson, J. L. and Tolman, R. M. (1992) *Intervention for Men who Batter. An Ecological Approach*. Newbury Park: Sage.
Edelson, J. (1999) 'Children's Witnessing of Adult Domestic Violence', *Journal of Interpersonal violence*, vol. 14, pp. 839–70.
Ezell, E., McDonald, R. and Jouriles, E. N. (2000) 'Helping Children of Battered Women: A Review of Research, Sampling of Programmes and Presentation of Project Support', in J. P. Vincent and E. N. Jouriles (eds), *Domestic Violence: Guidelines for Research Informed Practice*. London: Jessica Kingsley.
Farmer, E. and Owen, M. (1995) *Child Protection Practice: Private Risks and Public Remedies*. London: HMSO.
Farmer, E. and Pollock, S. (1998) *Substitute Care for Sexually Abused and Abusing Children*. Chichester: Wiley.

Forman, J. (1995) *Is there a Correlation between Child Sexual Abuse and Domestic Violence? An Exploratory Study of the Links between Child Sexual Abuse and Domestic Violence in a Sample of Interfamilial Child Sexual Abuse Cases.* Glasgow: Woman's Support Project.

Frude, N. (1993) *Understanding Family Problems: A Psychological Approach.* Chichester: Wiley.

Gilligan, R. (2001) *Promoting Resilience: A Resource Guide on Working with Children in the Care System.* London: BAAF.

Grych, J. H. (2000) 'Children's Perspectives of family violence: implications for research and interventions', in J. P. Vincent and E. N. Jouriles (eds), *Domestic Violence: Guidelines for Research Informed Practice.* London: Jessica Kingsley.

Hague, G., Malos, E., Mullender, A. with Debbonaire, T. (1996) *Children, domestic violence and refuges: A study of needs and responses.* Bristol: Women's Aid Federation.

Hanmer, J. and Griffith, S. (2000) *Policing Domestic Violence.* London: Home Office.

Harbison, J. (2000) 'The Repudiated Self: The Failure of Social Welfare Policy for Older People', in U. McCluskey and C.-A. Hooper, (eds), *Psychodynamic Perspectives on Abuse.* London: Jessica Kingsley.

Hearn, J. (1996) 'The Organisation of Violence: Men, Gender relations, Organisations and Violence', in B. Faucet, B. Featherstone, J. Hearn and C. Toft C. (eds), *Violence and Gender Relations,: Theories and Interventions.* London: Sage.

Hester, M. and Pearson,C. (1998) *From Periphery to Centre – Domestic Violence in Work with Abused Children.* Bristol: Policy Press.

Hester, M., Pearson, C and Harwin, N. (2000) *Making an Impact: Children and Domestic Violence; A Reader.* London: Jessica Kingsley.

Home Office (1990) *Circular 60/90, Domestic violence.* London: Home Office.

Humphreys, C. (2000) *Social Work, Domestic Violence and Child Protection: Challenging Practice.* Bristol: Policy Press.

Humphreys, C., Mullender, M. Lowe, P., Hague, G., Abrahams, H. and Hester, M. (2001) 'Domestic Violence and Child Abuse: Developing Sensitive Policies and Guidance', *Child Abuse Review,* vol. 19, pp. 183–97.

Humphreys, C. and Mullender, A. (in press) in Howarth and Stanlow (eds) *Making Links: Assessment and Roses across Social Work Specialisms.*

Jukes, A. (1999) *Men Who Batter Women.* London: Routledge.

Kelly, L. and Humphreys, C. (2000) *Outreach and Advocacy Approaches.* London: Home Office.

Kelly, S. (2001) *An Exploratory Study of Child and Adolescent Mental Health Workers Practice and Approaches with Child Witnesses of Domestic Violence and Their Families.* MSW dissertation, York: University of York.

Lorenz, K. (1966) *On Aggression.* New York: Harcourt, Brace and World.

Mcgibbon, A., Cooper, L. and Kelly, L. (1989) *What support? Hammersmith and Fulham Council Community police Committee Domestic Violence Project.* London: Polytechnic of North London.

Mezey, G. C., and Bewley, S. (1997) 'Domestic Violence and Pregnancy', *British Medical Journal,* 314.

McGee, C. (2000) *Children's Experiences of Domestic Violence.* London: Jessica Kingsley.

Milner, J. (1996) 'Men's Resistance to Social Workers', in B. Fawcett, B. Featherstone, J. Hearn and C. Toft, (eds.) *Violence and Gender Relations: Theories and Interventions.* London: Sage.

Mirlees-Black, C. (1999) *Domestic violence: Findings from the New British Crime Survey Self Completion Questionnaire.* London: Home Office.

Moran, D. and Wilson, M. (1999) 'Working with Men who are Violent to Partners – Striving for Good Practice', in H. Kemshell and J. Pritchard, (eds), *Good Practice in Working with Violence.* London: Jessica Kingsley.

Mullender, A. (1996) *Rethinking Domestic Violence: The Social Work and Probation Response*. London: Routledge.

Peled, E. (1997) 'Intervention with Children of Battered Women: A Review of Current Literature'. *Children and Youth Services Review*, vol. 19(4), pp. 277–99.

Ptacek, J. (1988) 'Why do Men Batter their Wives', in K. Yllo and M. Bograd (eds), *Feminist Perspectives on Wife Abuse*. Newbury Park: Sage.

Saunders, D. G. (1995) *It hurts me too: children's experiences of domestic violence and refuge life*. WAFE/Childline/NISW, Bristol.

Schreiber, (1996)

Scourfield, J. (1995) *Changing men*. Norwich: University of East Anglia.

Sinclair, D. (1985) *Understanding wife assault: a training manual for counsellors and advocates*. Ontario: Toronto.

Stanley, N. (1997) 'Domestic Violence and Child Abuse: Developing Feminist Social Work Practice', *Child and Family Social Work*, vol. 2, pp. 135–45.

Sylvern, L. Karyl, J. and Landis, T. (1995) 'Individual Psychotherapy for the Traumatised Child of Abused Women', in E. Peled, P. Jaffe and J. L. Edelson (eds), *Ending the Cycle of Violence: Community Responses to Children of Battered Women*. Newton Park: Sage.

Robertson, N. (1999) 'Stopping Violence Programmes: Enhancing the Safety of Battered Women or Producing Better Educated Batterers', *New Zealand Journal of Psychology*, vol. 28(2), pp. 68–78.

Walby, S. and Myhill, A. (2000) *Reducing Domestic violence...what works? Assessing and managing the risk of domestic violence*. Crime Reduction Series, London: Home Office.

Wallace, A. (2001) *Interventions with men who use violence against their female partners/wives*. MSW dissertation, York: University of York.

10

Working with Families who Neglect their Children

Dorota Iwaniec

Introduction

Current knowledge relating to child neglect points to the existence of a rather absurd paradox. On the one hand, child neglect has consistently been shown to have a markedly higher incidence rate than either physical or sexual abuse, and furthermore has been found to result in more profound developmental deficit than other forms of child maltreatment. On the other hand, however, child neglect is the most understudied and consequently the least understood type of child maltreatment. Given that so many children experience neglect of one sort or another, and that its outcomes can be profoundly harmful, there is an urgent requirement for practitioners and the decision-making forums to re-evaluate current practices and policies in relation to neglected children.

This chapter will discuss the thorny question of definitions of neglect as a complex and multi-faceted phenomena, and will review literature which points out that neglect of children by their carers is a long-term developmental issue, which creates many problems for practitioners and managers as evidence of long-term negative effects might be difficult to prove. The range of various practice issues facing practitioners working with families who neglect their children will be discussed. The case study will illustrate some methods and services used in parent-training and processes involved in dealing with such cases.

Definitions of child neglect

Zuravin (1999) stated that more than a decade ago the lack of a standard definition of child neglect was recognised as a fundamental problem in developing knowledge and better understanding of this type of child abuse. The fact that this problem prevails today is indicative of the lowly position that child neglect has held within the field of child abuse and neglect relative to physical and sexual abuse and, consequently, of the lack of substantive research that has specified this issue.

Definitions of child neglect vary considerably and reflect the diverse notions held by professionals, policy-makers, researchers and non-professionals as to what constitutes child neglect, and when it requires professional intervention. Some definitions focus upon the conditions of the child and exclude parental contribution (fault), while others hold the parents responsible due to their action or inaction for the child's neglected state. The Department of Health (DoH, 1999) defines neglect as

> the persistent failure to meet a child's basic physical and/or psychological needs, likely to result in the serious impairment of the child's health or development. It may involve a parent or carer failing to provide adequate food, shelter, and clothing; failing to protect a child from physical harm or danger; or the failure to ensure access to appropriate medical care or treatment. It may also include neglect of, or unresponsiveness to, a child's basic emotional needs.

The problem with the above definition is its generality. It gives a good description of the issues involved, but does not operationalise specific parental behaviours or child outcomes. One can argue that practitioners and decision-makers are left with substantial freedom to interpret the affects of neglectful parental behaviour and its harmful effects on the child's development and well-being. It is presumed that professional knowledge regarding child development and behaviour is good enough to judge whether the quality of parenting and parental conduct generally is adequate to protect child welfare, or, if it is not, then some action needs to be taken to deal with parenting deficiencies or harm inflicted on the child.

In order to overcome the numerous ambiguities, researchers often develop their own definitions which allow them to investigate various factors in a more independent and measurable way. Rose and Meezan (1993) identified nine components of neglect – inadequate food, clothing, shelter, supervision, medical care, emotional care, education, exploitation and unwholesome circumstances. Furthermore, neglect is described by them as a chronic form of maltreatment, unlike physical abuse which tends to be episodic. Erickson and Egeland (1996) suggested that neglect represents persistent failure on the part of parents to meet the basic needs of the developing child, in both the physical and psychosocial domains, and English (1998) described neglect as an act of omission by a parent or caregiver that involves refusal or delay in providing healthcare, failure to provide basic needs such as food, clothing, shelter, affection and attention, inadequate supervision or abandonment. This failure to act holds true for both physical and emotional neglect.

Iwaniec (1995) argued that as emotional neglect has a profound effect on child development, in particular self-esteem, self-confidence and social competence, practitioners need to pay careful attention when assessing the child and the parents. Emotional neglect refers to passive omission of children's emotional needs in terms of warmth and supportive nurturing, giving attention to signals of distress and responding to these signals promptly and consistently. Providing stimulation by talking, playing and doing things with the child, providing encouragement, praise, guidance, control and protection from danger and creating an atmosphere where the child feels secure, safe and welcomed. Emotional neglect and abuse are interlinked and are common features in chronically neglectful families. This is particularly observed in alcohol-abusing and violent families. Emotional abuse, therefore, should be taken into consideration as a possible factor when assessing neglect, especially in the areas of interpersonal relationships and a child's attachment behaviour to primary care-givers.

Parents and carers who persistently criticise, shame, rebuke, threaten, ridicule, humiliate, put down, induce fear and anxiety, who are never satisfied with the child's behaviour and performance, are emotionally abusive. Equally, those who distance themselves from the child – by ignoring signals of distress, pleas for help, attention, comfort, reassurance, encouragement, and acceptance – are emotionally abusive and neglectful. Their behaviour towards the child can be described not only as neglectful but overtly abusive, actively painful, and emotionally and cognitively damaging (Iwaniec, 1995).

The key problem in defining neglect is in establishing what may be considered minimally adequate levels of care. There is general agreement as to what constitutes inadequate care, however when it comes to defining at what point it should be considered as unacceptable and harmful to the child on a short- and long-term basis, it remains still unresolved and also controversial. Difficulties in establishing universal criteria for the thresholds of minimal care make decision-making and planning for these children hard to do, as these may vary depending upon the child's age, resilience or vulnerability, or the values that a particular community may hold.

Additionally, defining child neglect at any given time or context will depend heavily upon current political and moral ideals regarding what is considered adequate care for children and the strength of social policy or political will to ensure that these ideals are met. It also depends on the professional's ideology and interpretation of the childcare legislation. If practitioners, managers and policy-makers strongly believe that children are better off at home in spite of very poor care they receive, then their decision in respect of neglected children will be different to those who regard ongoing neglect as developmentally harmful and detrimental to achieving potentials and preparing them for life and adequate functioning. Equally, if neglected children will be considered, as they often are, as the last in the queue to get appropriate allocation of services, then the duty of protecting their welfare and facilitating positive change will not be fulfilled.

Stone (1998) stated on the basis of his study of 20 neglect cases that neglect is a complex and multifaceted phenomenon which cannot easily be defined. It is generally found that there is not one specific factor which, looked at in isolation, could be said to define neglect or detect its presence or absence. Cases studied tend to have a long history of social work involvement and, furthermore, it was observed that an accumulation of worrying factors over time had led to registration. Additionally, it was found that factors relating to parents were very commonly cited by practitioners and thus seem central to the way neglect is defined in practice. Many parents were found to have a history of neglect and abuse, and over a half had been through a care system. Furthermore, substance abuse, mental illness and learning difficulties were commonplace. Research and practice evidence suggests that neglectful parents are ill-prepared emotionally and practically to care for children, and are significantly damaged.

Failures in parenting

To understand why neglectful parents are unable to meet even the very basic developmental needs of their children, we need to look at their characteristics and functioning as individuals and parents. Firstly, their life experiences from early childhood have not given them opportunities to learn appropriate caring behaviours, which would inform their own parenting and learning of interpersonal skills which are essential for good-enough parenting.

Sroufe and Fleeson (1986) noted that care-giving deficiencies may result from parents' own experiences of neglect and abuse. The most consistent finding in research and practice is that abusive and neglecting mothers regularly report that they themselves were physically, sexually or emotionally abused, and/or neglected as children (De Panfilis and Salas, 1992). This is consistent with the early work of Maslow (1970) which suggested that when an individual does not have his/her own developmental needs met, then they in turn may find it very difficult to meet the needs of their own children.

Secondly, neglectful parents usually grow up and raise their own children in a socio-economic environment which inhibits or neglects the needs of families living in deprived communities, thus preventing them from learning new behaviours which would facilitate positive parenting. Thirdly, they tend to be undereducated and of modest intellectual abilities, have little insight of what is missing from their approach to child-rearing and are living in a social system that is materially, socially and emotionally impoverished. Fourthly, neglecting parents tend to be unresponsive and withdrawn and never apply discipline. Children, in turn, imitate parental apathy and initiate their own stimulation which tends to be destructive and at times dangerous. Christensen (1999) stated that neglectful parents were incapable of interpreting verbal and physical signals made by their children, and were unable to distinguish between their own and their children's needs. They generally present themselves as socially and emotionally immature.

Fifthly, findings based on research and practice data postulate that neglectful mothers have significantly lower self-concepts, lower perceptions of moral self-worth and adequacy as family members. Furthermore, they show negative perceptions of their identities and low self-concepts in relation to interpersonal relationships.

Urquiza and Winn (1992) pointed out that neglecting mothers may have problems coping with the demands of an intimate relationship and may not comprehend the required cues and interactions, given their own emotional instability. As a result the attachment relationship with their children is damaged. Consequently, the children do not acquire basic social skills and thus go on themselves to perpetuate the same dysfunctional child/parent relationship. Furthermore, Main and Goldwyn (1984) found that women who had been maltreated as children but were not neglecting their own children had strong marriages, high self-esteem and had consciously acknowledged their past abusive experiences. These findings suggest that the maintenance of intimate relationships in adulthood and a recognition of childhood neglect and abuse may protect against intergenerational transmission of neglect. These can be accomplished by appropriate intervention and treatment as well as life chances, such as meeting a caring and understanding partner, or coming to live in a socially and emotionally supportive environment.

Sixthly, frequent bouts of depression and general apathy contribute to an inability to engage physically and emotionally with their children. More importantly, they do not believe that they are capable, through their own efforts, of making positive changes. Neither do they believe that anyone can help them to produce the necessary change. There is an air of helplessness, a lack of purpose, goals, motivation and drive.

To compensate for the emptiness in their lives they tend to revert to drinking, drug use and engaging in short-term cohabitations which often leaves them even more debilitated as individuals and parents, as these relationships are often violent and exploitive both for the mother and children. Poor ability to form and maintain positive relationships does not facilitate an enormous need to be loved, wanted, appreciated or to belong. It is often seen that they care more for their co-habitees than they do for their children (Polansky, 1992; Oliver and Buchanan, 1979). Furthermore, they tend to repeat the same wrong choices over and over again, which leaves them and their children devoid of any stability, continuity and permanency, which are essential for emotional and social development.

Consequences of child neglect

The seriousness of child neglect is not always appreciated at early stages of professional involvement. This is not surprising since the consequences of neglect considered as reaching significant harm are not always obvious at the referral and assessment phase. There is also professional optimism and conviction that things can change and the quality of parenting can improve if there is some involvement and some service provision (I will come to discuss these points later). The research and practice literature tells us, however, a different story, highlighting that neglect of children by their carers is a long-term developmental issue and needs to be dealt with by looking at long-term prediction as the evidence confirms that it has the poorest long-term prognosis. Let us look at some research findings.

Egeland, Sroufe and Erickson (1983) found that children who were neglected had higher performance deficits on a range of tasks at both 42 and 56 months than a control group, and higher than those who were sexually or physically abused. By early school age it was found that the neglected group were exhibiting deficits in cognitive performance, academic achievement, classroom behaviour and social interactions. Egeland (1991) also found that by the second grade every neglected child was involved in some special remedial programme. The neglected children demonstrated greater developmental problems than any other maltreated group. Similarly, Eckenrode, Laird and Doris (1993) found that neglected children, when compared with children who had been physically or sexually abused, had the poorest school performance throughout the school years.

English (1998) argued that maltreating behaviours which are associated with ongoing neglect and with repeated emotional abuse result in cumulative harm, so the child's well-being and developmental trajectory is impaired. It is not surprising that neglected children suffer academically, emotionally and socially given that neglect may occur over a long time, and intellectual and psycho-social development is heavily dependent upon the ongoing quality of parent–child interaction and parental interest in a child. Carers' low educational aspiration, lack of encouragement for learning, a paucity of language stimulation, non-participation in school activities, and unresponsiveness to the child's achievements, all undermine school success and development of good self-esteem and a sense of achievement. Given the well-documented detrimental effects of poor school performance and lack of preparation for life in the home environment it is easy to see why neglected children face a future of marginalisation and poverty, such as unemployment because of lack of skills, poor housing, and living on a very low income.

Gauthier et al. (1996) found that physical and emotional neglect was significantly related to the range of psychological and relational problems such as anxiety, depression, somatisation, paranoia and hostility compared with those who reported physical abuse. These results suggested that neglect may be a stronger predictor of some psychological dysfunction in adulthood. The effects of emotional neglect and abuse are equally worrying. McCord (1983) carried out a longitudinal study, which compared abused, neglected and rejected boys with a group who had experienced love and nurturing over a 40 year period. It was found that maltreated boys had significantly higher levels of juvenile delinquency, with approximately 50 per cent of the abused and neglected boys being convicted of serious crimes, becoming alcoholics or suffering from mental illness. Similarly, Ney, Fung and Wickett (1994) found that emotional neglect may be more closely related to later development of psychiatric illnesses than any other form of abuse.

The long-term effects of neglect are beginning to emerge from various studies. Iwaniec (2000) and Iwaniec and Sneddon (2001) found from a 20-year follow-up of subjects who failed to thrive as children, that those who were neglected in childhood tend to neglect their own children as well. The long-term effect of the failure to thrive could still be seen 20 years after the initial referral, with these individuals being slightly shorter and lighter than average. Cognitive ability also appeared to be somewhat affected, with poorer educational attainments, high levels of unemployment, or inability to maintain work. However, not all subjects showed the same outcomes. Those who were referred during the first year of life for assessment and intervention and received help have done well, but those who came to attention between three and seven years of life and remained at home have shown poorer outcomes. This research suggests that early and decisive intervention is essential to break the cycle of neglect.

Practitioners' views of child neglect

A number of studies have demonstrated that social workers and managers often underestimate neglect and the long-term damage that it can have on children (Stevenson, 1996; Tomison, 1995; Stone, 1998). This is despite the fact that within the United Kingdom neglected children account for between one-quarter and one-half of all inter-agency child protection plans. It is also argued that neglect appears to be poorly understood in terms of theory which is reflected in the paucity of literature and empirical studies that deal specifically with neglect, and in the lack of child-neglect training for practitioners at different levels. Stone (1998) noted that neglect has a low public profile relative to physical and sexual abuse, and argues that this might be due to the fact that neglect tends to be a long-term developmental issue rather than an event-specific crisis; that there is not immediate danger and neglect, both of the physical and emotional kind; that it does not attract attention by the media or the general public in contrast to serious physical or sexual abuse; and that there is no sense of urgency also amongst professionals.

The problem of when and how to intervene in cases of emotional and physical neglect, including failure to thrive, was grossly overlooked prior to the Children Act and has continued to be marginalised in post-Act policy and practice. Neglected children do not get the attention they need (although they come under the category of children in need), and even when they do they tend to be dealt with briefly as a response to crisis, or worrying referrals of health visitors, teachers or neighbours and then are patched up and left without appropriate assessment and long-term action

(Iwaniec and Hill, 2000). Wilding and Thoburn's (1997) study found that although physical neglect was the largest category of child abuse, such cases were the lowest in resource allocation for family support. Equally, emotional abuse and neglect is seldom investigated in spite of the serious effects it has on children's self-esteem, self-confidence, social adjustment and emotional stability in general (Doyle, 1997; Glasier and Prior, 1997; Iwaniec, 1997a).

Minty and Pattinson (1994) also argued that neglect referrals are not dealt with promptly, in spite of the large body of evidence that neglect may have many negative outcomes and may increase the risk of the child being injured or killed. They pointed out that a significant number of child fatalities have been attributed to parental or care-giver neglect, but that professionals had failed to recognise the risk even in cases of severe neglect. Serious errors of judgment on the part of social services in leaving highly at-risk children with their parents are not infrequent. Fogarty (1993) noted that one of the main problems in these cases is that social workers can at times focus upon the rights of the parents to the detriment of the rights of the child, with the parents being given numerous opportunities to improve the family functioning which as a rule have little affect in chronic neglect cases. The emphasis upon family preservation is a fundamental tenet of the Children Act 1989, as well as working in partnership with parents. Those two legal requirements sit uncomfortably, create tension, and pose difficulties for those who work with families who neglect children. Some neglectful carers have no capacity to work constructively and systematically with social workers or others who try to help them. Some are unwilling and refuse to have any involvement with social workers, they do not open a door, are not home in spite of arranged visits to take a child to see the GP, for a hospital appointment, group work, attendance at a family centre and so on. They quite often refuse to have anybody advising them or directly trying to help them with parenting skills, and additionally they are often aggressive, both physically and verbally. While the hopeless struggle goes on between Social Services and the parents in question, the child's situation is as bad as it was before, so the concerns about the child which brought the attention of the Social Services in the first place are not dealt with, quite often because of parental lack of cooperation and Social Services' reluctance to accept that there is no point in going on trying to change the unchangeable over and over again.

It would appear that less attention is paid to the other requirements of the Children Act, such as parental responsibility, or that child welfare is paramount, and that delays in decision-making to secure child welfare should be avoided. Children cannot wait indefinitely, simply because ongoing serious neglect will affect their development and behaviour, which will be difficult to make good if it lasts a long time. It is useful to keep in mind that as the child grows the problems grow as well. Social workers tend to worry that they do not have enough evidence to prove that the criteria of significant harm have been met in order to take the case to Court. Let me quote Judge Martin Allweis (1999):

In my experience, once the evidence has been gathered, the problem is rarely whether the child has suffered harm or is likely to suffer harm, even significant harm. The evidence of neglect or emotional abuse is often overwhelming, so that the only real issue is not what has happened, but what should happen. In other words, is the care plan in the interest of the child. This often involves an assessment of whether the parents or extended family have the capacity or potential, with professional support, to change and be in a position to meet the child's needs within the child's time-scale.

The child's time-scale is of the essence. There must be a time limit set up for trying to improve the quality of childcare at home and general family functioning. If there is no improvement within the time-scale set by the case conference, with appropriate services in place, then removal from the home should be considered.

However, most cases of neglect do not need to go to Court, and we should be mindful that many children and their parents can be helped in the community, if appropriate services are provided based on assessed needs of the child and the parents. I say appropriate, as so often service provision does not match the child's needs and occasionally can do more harm than good; for example, a neglected child being placed in a short-term foster home where there are already four children, and the foster mother being unable to spend the required time with this particular child who needs a lot of stimulation and personal attention to deal with developmental deficit and disturbed behaviour.

It is now widely recognised (and this awareness is based on research studies and inspections of practice) that there needs to be a refocusing of children's services to embrace both child protection and services to children in need. The emphasis on child protection investigations at the expense of family support work has prevented practitioners from following through for the required time intervention to meet the family, and children's needs. In other words 'the cake must be sliced fairly' if the needs of vulnerable children are to be met. There must also be recognition that family support for some of those children and their parents will be required for years to come if they are to remain with the parents. Neglected children do not get a fair deal at present either from the Child Protection System or Family Support, as they are considered in the former as not serious enough and in the latter as not urgent enough. Generally, the 'wait and see' approach has been adopted when allocating services and processing referrals for action. When assessing parenting practitioners need to address the questions listed in Table 10.1.

TABLE 10.1 Assessment of parenting

The following questions need to be asked when assessing parenting:

1. Is there evidence which would indicate:

   (a) Acceptable/unacceptable physical care, e.g. feeding, dressing, changing nappies, bathing, keeping clean and warm, acceptable sleeping arrangements, safety;
   as evidenced by
   (b) positive/negative attitudes towards parental duties and responsibilities;
   as evidenced by
   (c) positive/negative attitudes towards the child;
   as evidenced by
   (d) parental lifestyle which might be contributing to the child's neglect and abuse: lack of routines, planning, communication, frequent changes of partners, poor management of money, chaotic daily functioning, hygiene;
   as evidenced by
   (e) harmful habits (alcohol, drug-abuse, criminal behaviour, prostitution, family violence, frequent changes of accommodation and places of living;
   as evidenced by
   (f) personal circumstances affecting positive parenting (single parents, poor housing, poverty, social isolation, poor health, unemployment, mental illness, immature personality);
   as evidenced by
   (g) parents' intellectual and cognitive functioning abilities of problem-solving;
   as evidenced by
   (h) passivity, withdrawal, inertia – learned helplessness affecting child's development and well-being;
   as evidenced by
   (i) parental childhood experiences of being parented.

2. Are parents aware of their children's developmental needs, i.e. importance of stimulation, supervision, regular schooling, boundaries of behaviour, regular meals, affection, protection?
   as evidenced by:
3. Are they concerned about the child's physical and psycho-social well-being? Do they ask for help;
   as evidenced by
4. Do they show affection and demonstrate a positive bond with the child?
   as evidenced by
5. What is the level, content, and quality of parent-child interaction?
   as evidenced by
6. What help and assistance were provided for parents to overcome parenting difficulties?
   as evidenced by
7. What use did they make of the help available to them?
   (a) level of cooperation with workers
   (b) working constructively towards set goals
   as evidenced by
8. Are they able to understand what is going wrong in their parenting and are they able and willing to work at it?

Practice issues

Child neglect, as we have seen, involves a complex spectrum of shortcomings in the care of children. Because competence and care-taking deficiencies are multidimensional, social work assessment should consider multiple domains, for example the level of stimulation; supervision; emotional availability and interest in the child; medical care and education; food; clothing; and other daily requirements to promote child health, development and well-being. As there are serious shortcomings in the way children are looked after, which can often result in extremely poor developmental outcomes, serious injuries or even death, assessment must cover both parental behaviour and the child's outcomes.

It is essential to examine the two sides of the coin:

(a) the quality of parenting and what stands in the way of adequate care provision; and
(b) how children are affected, or are likely to be affected, in terms of physical, emotional, cognitive, social and educational development.

It is also necessary to assess realistically whether parents are able to change or to learn better ways of caring for their children. Many types of neglectful behaviours are resistant or impossible to change, such as substance abuse, immature personality, mental illness and learning disabilities. When some of these factors are compounded with chronic poverty, lack of support and social isolation, then the likelihood of necessary change within the required time to facilitate developmental needs of a rapidly growing child is slim, if not impossible. The question we need to ask ourselves is 'is it fair to leave a child in the home which is hurtful and damaging to his/her development on a short- and long-term basis and stands in the way of achieving the child's potential?' Sadly, we often consider parents' needs first; and feel sorry for them because of the many problems that they are wittingly or unwittingly experiencing. But feeling sorry does not often help the acutely emotionally disturbed and unsocialised child, trapped in the parents' and his/her own misery. Children cannot wait indefinitely, and parents have a responsibility, as required by law, to provide a reasonable quality of care and to protect them from harm. If parents are unable to provide care because of their limitations or have difficulties which they find hard to overcome, then the State must step in to take parental responsibility or assist them on a regular basis to provide good enough care for their children.

Naturally, neglect has to be assessed in the same way in terms of significant harm criteria as other forms of abuse. We know enough about developmental norms to be able to judge how bad developmental attainments are impaired for a child's chronological age; we are quite capable of identifying various types and severity of emotional disturbances, for example enuresis, encopresis, compulsive stealing, lying, bizarre eating patterns, or depressive moods, withdrawal and severe inhibition. We know that persistent non-attendance at school will seriously curtail education, which in the long run will have an effect on employment and quality of life. We know that inadequate provision of nutrition can lead to malnutrition and failure to thrive which, when severe and persistent, can affect physical development in terms of weight, height and brain growth, and psychosocial attainments. We are aware that child health might be impaired or irreversibly damaged if medical care is not provided. We also know that many important psychological outcomes can be disrupted by deficiencies in parental care, such as cognitive development, socio-emotional competence, peer relationship and academic achievements. We know that neglected children tend to present behavioural problems and conduct disorders, problems in social relationships and less-competent behaviour.

Additionally, these children suffer from low self-esteem and self-confidence and appear to be socially isolated or are being bullied at school and in the neighbourhood. As a rule this is because of their shabby and dirty appearance and poor academic performance at school so they are considered as not worthwhile to be with.

A case study

Liza (6 years of age) and Ann (aged 4) were referred to Social Services by the school headteacher and a week later by the GP. The headteacher was concerned about Liza's poor school attendance, being late, very poor academic attainments, shabby unkempt appearance, and concerns that she came to school being hungry. The GP was concerned about the children's health in terms of Liza's asthma and eczema, which were not attended to, prescribed medication was not applied regularly, and follow-up appointments were not kept, and Ann's failure to thrive. There was also an anonymous telephone call from one of the neighbours, stating that the children were unsupervised, appeared to be starved and looked dirty. There had been a succession of boyfriends, but no-one had stayed long.

The assessment revealed that the mother was divorced due to her husband's alcoholic abuse and frequent domestic violence, which the children often witnessed. The mother presented herself as an immature person with moderate learning difficulties who constantly looked for new relationships and tended to get involved with men who had alcoholic dependency and little sense of responsibility towards her and her children. The house was dirty and chaotic, with dozens of empty beer and vodka bottles scattered around. The children's beds had only blankets and dirty pillows.

The children presented themselves as withdrawn, apathetic, looking tired and drawn, dressed shabbily and being dirty. Both of them were developmentally delayed for their chronological age in cognitive, emotional and social areas. Their socialisation was poor, lacking basic skills such as washing, bathing, toileting, eating and interacting appropriately with the peer group, for example observing rules of play, sharing, knowing how to respond to questions and how to react to social cues. Emotionally they were both unstable and volatile, lacking in confidence and reacting when frustrated either by throwing temper tantrums or becoming withdrawn, fearful and inhibited. Mother–daughter relationships were warm and they appeared to be attached to her, although in a rather insecure way. The quality and frequency of interactions was determined by the mother's different boyfriends' attitudes towards the children. Since the death of the grandmother they had no-one to turn to when things were difficult at home, either because of the mother's depression or because of her preoccupation with her boyfriends. General family support until two years ago came from the grandmother who lived nearby. Since her death the situation deteriorated and reached the point of everybody's concern regarding childcare and the mother's behaviour.

The health visitor who knew the family felt that the mother might respond to intensive family support and ongoing supervision, as deep down she loved her children and had simply lost a sense of direction in her life after a difficult marriage and the loss of her mother.

Problems identified at the case conference which required urgent attention were as follows:

1. both girls were developmentally delayed;
2. Ann was failing to thrive – her weight being under the third centile for over a year now;
3. both girls lacked basic social skills;
4. their hygiene and attention to basic needs like food, sleeping arrangements and stimulation were below minimum standards;
5. the girls' behaviour was emotionally volatile and they had frequent temper tantrums and outbursts of aggression;
6. Liza was socially isolated at school because of being dirty and being infested with lice;
7. Liza has missed about 45 per cent of schooling as she often refused to go to school, or her mother did not get up on time to send her to school.

Several parenting problems were identified:

1. poor parenting skills and lack of awareness of the children's developmental needs;
2. inability to organise daily routines, rules and tasks to promote predictability and a sense of security for children;
3. putting her emotional needs first, instead of the needs of the children;
4. frequent changes of partners, affecting stability and a sense of belonging for everybody concerned;
5. poor model of behaviour and lack of guidance and supervision required for young children;

6. little attention paid to hygiene and health of the children;
7. mother's bouts of depression;
8. low self-esteem and social isolation in the community;
9. poor management of money, for example buying ready-made meals instead of cooking, or buying alcohol which left her short of money by the middle of the week.

Certain strengths were identified such as:

1. protectiveness of children, if mother's partners were harsh to them;
2. deciding to get divorced because of domestic violence and alcohol abuse which was affecting the children's behaviour;
3. a good relationship between mother and children;
4. mother's admission that she has neglected her children in terms of cleanliness, provision of regular food, and not attending to the medical needs of Ann. She acknowledged that she had failed to see the value of supervision, stimulation, regular school attendance and spending quality time with them.

Helping strategies for parents

Various research findings tell us that, more than anything, neglecting parents lack a belief in the efficacy of their own efforts. They also lack skills in parenting and problem-solving in their lives generally. It seems appropriate, therefore, that intervention efforts be focused on parent training using positive reinforcement to shape and encourage emerging skills. Parent training should include developmental counselling to raise parental awareness of what are those developmental needs of children and how parents can facilitate their achievement.

Additionally, cognitive counselling would be of benefit here to help parents to begin viewing things in a way which generates positive thoughts, beliefs and feelings about their capabilities of finding a way out of a problem, and to generate emotional energy to take action based on the conviction that they are able to produce change. This can be achieved only if parents experience some level of success by practising newly-introduced skills and be given credit for it by massive reinforcement provided by the practitioner.

Repetitions of small achievements produced by the successful reenactment of the performance of tasks will lead gradually to stronger self-esteem. The heightened self-efficacy leads to more vigorous, persistent and probably more successful attempts to cope with problems, while successful problem-solving further increases perceived self-effectiveness. Thus, if a mother succeeds in changing one problem, for example providing regular meals for her children or sending them to school clean on a regular basis, then her expectation of further success should increase. Such self-observed

TABLE 10.2 Helping neglected children and neglectful parents

Prevention and family support are thought to be the best helping strategies.

1. Attending to the family's material needs, housing, benefits, heating, clothing etc.
2. Provision of long-term family support in terms of meeting children's basic needs by provision of outside and home-based services.
3. Provision of day-care for preschool children, and recreational activities for school-age children – in order to receive sensitive responses to his/her own behaviour and to engage in cognitively stimulating experiences.
4. Training parents in parenting skills, regarding physical and psycho-social care of their children;
   (a) attending Family Centres or other family support training sessions;
   (b) getting individual training at home;
   (c) ongoing supervision and demonstration of parenting skills.

Training parents might include:

1. Developmental counselling exploring psycho-social care of children, the physical environment and unrealistic expectations.
2. Helping parents to set up routines of everyday living, proper boundaries of behaviour, family rules and expectations.
3. The importance of stimulation, communication, reasoning and exploration.
4. Personal and couple counselling regarding their aims and goals in life, understanding their own and their childrens' needs and feelings.
5. Increasing mother's self-efficacy by using positive reinforcement to shape emerging parenting skills.
6. Cognitive work to enable parents to recognise and label their own feelings, beliefs and thoughts, and later the emotions and beliefs of others.
7. Intervention should be directed to the community at large where poverty and disadvantage is widespread.

success is the most potent and rewarding source of increased self-confidence and motivation.

Neglectful parents appear to be unaware of their partners and children's feelings. The absence of appropriate affective display prevents the mutual flow of communication between family members. Training parents to enable them to feel, show and recognise their own and later others' emotions is needed, and some family therapy techniques would be useful here. Table 10.2 shows some possible helping methods for neglectful parents.

Intervention plan for the mother and children

Helping strategies in respect of Liza, Ann and their mother were organised on a crisis-intervention basis to start with and then longer-term family support. The mother played an active role in discussing what was needed in order to minimise developmental deficit and to promote her chuldrens' welfare on a daily basis. The mother was told very clearly and openly that the way she looked after her children was unacceptable, and if she wanted them to remain at home she would have to pay more attention to their needs and change the pattern of her behaviour and functioning. The mother was asked what she thought she needed to help her become a better parent and a happier person herself. Several suggestions were put forward which were in line with the assessed needs, so she could choose what seemed most comfortable, acceptable and workable for her. An agreement was made between Social Services and the mother to evaluate progress on a weekly basis and targets were set as to what needed to be done to help the children and the mother and what had to be done to provide necessary change.

Crisis intervention

The first step in the helping package was to arrange a Family Centre placement for Ann to deal with developmental deficits. The daily attendance was meant to provide, firstly, appropriate stimulation, good quality physical and emotional care, and provision of attention to facilitate her unmet needs, such as acquiring various socialisation tasks like playing, learning to share with other children, eating and toileting behaviour, dressing, washing and communicating, and so forth. Secondly, it was intended to build-up self-confidence by creating opportunities for gradual achievements and providing praise to boost the child's motivation to do even better.

It was agreed that the mother would attend a parent training group twice a week and would be seen there by a social worker to discuss personal issues regarding her problems and needs. It was agreed that the mother would bring Ann to the nursery and collect her at the end of the day, since it was a short walking distance from where they lived. It was felt that taking Ann to the nursery, would give the mother a sense of responsibility and a tangible task to do each day.

Liza's medical problems, such as dealing with eczema and asthma, were to be addressed by the health visitor and supervised for the first two weeks. The mother was asked to take Liza to the school bus each morning in clean clothing after having breakfast. She was to meet her after school, provide tea, and play with both of them for a little while. She was instructed how to apply ointment for Liza's eczema and medication for asthma. It was agreed that Family Aid would come twice a week to help with setting up routines, advising on budgeting and housework. It was envisaged that it was a short-term arrangement to start the mother off and to support her during the early stages of intervention.

It was necessary to provide some financial help in terms of getting some clothing and bedding for the children and to provide home help (3–4 times) to help mother clean the house and bring it to a reasonable level of hygiene.

Although services were provided it was not a passive exercise; mother was involved in every task, had to play a part and take responsibility for the work to be accomplished.

The families like the one we are discussing might require ongoing long-term family support. Some of them are unable to function adequately as parents without help because of their limitations such as learning difficulties, mental health problems, immaturity or substance abuse, and quite often because of their damaged up-bringing. Additionally, low self-esteem, social isolation and accompanying depression do not facilitate adequate provision of parenting and meeting minimum standards of children's developmental needs. It is therefore essential to provide help and supervision for more severe cases until the children reach the age when they can look after themselves and are able to communicate their needs to helping professions such as doctors, social workers, teachers, or people and organisations in the community. Premature closing of the case might lead to rapid deterioration. It is advisable, therefore, to monitor the case for while.

Ongoing long-term family support

In order not to let things drift back, fortnightly home visits might be needed to maintain new routines and to give encouragement and advice. There is also a necessity for coordination between the school, health visitor, GP and Family Centre. It is advisable to do regular case reviews to monitor progress and the necessity for either reducing or increasing services.

It is advisable, whenever possible, to find organisations, clubs or interest groups for the children to provide extra stimulation and to give them opportunities for appropriate social interaction and various learning and leisure activities. School teachers are very good at making such arrangements as they know what is available and what would be suitable for a particular child. Liza, for example, joined a 'drawing club' and showed considerable talent in drawing animals. She won a painting competition in the school, which accelerated her self-esteem and in turn improved her position in the classroom.

It is also important to link parents to some worthwhile community activities. Organisations attached to churches can quite often offer some participation in the parish activities. Ann and Liza's mother helped in preparing a garden fête and then selling lottery tickets. She was so pleased that people talked to her and that they commented that both girls looked well and were very nice. These experiences, rare as they might be, provide powerful morale boosters and can energise people to do more and to deal with more complicated tasks especially if some cognitive work is provided as well. As we know, the common characteristics of neglectful parents are their low self-esteem and conviction that they cannot do anything themselves and that they have no control over what happens to them. These dysfunctional thoughts lead to dysfunctional feelings, and consequently to negative outcomes for the parents and for the children. It is important, whenever possible, to create opportunities for these parents so they can experience pleasure, deriving from accomplished tasks, so they can generate emotional energy to take action based on the conviction that they can produce good change in their own and their children's lives.

There is ample evidence to suggest that continuity of family support would prevent many children coming into care (Wilding and Thoburn, 1997; Pinkerton, Higgins and Devine, 2000). There is also ample evidence that 'quick fixing' and premature closure of chronic neglect cases invariably does not solve the problems; the case will come back with bigger and more serious problems to be dealt with. In many instances children at that stage are so damaged that there is little hope for effective intervention in the community; they will become the next generation of neglectful and abusive parents, leading unsatisfactory and empty lives. To prevent this happening we need to help their parents for as long as is necessary if they show some commitment and willingness to improve childcare practices and if they have the capacity to do so. However, if attempts to help and engage parents in better parenting fail, the decision to remove the child from home should be dealt with promptly and decisively.

Conclusion

Every practitioner and researcher finds child neglect difficult to deal with. In order to establish that neglect is harmful and then to take action, evidence has to be gathered in a systematic way over a period of time, rather than at a specific point in time. Very often abuse and neglect are treated as if they are one and the same, which results in abuse being more thoroughly studied, because it is easier to identify. Cases of neglect are often minimised or ignored, partly because of difficulties in substantiating anything but severe neglect. It is suggested that neglect of neglect occurs because cases do not contain enough 'drama' to spark the child protection system into action.

What is abundantly clear is that child neglect has been starved of recognition relative to other forms of child abuse and that this imbalance needs to be addressed as a matter of urgency. What is also clear is that neglect can result in more profound cognitive, social and psychological deficit than is the case for physical and sexual abuse, and these facts need to be accepted so that appropriate interventions are put in place at an early stage. Identifying neglect in its infancy, however, requires that practitioners first of all recognise neglect when it is present, and secondly feel compelled to do something about it. If neglected children and neglectful families are to be rescued from the ravages of cyclical neglect, it is imperative that neglect ceases to be the poor relation within the field of child maltreatment.

References

Allweis, M. (1999) *Neglect and Assessment – A Judicial Perspective*. Conference Paper, Rochdale Area Child Protection Committee.

Christensen, E. (1999) 'The Prevalence and Nature of Abuse and Neglect in Children under Four: A National Survey', *Child Abuse Review*, vol. 8, pp. 109–119.

De Panfilis, D. and Salas, M. K. (1992) *A Co-ordinated Response to Child Abuse and Neglect: A Basic Manual*. US Department of Health and Human Services, DHHS Publications no. (ACF) 92-30362, pp. 1–66.

Department of Health (DoH) (1999) *Working Together to Safeguard Children*. London: The Stationery Office.

Doyle, C. (1997) 'Emotional Abuse of Children: Issues for Intervention', *Child Abuse Review*, vol. 6, pp. 330–42.

Eckenrode, J., Laird, M. and Doris, J. (1993) 'School Performance and Disciplinary Problems Among Abused and Neglected Children', *Developmental Psychology*, vol. 29, pp. 53–62.

Egeland, B. (1991) 'A Longitudinal Study of High-Risk Families: Issues and Findings', in R. H. Starr and D. A. Wolfe (eds), *The Effects of Child Abuse and Neglect: Issues and Research*. New York: Guilford, pp. 33–56.

Egeland, B., Sroufe, L. A. and Erickson, M. (1983) 'The Developmental Consequences of Different Patterns of Maltreatment', *Child Abuse and Neglect*, vol. 7, pp. 459–69.

English, D. J. (1998) 'The Extent and Consequences of Child Maltreatment', *The Future of Children*, vol. 8(1), pp. 31–53.

Erickson, M. and Egeland, B. (1996) 'Child Neglect', in *APSAC Handbook on Child Maltreatment*. American Professional Society on the Abuse of Children, ed. J. Brier, L. Berliner, J. A. Buckley, C. Jenny and T. Reid. Thousand Oaks, Cal.: Sage, pp. 4–20.

Fogarty, J. (1993) *Protective Services for Children in Victoria: A Report by Mr Justice Fogarty*. Health and Community Services Victoria, Melbourne.

Gauthier, L., Stollak, G., Messe, L. and Aronoff, J. (1996) 'Recall of Childhood Neglect and Physical Abuse as Differential Predictors of Current Psychological Functioning', *Child Abuse and Neglect, vol.* 20(7), pp. 549–59.

Glaser, D. and Prior, V. (1997) 'Is the Term Child Protection Applicable to Emotional Abuse?', *Child Abuse Review*, vol. 6, pp. 315–29.

Iwaniec, D. (1995) *The Emotionally Abused and Neglected Child: Identification, Assessment and Intervention*. Chichester: Wiley.

— (1997) 'Evaluating Parent Training for Emotionally Abusive and Neglectful Parents: Comparing Individual Versus Individual and Group Intervention', *Research on Social Work Practice*, vol. 7(3), 329–49.

— (2000) 'From Childhood to Adulthood: The Outcomes of a Twenty-Year Follow-up of Children who Failed to Thrive', in D. Iwaniec and M. Hill (eds), *Child Welfare, Policy and Practice: Issues and Lessons Emerging from Current Research*. London: Jessica Kingsley Publishers.

— (2000) 'Issues Emerging from Child Care Research: Post-Implementation of the Children Act 1989', in D. Iwaniec and M. Hill (eds), *Child Welfare, Policy and Practice: Issues and Lessons Emerging from Current Research*. London: Jessica Kingsley Publishers.

Iwaniec, D. and Sneddon, H. (2001) 'Attachment Style in Adults who Failed-to-Thrive as Children: Outcomes of a 20-Year Follow-up Study of Factors Influencing Maintenance or Change in Attachment Style', *The British Journal of Social Work*, vol. 31(2), pp. 179–95.

McCord, J. (1983) 'A Forty Year Perspective on Effects of Child Abuse and Neglect', *Child Abuse and Neglect*, vol. 7, pp. 265–70.

Main, M. and Goldwyn, R. (1984) 'Predicting Rejection of Her Infant from Mother's

Representation of Her Own Experience. Implications for the Abused-Abusing Intergenerational Cycle', *Child Abuse and Neglect*, vol. 8, 203–17.

Maslow, A.H. (1970) *Motivation and Personality*. New York: Harper & Row.

Minty, B. and Pattinson, G. (1994) 'The Nature of Child Neglect', *British Journal of Social Work*, vol. 24, pp. 733–47.

Ney, P. G., Fung, T. and Wickett, A. R. (1994) 'The Worst Combinations of Child Abuse and Neglect', *Child Abuse and Neglect*, vol. 18, pp. 705–14.

Oliver, J.E. and Buchanan, A. H. (1979) 'Generations of Maltreated Children and Multi-Agency Care in One Kindred', *British Journal of Psychiatry*, vol. 135, pp. 289–303.

Pinkerton, J., Higgins, K., and Devine, P. (2000) *Family Support, Linking Project Evaluation to Policy Analysis*. Aldershot: Ashgate.

Polansky, N. (1992) 'Family Radicals', *Children and Youth Services Review*, vol. 14(1/2), pp. 19–26.

Rose, S. J. and Meezan, W. (1993) 'Defining Child Neglect: Evolution, Influences, and Issues', *Social Services Review*, vol. 67, 279–93.

Sroufe, L. A. and Fleeson, J. (1986) 'Attachment and the Construction of Relationships', in W. W. Hartup and Z. Rubin (eds), *Relationships and Development*. New York: Cambridge University Press.

Stevenson, O. (1996) 'Emotional Abuse and Neglect: A Time for Reappraisal', *Children and Family Social Work*, 1, 13–18.

— (1998) *Neglected Children: Issues and Dilemmas*. Oxford: Blackwell Science.

Stone, B. (1998) 'Child Neglect: Practitioners' Perspectives', *Child Abuse Review*, vol. 7, pp. 87–96.

Urquiza, A. J. and Winn, C. (1992) *Treatment for Abused and Neglected Children: Infancy to Age 18*, US Department of Health and Human Services. The Clearinghouse on Child Abuse and Neglect Information, pp. 1–131.

Wilding, J. and Thoburn, J. (1997) 'Family Support Plans for Neglected and Emotionally Maltreated Children', *Child Abuse Review*, vol. 6, pp. 343–56.

Zuravin, S.J. (1999) 'Child Neglect: A Review of Definitions and Measurement Research', in H. Dubowitz (ed.), *Neglected Children: Research, Practice and Policy*. London: Sage, pp. 24–46.

11

Foster Care: Policies and Practice in Working with Foster Families*

Kate Wilson and Ian Sinclair

Foster care refers to a situation in which children and young people live in other people's families. The majority of foster carers are ordinary families in the community who are recruited, assessed, trained and supported in caring for looked-after children on behalf of the local authority. Most of them have children of their own, either living with them or grown up. A foster placement can be for a single weekend to relieve a family crisis, or may provide a permanent home for a child who cannot be cared for by her/his birth family. It may be undertaken by relatives of the child under an arrangement with the local authority (Waterhouse, 1997, suggests 12 per cent of foster carers are relatives or family friends). The majority of the children fostered have experienced difficult and potentially damaging situations in their own families; many although not all wish nonetheless to return to them or remain at least in contact with them. In their foster families they often lack the sense of 'entitlement to be there' which usually characterises members of a family. Foster families therefore both resemble and differ from the families described in most other chapters in this book. This chapter describes the legal, statutory and policy basis for foster care, considers factors which the research suggests may make for successful fostering, and the role of social workers in contributing to this. It concludes with an illustrative case study.

---

* Some of the content of this chapter was developed for a report on foster care research for the then Department for the Environment, Trade and the Regions under the Beacon Councils initiative. The report was written by the present authors together with colleagues from the University of East Anglia, Gillian Schofield, Clive Sellick and June Thoburn, and we are grateful to them for allowing us to use the material.

Background

Historically, local authority services to children in need have been dominated by foster and residential care. Only since the war has much attention been given to prevention and to children in the community. The Children Act 1948 emphasised foster care as *the* alternative provision for children who cannot be cared for by their own families, underlining the responsibility of the State to provide good alternative homes where necessary. Traditionally, foster parenting, as the name suggests, was regarded as a replacement for a child's life within her or his birth family, and was seen as providing a total, substitute experience in which children would probably have minimal contact with birth relatives, and would form primary attachments with their foster parents. However, greater awareness from the late 1960s on of the deficiencies of the state as parent, and the complexity of relationships between children, their birth families and foster parents, highlighted the ambiguities of what foster care could and should offer. Foster care began to be perceived less homogeneously than before, since it needed to address such a variety of children's placement needs: many admissions to care were short-term, some were intended to be so but lasted longer than planned, many children 'drifted' in care with no clear plans for their future, and were leaving care ill-equipped to cope with the adult world (Stein and Carey, 1986).

Since foster care was unsatisfactory and impermanent, an alternative model was put forward: permanence for children unable to return home began to be equated with adoption, and foster care should be based on a series of tasks, preparing children either for this, or for a return home. Only very recently has the existence and legitimacy of long-term foster care, in which children may or may not retain contact with their birth families while developing core attachment relationships within their foster families, been recognised. (Schofield *et al.*, 2000). Understanding and managing these diverse expectations of family relationships within foster families is thus one of the key tasks of foster care.

Most children and young people separated from their families and who are looked after by local authorities live in foster families. On the most recent figures, around 55,000 children are looked after by English local authorities at any one time. Around two-thirds of these live in foster families, a proportion that has been growing steadily since the 1970s, although their actual numbers have remained constant, as has the estimated number of carers (around 25,000) (Berridge, 1997). Fostering is an important service for young people as well as for children: over half are aged 10 or over, although two-thirds were under 10 when they came into 'care'. Most of these foster children have been looked after for a long time, and can be expected to stay longer. Eight out of 10 of those in the looked-after system have been there for six months or more, and of the 29,800 children in non-relative foster care on 31 March 1999, roughly a third had been in foster care for over four years. These lengthy periods 'in care' constitute a major official intervention in the lives of vulnerable children and young people. These figures suggest a certain stability, but this is misleading, reflecting the fact that in a cross-sectional survey a child who spends a year in foster care is 52 times as likely to appear as one who spends one week. In practice the majority of foster placements from the community are brief. Around 30 000 children enter the care system each year and a similar number leave – around a quarter having spent less than two weeks, and two-thirds less than a year.

In addition there is considerable turnover among the longer-staying children within the care system, with a minority of mainly older children acquiring a large number of placements. Around one in seven of those leaving at 18 or over have had 10 or more placements. Even those who have stable care careers tend to leave 'home' at a much earlier time than is common for their age group (Biehal *et al.*, 1992; Sinclair *et al.*, 2000). The service is therefore characterised by a good deal of movement and change, which is likely to prove stressful for the participants as well as making for complexities in provision and management.

Key factors affecting foster care

Factors which affect most aspects of foster care include the legislative framework, the needs of children and the views of children and their families.

The legislative and statutory framework

The legal basis for fostering in England and Wales is laid down in the Children Act 1989. Recent key policy and legislative developments include the *Quality Protects* Initiative, the government *Objectives for Social Services* and the publication of the UK *National Standards for Foster Care*. Standards are buttressed by guidance, regulation and the Looked-After Children Assessment and Action records, developed with funding from the Department of Health, which are intended to measure whether children's day-to-day needs (on five dimensions of health, education, identity, family relationships and social presentation) are being met. In 1997, Sir William Utting's report *People Like Us* raised the issue of the safety of children living away from home, and proposed a series of measures which could be implemented to protect children. These have significantly affected both foster care policy and practice, leading amongst other things to the provision of a framework through which councils can deliver high quality and safe foster care services.

Taken together, these documents suggest the service, practice and professional considerations which need to be kept in mind in providing foster care. They relate to:

- *Values*: the paramount importance of the welfare of the child, the need for a partnership approach embracing parents, carers, social work services and the children themselves, and birth families and the need to value diversity in ethnicity, culture religion and gender.

- *Placements*: the need for placement choice if children are to be protected and their development enhanced.
- *Fostering*: the need to provide *stable placements* and to develop foster children's *physical and mental health, education, sense of identity including racial identity, family relationships, and ability to present themselves in social situations.*
- *Moving on*: the need to maintain *family relationships* where possible, to consider *adoption* in all appropriate cases and to maintain contact with *children graduating out of the care system* and support them as far as possible.

The needs of foster children

The needs of foster children are partly those which are common to all children – for example, for a stable, loving home where children are listened to, encouraged and given clear guidance when needed. Most children in the care system have lacked such backgrounds. They are 'looked after' because their birth families are for various reasons unable to care for them at home. They tend to come from broken and troubled families. A very high proportion – three-quarters to nine out of ten – of those looked after at any one time are thought to have been abused or neglected (Schofield *et al.*, 2000; Sinclair *et al.*, 2000). Others enter because they are disabled (Morris, 1995, 1998) because family relationships have broken down, or because they are orphaned or abandoned.

Unsurprisingly foster children tend to be much more disturbed (McCann *et al.*, 1996, Quinton *et al.*,1997, Rowe *et al.*, 1984) and somewhat less physically healthy than their peers. A significant minority have some physical disability, and a sizeable proportion, perhaps around a quarter, have a learning disability, in a minority of cases a serious one (Lyon, 1990; Morris, 1998b). They also perform much less well than their peers at school (Heath *et al.*, 1994; Cheung and Heath, 1994; Triseliotis, 2000). Many display 'challenging' behaviour, including sexualised behaviour which may present risks to other children (Macaskill, 1991). Many have difficulty in forming close relationships (Delaney, 1991; Quinton *et al.*, 1998; Schofield, 2000).

The perspectives of foster children and their birth families

Studies of children's views are bedevilled by problems of poor response rates, and the marked underrepresentation of young children and those who spend brief periods in the care system. They therefore do not provide a clear overview of the proportions of foster children who feel positive or negative about their care. They do, however, give a clear picture of the range of issues which are important to children.

Generally, relationships with birth families seem to be a key issue. Some feel that being away from their families is 'the worse thing about foster care' (Shaw, 1998). Some desperately want to return home. Some would like to return home but realise that this is impossible. Others accept that the foster family is 'more healthy' or value the lower levels of stress and better amenities (Kufeld *et al.*, 1995; Colton, 1988). Some do not want to return to their families but do want continuing contact, some find that absence makes the heart grow fonder (Fisher *et al.*, 1986), some want to be adopted. Others object to foster care which seems to compete with their families and to feel more like adoption (Sinclair *et al.*, 1995). Whether or not they wish to stay in their placement many seem preoccupied with producing an account they can accept of why they are in the care system and who is to blame.

The second key issue for the children concerns their care career and the quality of their relationships with the current foster family. Generally they feel a need to belong somewhere. They do not like uncertainty about their future, wanting their care careers to be predictable and to have a say in them. Moves are stressful. They may involve changes of school, a sense of failure if the previous placement broke down, and adaptation to a new family and rules. As for this family children want to feel fairly treated and part of it (provided this is not seen as being in competition with their own). They wanted foster care to be as like normal family care as possible. The best thing is being loved and cared for. However, it is also important to be encouraged, not put down and expected to perform to a high standard (Sinclair *et al.*, 2001).

Birth parents also vary in their views of foster care. Removal of a child is associated with grief, guilt, embarrassment, anxiety and relief in varying proportions. Some parents are determined to get their child back and fight to achieve this. Others (more commonly) are dismayed to find that a request for accommodation is refused and alternative help not offered. Many are inured to separations from their children and do not regard this as an irreparable rift in family life (Fisher *et al.*, 1986).

How successfully does foster care meet its tasks?

The policy framework, the needs of children and their views set the implicit criteria against which foster care is judged. How far does current provision meet them? The answer seems to be 'partially'. On several measures, including the consumption of a healthy diet and help with homework, 'looked-after' children receive parenting which is the same or better than those living in families from similar backgrounds (Sellick and Thoburn, 1996). Both parents and children commonly appreciate the care provided. Respite care is particularly popular with parents and children, too, come to appreciate its benefits for themselves as well as their parents (Aldgate *et al.*, 1999). Other short-term care also seems to meet its aims – at least in the eyes of social workers (Rowe *et al.*, 1989).

Even more importantly, foster care seems to be 'better' in some circumstances than return home. Its generally poor outcomes are 'not its fault'. Longitudinal studies suggest that children's disturbance and educational deficits precede rather than follow entry to the care system. Young children who have been abused or neglected seem to put on weight and be less disturbed if they remain in foster care than if they return home. Length of stay in foster care seems to be associated with 'good outcomes' (although this may reflect differences between early and late entrants). Comparisons of educational and psychological progress of foster children with similar samples in the community is, if anything, in favour of the former. The outcomes of long-stay stable fostering are typically good (See Minty, 1999). A European study suggests that even if foster children have troubled outcomes in early adulthood they may settle later (Dumaret *et al.*, 1997).

Less positively, foster care generally does not reverse the difficulties of children entering the care system. There are problems relating to lack of placement choice, particularly for teenagers and for those from ethnic minority backgrounds, placement instability, low expectations of educational achievement, and shortages of foster carers. Outcomes are not encouraging, particularly for those with unstable careers. Foster children are more likely than their peers to be unemployed, in prison, homeless or unsupported parents.

Practice issues in providing and maintaining good foster placements

So far we have considered the historical and policy background of foster care, the perspectives and needs of children and their families, and the evidence on outcomes of foster care. We now consider what those involved in providing and managing the service and those working with the individual foster and birth families can do to improve the success of foster care. Some areas which we consider relate to the way foster care is organised and delivered (for example having enough carers to provide a choice of placements), some relate to individual planning for the child (such as matching, moving a child home or to a long-term placement or adoption), and some to work with the foster family itself (for example helping foster carers use a range of approaches with the children in their care).

Placement choice, matching and moving

Placement choice depends, unsurprisingly, on the recruitment and retention of adequate numbers of carers. It also depends on the provision of an appropriate range of placements and on practice which allows some matching between child and placement. In terms of range, foster care has been classi-fied by its length, purpose and the type of children it serves. One study (Sinclair *et al.*, 2000) distinguished between short-term care, respite/revolving care, treatment/project foster care, long-term fostering and relative fostering. This classification relates to differences in the purpose (Rowe *et al.*, 1989) and outcome criteria (Sellick and Thoburn, 1996). However, many carers provide mixed forms of care (for example both long-term and short-term). Moreover, this classification ignores the real distinc-tions between placements for teenagers, those for babies, those made with a view to adoption, those for disabled children, remand fostering (rare), and so on.

In general, the evidence suggests that authorities need to provide:

- Robust short-term placements – which can take a wide range of children until appropriate placements become available
- Treatment/teenage fostering capable of managing the difficult adoles-cents for whom residential care is no longer available (Barrows, 1996; Bondy *et al.*, 1990).
- Long-term placements – these exist in all authorities but are not always acknowledged as a legitimate placement choice and are often in short supply.
- Placements for special groups – children with disabilities, siblings, chil-dren from ethnic minorities.

In terms of practice, social workers and managers have sought 'rules of thumb' to guide their choice of placement – that children should be placed with siblings, where there are no children of the foster carers close in age, with relatives or in placements of the same ethnicity. The evidence on the relationship between outcomes and these placement choices is either conflicting (for example on placements with siblings) or largely negative (for example on the need for same-race placements (Thoburn *et al.*, 2000). The evidence suggests that the rules do reflect key issues (for example that the attitude of carers' children to the child is important, but this can work for good or ill). In most cases there is a moral presumption in favour of the 'rules' (for example that children should be placed with siblings or in same-race placements). This has to be backed by practitioners' willingness to pay careful attention to what the children want and to particular factors in the situation (such as a child's extreme jealousy of a sibling or conflicts within the extended birth family).

The decision to move a child also requires professional judgement. In general children crave stability, and there is therefore a moral presumption against movement. However, some moves are more serious than others (such as those where a child has been settled for some years), some children want to be moved, and some moves in late teens may be necessary to maintain a relationship with carers, albeit at a distance. In terms of outcome there is strong evidence that disturbed children are likely to have disrupted placements and hence more placements. The evidence does not suggest that more placements *per se* lead to disturbance (Sinclair *et al.*, 2000) and many practitioners will have experienced situations when they have moved a child, reluctantly, after a lengthy time in a placement only to find that the new placement provides unlooked-for success.

Similar dilemmas arise over whether to leave children in placements in contradiction to an existing plan. A child may need to move when the placement lasts longer than the carer expected or wishes. However, some children and carers bond in short-term care, and there is a strong case, here as elsewhere, for profiting from these mutual choices. Children given placements which are not seen as fully satisfactory are more likely to have placement breakdowns in the first year. If they survive this they are no more likely to disrupt than other foster children, suggesting the wisdom of an 'if it ain't broke don't fix it' approach at this stage. Since this may have unwelcome consequences for the system (for example by 'blocking' a short-term placement) practitioners need to be confident in arguing for it.

There is overwhelming evidence that difficult behaviour disrupts placements. Conversely 'appealing' children are less likely to disrupt (Rowe *et al.*, 1989, Sinclair *et al.*, 2000). The accounts by carers, social workers and children suggest that children's motivation in being in the placement can be a key factor in its success: if they want a placement to work they can make it do so (or conversely if they wish disrupt it). A foster carer interviewed for Sinclair *et al.*'s study, for example, attributed the success of the placement (initially a short-term one, which changed to adoption) to the four-year-old child's commitment:

> He wanted to move – its funny that – he wanted to be here. But I had to need a Casper. I had to keep telling him – He kept saying – do you need a Casper – and I kept saying – I do – I'm waiting for a Casper to move in ... and he's made it work. I don't know how but he has. He's a beautiful child. I mean he had a lot of problems, which took it out of us a bit, but ... he's got a lot of love to give. (Sinclair *et al.*, 2000)

It therefore makes sense for practical as well as moral reasons for social workers to attend closely to what children say about their placements.

Other key issues for practitioners involve helping children moving out of foster placements, whether back to birth families, to adoptive families or to independent living; helping sustain long-term foster placements; and working with carers, birth families and children to improve the quality of relationships, behaviour and social skills. We consider these now.

Return to birth families

As we indicated at the beginning of this chapter, most of those entering the system return rapidly to their own families. Good social work practice has been associated with the successful return home of the child (Bullock et al.,1993; Thoburn, 1995, 1998), and avoidance of multiple moves in the care system. Such practice promotes good contact between the birth parents, foster carers and the child, supports the foster carers and the birth parents and coordinates a multi-agency approach to treatment of the child and parents before, during and after placement. Key aspects of this work by social workers probably include the identification of specific problems that the family needs to resolve, and helping the birth parents keep a place within their home for the child. One useful approach is to offer both foster carer and birth parents training in the same parental skills – an approach that should ensure consistency of approach and outcome. (An American project described and validated by Chamberlain, 1998 provides a model which might well be pursued over here.)

Implementing contact between children and birth families

In general, the maintenance of contact between parent and child is required, wherever practicable, by the Children Act. Research prior to the Act reported a desire on the part of children for more contact, difficulties in providing it, and an association between contact and return home. More recent research shows an increase in contact. While the moral case for it remains unimpaired there is now doubt that it produces the outcomes claimed for it (Quinton et al., 1997). Moreover, there is evidence that it can be distressing to children or foster carers. One study showed that prohibitions on contact with at least one individual were associated with better outcomes when the child had been abused (Sinclair et al., 2000).

So again this seems an area calling for sensitive professional decisions rather than blanket rules of thumb. Certainly practitioners should operate with a presumption in favour of contact and be prepared to put time into making it happen. They need to clarify the purposes contact serves in particular situations (for example question the value of twice-weekly contact with his birth mother for an abused 10-month-old being placed for adoption, as in one case we encountered). They should also listen carefully to what both children and carers have to say about timing and frequency, and consider whether and how the contact needs to be supported or supervised. Equally there is a need to distinguish between contact with different members of the family (for example with grandparents) some of which may be beneficial and others not (Sinclair et al., 2000). Siblings are often sorely missed. Contact with previous foster carers is known to be desired by a number of foster children and may be vital in building a sense of identity, but in practice seems often to be discouraged or to be difficult to achieve (Palmer, 1996; Fanshel, Finch and Grundy, 1990;

Kufeldt *et al.*, 1995). Some foster carers, for example, in our study felt that it would be 'interfering' or unprofessional to keep in touch with foster children who had left. Social workers have a role to play in promoting such contact, again where it fits with the wishes and needs of the child or young person.

Adoption and long-term fostering

The likelihood of adoption drops rapidly with age, and this is sometimes attributed to a negative attitude by social workers to adoption. Certainly there is wide variation in the use made of adoption by different authorities. However, the choice between adoption and long-term fostering as an option for children unable to return to their birth families also depends on a range of factors. These include age, sibling groups, disturbed behaviours, close family ties, the need for high levels of contact or, quite commonly, combinations of these factors. In Schofield *et al.*'s (2000) study of 58 children aged between 4 and 12 in long-term foster families, adoption would have been an option for only a small minority. Sellick and Thoburn (1996) concluded that when age at placement was held constant, breakdown rates were not dissimilar between adoption and foster care. They go on to say that there is insufficient evidence on the desirability of adoption, permanent fostering or residence orders from the child's point of view, so that all placement options must be made available by local authorities to suit the needs of different children. Schofield's study also showed that just as there is a wide variation in the use made of adoption by different authorities, so there is a wide variation in the systems set up to ensure good planning and placement support for long-term foster placements. Social workers have again an important role in supporting the relationships which can develop in such placements between skilled foster carers and children, thereby encouraging the development of secure attachments, a sense of identity and self–esteem.

Independent living

Generally foster children move to live independently at a much younger age than their peers (Jones, 1987). It is not clear why this is. Some social workers may wish to have got the move out of the way before the child reaches age 18; some children may wish to go; some carers may wish them to go also. There are also financial considerations with a potential loss of fostering allowances. There may be a perception that it is professional to let a child go; to keep them would smack of adoption. And local authorities may need the placement for other children. Nonetheless, it is apparent that many more foster children expect and want to stay on in foster care than actually do so (Sinclair *et al.*, 2000). Social workers and agencies need not only to develop schemes to increase the proportion of those who do (Biehal *et al.*, 1992) but also to recognise that this may have consequent costs and, for example, be prepared to provide financial and emotional support when the young person and the carers wish the young person to remain as part of the household after the age of 18.

Improving the quality of relationships in foster families

One of the key concerns for those working with foster families is the extent to which it is possible to improve outcomes in foster placements. We have highlighted some of the broader issues with which practitioners and managers need to concern themselves, for example those to do with supply, retention or matching (by age or ethnicity, for example). We now consider issues to do with the interactions between the key players, and how it may be possible to work with these to provide better foster placements.

The basic qualities required by carers seem to be those needed by all parents – warmth, firmness, consistency, willingness to encourage and so on. There is a case for building on these qualities by using carers as the key providers of treatment, with a number of examples of innovative approaches to this. An American project trained parents and carers in parenting skills using an approach pioneered with birth parents (Chamberlain *et al.*, 1992). The approach emphasised the need to reward 'good behaviour', intervene early with difficult behaviour, develop skills in negotiation and use concrete rewards. The project was positively evaluated using a rigorous design and it is one of a number of American projects which use explicit theories and claim reasonable success with a positive rating by young people and some improvement in their well-being (Hill *et al.*, 1993; Clark *et al.*, 1994). The project described by Chamberlain and her colleagues emphasises the need for individual work with children, and, when children were returning home, the importance of working with birth parents so their approach was as consistent as possible to that of the foster carers. Schools, therapists of various kinds, and social workers may all provide this work. Another study (Sinclair, Gibbs and Wilson, in press) found evidence that behavioural interventions reduced problem behaviours, that life-story work was associated with improved adjustment, and that contact with an educational psychologist was strongly associated with perceived placement success and the avoidance of placement breakdown.

Gilligan (2000) considers resilience as a protective factor, and suggests that by enhancing this foster carers and social workers can help children and young people counteract the risk factors in their lives. He suggests a set of specific actions which foster carers might usefully take to promote resilience in the young person in their care, and to develop in the child three key qualities of *belonging* (having a secure base), *mattering* (enhanced self-esteem) and *counting* (a sense of self-efficacy and some choice in decisions about their lives). He points out that it is often the detail of what foster carers and others – social workers, teachers and other mentors – do which is important, cumulatively.

In their study of a large sample of foster placements, the present authors with Gibbs (Wilson, Sinclair and Gibbs, in press) develop a model of successful foster care based on quantatative and qualitative material and case studies. The model involves a specification of the relevant factors and the ways in which they bring about a given outcome. It is hoped this may be useful in assessing placements and suggesting directions for work with carers, foster children and others. The model contains two main components:

- *Responsive parenting*: the way in which the carer deals with the child.
- *Conditions*: the prior conditions which make this kind of interaction more or less likely. Two types of conditions are distinguished:

  - conditions to do with the characteristics of the child, the carer and the compatibility between them;
  - conditions to do with the wider context.

Responsive parenting is a necessary attribute of a successful placement. The various conditions are not necessary or sufficient for success, but they do make it more or less likely. These conditions relate to the characteristics of the foster child, particular attributes of the foster carer (for example her/his general skills and the presence/absence of a sense of being stressed), and the compatibility between the carer and the child in question. Other conditions reflect the wider context, including the local authority's care plans for the child, support from other agencies such as the school, and the involvement of the birth family members and members of the foster carer's own family.

Each of these components may be divided into different sub-elements. Thus, to show the child *responsive parenting*, carers must:

- Handle attachment appropriately; for example,

  - deal sensitively with previous attachments and losses,
  - offer security with persistence and avoid threats of rejection,
  - offer tolerable closeness,
  - be sensitive to attachment times and approaches,
  - deal sensitively with jealousy and exclusiveness,
  - go out of their way to make the child 'feel at home'.

- Reinforce socially acceptable self-esteem/identity; for example,

  - praise success of whatever kind,
  - avoid dwelling on failure,
  - set realistic expectations, and
  - maintain a positive but realistic picture of the child.

- Handle difficult behaviour appropriately; for example,

  - analyse motives/reasons for behaviour,
  - avoid increasing these motives,
  - set clear limits,
  - negotiate in ways that avoids humiliating the child,
  - offer alternative ways of meeting needs,
  - avoid reinforcing difficult behaviour itself, and
  - reinforce competing behaviour.

Some of the *conditions* which make appropriate interaction more or less likely relate to the child, the carer and the compatibility between them. Relevant conditions include:

- The child's

  - attractiveness (to most people and the carer in particular),
  - motivation to make the placement work, and
  - propensity to difficult or easy behaviour.

- The main carer's

  - general skill and motivation,
  - commitment to the particular child,
  - sense of professional limits, and
  - degree of sense of being stressed.

- Compatibility between the carer and child in relation to

  - attachment/closeness needs,
  - definitions of success (e.g. academic),
  - expectations over behaviour.

Other *conditions* may impinge on the placement from its wider context. These include the carer's family, birth family, social services, school and so on. Placements are more likely to go easily where:

- the carer's family is committed to the placement,
- there are not clashes between the child and particular members of the family,
- members of the birth family are not seeking to disturb the placement,
- Social Services support the carer's preferred view of the placement's purpose, and
- the child's social world (school, friends, etc.) supports the placement expectations.

A short case example provides an illustration of the model:

Robert, age 12 – 'it's as if he's been with us forever'

Robert came into care when he was seven, because his grandparents with whom he was living at the time were found to be neglecting him, and there were concerns about an uncle who was accused of sexually abusing a young girl. Robert made a planned move to his present foster carers (Mr and Mrs W) when he was eight, and has been there for nearly four years.

Mr and Mrs W are experienced foster carers, with two grown-up children, and consider they were chosen for Robert because they offered a home with firm but loving boundaries, enjoyed outdoor activities and sport, and wanted a long-term placement. Robert was eager to come – 'he kept on and on, and he was thrilled to bits when I went that Saturday morning and picked him up and brought him here and said, right – you're staying.' They see Robert as very much part of the family, and treat him as they treated their own children – indeed, Mrs W says her own children are a help in that they tell Robert their mother was just the same with them (for example in nagging him about homework, so that he does not feel he is being unfairly 'got at'). Mrs W speaks of him as a loved child, describing him as very popular, brilliant at sport, a brilliant artist and good at music.

They recognize that he will need academic qualifications to get anywhere, and are prepared to see him through college or university – 'he knows that whatever he wants to do, we'll support him'.

Along with their commitment to him, and his to them, they accept Robert's attachment to his birth family – 'when you foster, you know that you're fostering someone else's child. You don't actually want the child for yourself.' Robert has asked whether the Ws would adopt him, but Mrs W feels that his relationship with his birth family is too strong – 'for all their faults, they love him. And deep down inside, he loves them. There is that bond there. And I think it's something that should be encouraged. And when Robert's older, it's up to him what he does.'

In contrast to that of many foster children, Robert's behaviour before he came to the placement was not particularly difficult, so that the demands on Mrs W's parenting skills were not perhaps as great. Robert himself seems to have been highly committed to the placement, and to be an attractive child, qualities which in turn probably strengthened Mrs W's commitment to him. Having said this, she seems to have been able, in terms of the qualities identified above as promoting a secure sense of attachment, a sense of identity and self-esteem, to exercise a high level of skill. This includes her ability be clear about her role, to access support when she needs it – she is, for example, aware of what tasks it is appropriate for the social worker to carry out – and to use other supports, whether it be neighbours or her own grown-up children to help in her care for Robert. We can surmise that her acceptance of Robert's birth family, which is open, tolerant and shows a predominant concern for what he wants and she feels deep down needs, allows him to feel settled and at ease in the placement.

In terms of the model then, Mrs W demonstrates a degree of *responsive parenting*, and the *conditions* of the placement are such that this can occur: Robert is an attractive child, well-motivated to be in the placement, and rewarding. In terms of emotional closeness, the fit is a good one – he needs a sense of belonging and permanence, and the family provides this for him.

Mrs W offers a stable, committed and responsive environment for him. She combines her love and commitment to him with a professional approach to looking after him (for example in accessing social work support when she deems it appropriate, or encouraging contact with birth family members). He fits well into her family, who help her in her handling of him, and are neither threatened by nor in competition with him.

The second kind of condition, the *context* of the placement, supports what is happening in it, in that it is seen as long-term where it is appropriate for the child and family to develop close attachments and a sense of belonging. Carers, child and social workers seem to have the same goals for the placement, and those minor upheavals which could have unsettled the placement (for example, issues over contact with an abusing uncle, or loss by Robert of contact with two younger siblings when they were placed for adoption) seem to have been addressed by the social workers in an open and reassuring way.

The model, then, suggests areas, no doubt familiar to most if not all practitioners, on which they might usefully focus in working with foster families. These include thinking about the quality of *responsive parenting* and the detail of how the foster carers respond to their foster children, and if necessary working with them, for example by developing skills in promoting attachments. It also highlights the need to think through various aspects of the placement conditions, both when assessing its viability, and when working with the family after placement. Thus questions such as the child's motivation, the compatability between the child's and the family's expectations, the support from members of the family, become issues to consider.

Conclusion

This chapter has considered the policy background to foster care in the UK, and highlighted some of the issues which social workers, Social Services departments and other involved professionals need to consider in delivering foster care. We have focused particularly on what social workers need to promote at an organisational level, and also suggested areas for working with individual foster families, foster children and birth families. We concluded with an account of a model of foster care, illustrated with a short case study of a successful foster placement.

References

Aldgate, J. and Bradley, M. (1999) *Supporting Families through Short-term Fostering*. London: HMSO.

Berridge, D. (1997) *Foster Care: A Research Review*. London: HMSO.

Biehal, N., Clayden, J., Stein, M. and Wade, J. (1992) *Prepared for Living? A Survey of Young People Leaving the Care of Three Local Authorities*. London: National Children's Bureau.

Bondy, D., Davis, D., Hagen, S., Spritos, A. and Winnick, A. (1990) 'Mental Health Services for Children in Foster Care', *Children Today*, vol. 19, pp. 28–32.

Chamberlain, P., Moreland, S. and Reid, K. (1992) 'Enhanced services and stipends for foster parents: effects on retention rates and outcomes for children', *Child Welfare*, vol. 71, pp. 387–401.

Chamberlain, P. (1998) *Family Connections: A Treatment care Model for Adolescents with Delinquency*. Oregon: Northwest media inc.

Cheung, Y. and Heath, A. (1994) 'After Care: The Education and Occupation of Children who have Been in Care', *Oxford Review of Education*, vol. 20, pp. 361–74.

Colton, M. (1988) *Dimensions of Substitute Care: Comparative Study of Foster and Residential Care Practice*. Aldershot: Avebury.

Delaney, R. (1991) *Fostering Changes: Treating Attachment-Disordered Foster Children*. Colorado: Walter J. Corbett Publishing.

Fanshel, D., Finch, S. and Grundy, J. (1990) *Foster Care Children in Lifecourse Perspective*. New York: Columbia University Press.

Fisher, M., Marsh, P., Phillips, D. with Sainsbury, E. (1986) *In and Out of Care: The Experiences of Children, Parents and Social Workers*. London: Batsford.

Gilligan, R. (2000) 'Promoting Resiliance in Children in Foster Care', in *Issues in Foster Care*, ed. G. Kelley and R. Gilligan. London: Jessica Kingsley, pp. 107–210.

Heath, A., Colton, M. and Aldgate, J. (1994) 'Failure to escape: a longitudinal study of foster children's educational attainment', *British Journal of Social Work*, vol. 24, pp. 241–60.

Hill, M., Nutter, R., Gittinan, D., Hudson, J. and Galoway, B. (1993) 'A comparative survey of specialist-fostering in the UK and North America', *Adoption and Fostering*, vol. 17, pp. 17–22.

Jones, G. (1987) 'Leaving the parental home: an analysis of early housing careers', *Journal of Social Policy*, vol. 16(1), pp. 49–74.

Kufeldt, K., Armstrong, J. and Dorosh, M. (1995) 'How Children View their Own and their Foster Families: A Research Study', *Child Welfare*, vol. 74, pp. 695–715.

Lyon, C. (1990) *Living Away from Home: The Legal Impact on Young Children with Severe Learning Difficulties*. Keele: University of Keele/Barnardo's North West.

Macaskill, C. (1991) *Adopting or Fostering a Sexually Abused Child*. London: Batsford.

McCann, J., James, A., Wilson, S. and Dunn, G. (1996) 'Prevalence of Psychiatric Disorders in Young People in the Care System', *British Medical Journal*, vol. 313, pp. 1529–30.

Morris, J. (1995) *Gone Missing? A Research and Policy Review of Disabled Children Living Away from their Families*. London: Who Cares? Trust

— (1998) *Still Missing? The Experiences of Disabled Children and Young People Living Away from their Families*, vol. 1. London: Who Cares? Trust.

— (1998b) *Still Missing? Disabled Children and the Children Act*. London: Who Cares? Trust.

Palmer, S. (1996) 'Placement stability and inclusive practice in foster care: an empirical study', *Children and Youth Services Review*, vol. 18, pp. 589–601.

Quinton, D., Dance, C. and Rushton, A. (1998) *Joining New Families*. Chichester: Wiley.

Quinton, D., Rushton, A., Dance, C. and Mayes, D. (1997) 'Contact between Children Placed away from Home and their Birth Parents: Research Issues and Evidence', *Clinical Child Psychology and Psychiatry*, vol 2(3), pp. 383–413.

Rowe, J., Cain, H., Hundleby, M. and Keane, A. (1984) *Long-term foster care.* London: Batsford.

Rowe, J., Hundleby, M. and Keane, A. (1989) *Child Care Now – A Survey of Placement Patterns.* London: British Agencies for Adoption and Fostering.

Schofield, G., Beek, M., Sargent, K. (2000) *Growing Up in Foster Care.* London: BAAF.

Sellick, C. and Thoburn, J. (1996) *What Works in Family Placements.* Barkingside: Barnardos.

Sinclair, I., Gibbs, I. and Wilson, K. (2000) *Supporting Foster Placements: Research Report.* Available from the authors, SWRDU, Department of Social Policy and Social Work, University of York.

Sinclair, I, Wilson, K and Gibbs, I. (2001) 'A Life More Ordinary: What Children Want from Foster Placements', *Adoption and Fostering*, vol. 25(4).

Sinclair, I., Gibbs, I. and Wilson, K. (in press) 'Matches and Mismatches: the contribution of carers and children to the success of foster placements', *British Journal of Social Work*.

Sinclair, R., Garnett, L. and Berridge, D. (1995) *Social Work and Assessment with Adolescents.* London: Nation Children's Bureau.

Stein, M. and Carey, K. (1986) *Leaving care.* Oxford: Blackwell.

Thoburn, J., Norford, L. and Rashid, S. (2000) *Permanent Family Placement for Children of Minority Ethnic Origin.* London: Jessica Kingsley.

Triseliots, J., Borland, M. and hill, R. (2000) *Delivering Foster Care.* London: British Association for Adoption and Fostering.

Utting, W. (1997) *People Like Us: The Report of the Review of the Safeguards for Children Living Away from Home.* London: The Stationery Office.

Waterhouse. S. (1997) *The Organisation of Fostering Services: An Investigation of the Structural Arrangements for the Delivery of Fostering Services by Local Authorities in England.* London: National Foster Care Association.

Wilson, K., Sinclair, I. and Gibbs, I. (2000) 'The Trouble with Foster Care: The Impact of Stressful Events on Foster Carers', *British Journal of Social Work*, vol. 30, pp. 193–209.

Index

meanings – *continued*
  TFFT 112–13, 120–1
Meeting the Childcare Challenge
  25
Meezan, W. 210
men
  confronting violent men 177
  fathers 35, 41
  violent, stepfamilies and child
    abuse 151
  working with 35, 203–5
messages, expression and reception
  of 65, 78
mind-reads 115–16
Minneapolis Domestic Abuse
  Programme (DAP) 203
Minty, B. 216
misattunement 92, 107, 118
mixed economy of welfare
  169–70, 181–3
model of successful foster care
  240–3
*Modernising Health and Social
  Services* 5, 171
monitoring 198
mothers *see* women
moving on 232, 234–6
Mullender, A. 192
Murray, C. 20

National Childcare Strategy
  25–6, 41
National Family and Parenting
  Institute 34
National Health Service and
  Community Care Act 1990
  7, 169
National Standards for Foster Care
  231
Neale, B. 43, 45–6
needs
  of foster children 232–3
  working with women on
    understanding children's needs
    201
neglect 7, 10, 13, 105, 209–28
  case study 220–2, 223–6
  consequences of 213–15
  crisis intervention 224–5
  definitions 209–12
  failures in parenting 212–13
  helping strategies for parents
    222–3
  intervention plan for mother and
    children 223–4
  ongoing long-term family
    support 225–6
  practice issues 219–20
  practitioners' views 215–18
Neighbourhood Nurseries 32
Neil, A. 177
networks, wider family 35
New Deal 30–1, 35
New Labour 5, 10, 19–38
  approach to family policy 22–4
  communitarianism 40–1
  general support for families with
    children 24–7
  implications of policy for social
    work practice 33–6
  support for poor families with
    children 27–33
nominal divorces 138
non-directive play therapy 175,
  203

non-molestation orders 191
non-resident parent 156–7
non-verbal communication 86,
  87, 92–3, 100, 106–8
NSPCC 182
nursery provision 21, 32

Objectives for Social Services 231
occupation orders 191
Office of National Statistics (ONS)
  50–1
older children
  Connexions Service 5, 33, 35
  foster care 230, 235, 238–9
  targeted support 32–3
ongoing long-term family support
  225–6
Ontario model 203
organisational adaptability 62–3,
  76

paranoid–schizoid position 135–6
parent–child relationship
  The Family Assessment 68, 79
  predating couple relationship
    155–6
  see also child–parent relationship
parent coalition 156
parental leave 26
parental relationship 67–8, 79
Parental Responsibility 149, 157
parental system 95–6, 99–100
parenting
  assessment of 217, 218
  failures in 212–13
  The Family Assessment 62,
    63–4, 77
  responsive parenting 240–3
  skills: training in 222–3, 237,
    239; work on 200–1
parenting capacity 164
parenting deficit 40
parenting helplines 162
Parenting Orders 41
parenting programmes 162
Parentline Plus 162, 165
parents
  contactual commitment 44
  fathers 35, 41
  helping strategies for 222–3
  involvement in child protection
    work 175–9
  linking to community activities
    225–6
  mothers *see* women
  non-resident 156–7
  overinvestment in work 40,
    41
part-time stepfamilies 148
participation *see* involvement
partnerships
  local 33, 34
  working in partnership with
    parents and carers 175–9,
    216
past experience 144–5
paternity leave 26
Pattinson, G. 216
Pearson, C. 193
peers, exploratory interest-sharing
  with 93, 94, 100
persecutory anxiety 135–7
personal competence 92, 97
personal defence system 93, 95
personal safety plan 202

personal supportive environment
  96–7
physiological systems 88
Pikler, E. 174–5
placement choice 232, 234–6
play 90–1, 97
Playing for Success programmes
  32
policy 10, 19–38
  child protection 168–9, 170–2
  Conservative governments
    20–2
policy – *continued*
  context of family change 20
  domestic violence 191, 193
  foster care 231–2
  general support for all families
    with children 24–7
  historical background 2–3
  implications for social work
    practice 33–6
  Labour government approach
    22–4
  and stepfamilies 149–50
  support for poor families with
    children 27–33
  see also legislation
positive reinforcement 222–3
post-traditional society 42–3
poverty 60
  social inequalities and 50–2
  stepfamilies 159
  support for poor families with
    children 27–33
  see also child poverty
power, balance of 143–4
pragmatic feminism 45–6
primary intersubjectivity 93
problem-solving 63, 76–7
professional help 144
professional judgment 183
protest 133–4
Pryor, J. 153, 154, 165
psychological problems 214–15
Pupil Learning Credits 32
purposeful misattunement 92

Quality Protects 5, 6, 33, 36,
  171, 231

rainbow lizard 92–3
reception of feelings 68, 78
reception of messages 65, 78
refocusing initiative 171
refuges 189
regulation 36
relationships
  child–parent relationship 68,
    79
  couple relationship 67, 79,
    155–6
  IMERs 90, 117
  improving the quality of
    relationships in foster families
    239–43
  nature of 66, 78–9
  parent–child relationship 68,
    79, 155–6
  parental relationship 67–8, 79
  problems in 130–1; *see also*
    divorce
  pure relationship 42, 43
  sibling relationship 68, 79
  in stepfamilies 155–7, 158–9,
    165